ANNUAL REVIEW OF NURSING RESEARCH

VOLUME 32, 2014

SERIES EDITOR

Christine E. Kasper, PhD, RN, FAAN, FACSM
Department of Veterans Affairs
Office of Nursing Services, Washington, DC
and
Professor, Daniel K. Inouye Graduate School of Nursing
Uniformed Services University of the Health Sciences,
Bethesda, MD

VOLUME EDITOR

Patricia Watts Kelley, PhD, RN, FNP, GNP, FAANP, CAPT (ret) U.S. Navy
Department of Veterans Affairs
Office of Research and Development, Washington, DC
and
Associate Professor, Daniel K. Inouye Graduate School of Nursing
Uniformed Services University of the Health Sciences,
Bethesda, MD

Annual Review of Nursing Research

Military and Veteran Innovations of Care

VOLUME 32, 2014

Series Editor

CHRISTINE E. KASPER, PhD, RN, FAAN, FACSM

Volume Editor

PATRICIA WATTS KELLEY, PhD, RN, FNP, GNP, FAANP,
CAPT (RET) U.S. NAVY

Springer Publishing Company, LLC
11 West 42nd Street
New York, NY 10036
www.springerpub.com

Acquisitions Editor: Joseph Morita
Composition: Absolute Service, Inc.

ISBN: 978-0-8261-2807-2
E-book ISBN: 978-0-8261-2809-6
ISSN: 0739-6686
Online ISSN: 1944-4028

14 15 16/ 5 4 3 2 1

Printed in the United States of America by Gasch Printing

Contents

About the Volume Editor

Patricia Watts Kelley, PhD, RN, FNP, GNP, FAANP, CAPT (ret) U.S. Navy, holds the position of Health Sciences Officer, Department of Veterans Affairs, Office of Research and Development. Prior to her Navy retirement, she held the position of Deputy Director of Nursing and Allied Health Research, Navy Medicine Research and Development Center, Navy Headquarters, Bureau of Medicine and Surgery. She continues to hold an associate professor appointment at the Daniel K. Inouye Graduate School of Nursing, Uniformed Services University of the Health Sciences, Bethesda, MD. Dr. Kelley has held several nursing leadership and research positions. She served as the first Navy executive director of the TriService Nursing Research Program and director of Nursing Research Services, National Naval Medical Center, Bethesda, MD. Her research interests are in the areas of clinical knowledge development and continuity of care of wounded service members, evidence-based practice, health promotion and diabetes self-care management, and nursing retention and recruitment. She served as the specialty consultant to the U.S. Navy Surgeon General for Nursing Research. Captain Kelley had maintained a part-time nurse practitioner practice at the National Naval Medical Center, Bethesda, MD, specializing in diabetes and military health up until her recent retirement. Dr. Kelley is a board member, Navy Safe Harbor Foundation; the Navy Safe Harbor Foundation is dedicated to supporting the recovery of seriously wounded, ill, and injured sailors, coast guardsmen, and their families by assisting them with resources not currently provided by government or community resources. Dr. Kelley serves on the Board of the Reeder House, which exists to improve the living conditions of the most vulnerable people: the chronically homeless Veterans experiencing mental illness.

Dr. Kelley received her PhD in nursing from the Catholic University of America, a postmaster certificate in Family Primary Care from Northeastern University, a master of science from Boston University School of Nursing with a specialty in gerontology, a bachelor of science in nursing from American University, and an associate degree in science from Northeastern University. Dr. Kelley is board certified as a family and gerontological nurse practitioner and a Fellow of the American Academy of Nurse Practitioners.

Captain Kelley entered Naval Service from Boston as a family nurse practitioner in 1990 and since then has held various clinical research, operational, staff, and leadership positions overseas and within the United States. She was recognized for her service with various military awards and honors.

Prior to entering into Naval Service, Dr. Kelley held a number of civilian-nursing positions, including serving as executive director, assistant executive director, and gerontological nurse practitioner, Windsor House Adult Day Care, Cambridge, MA, and director of Nursing Senior Care Management. Dr. Kelley was responsible for the development of several innovative geriatric community Alzheimer's support services.

Dr. Kelley resides in Silver Spring, Maryland, with her husband Stephen.

Contributors

Janice Agazio, PhD, CRNP, FAANP, FAAN
LTC (ret), U.S. Army
Associate Professor
School of Nursing
The Catholic University of America
Washington, DC

Carolyn B. Allard, PhD
VA San Diego Healthcare System
University of California San Diego
San Diego, CA

Danielle Beck, MPH, CCRC
VA San Diego Healthcare System
University of California San Diego
San Diego, CA

Jill E. Bormann, PhD, RN, FAAN
VA San Diego Healthcare System
University of California San Diego
San Diego, CA

Elizabeth Bridges, PhD, RN, CCNS, FCCM, FAAN
Col. U.S. Air Force
Headquarters U.S. Air Force (SG1N)
Falls Church, VA
University of Washington School of Nursing
Seattle, WA

Jose A. Centeno, PhD, FRSC
Biophysical Toxicology Laboratory, Joint Pathology Center
Malcolm Grow Medical Clinic
Joint Base Andrews, MD

Lindsay Cosco Holt, PhD, RN
University of San Diego
San Diego, CA

Susan Dukes, PhD, RN, CCNS
Lt. Col. U.S. Air Force
U.S. Air Force School of Aerospace Medicine
Wright-Patterson Air Force Base, OH

Magaly Freytes, PhD
Research Health Scientist
Center of Innovation for Disability and Rehabilitation Research
Veterans Health Administration
North Florida/South Georgia Veterans Health System
Gainesville, FL

Joanna M. Gaitens, PhD, RN
Department of Veterans Affairs
VA Medical Center
Department of Medicine Occupational Health Program
University of Maryland School of Medicine
Baltimore, MD

Petra Goodman, PhD, WHNP-BC
COL (Ret), U.S. Army
Associate Professor
School of Nursing
The Catholic University of America
Washington, DC

Jennifer J. Hatzfeld, PhD, RN, APHN-BC
Lt. Col. U.S. Air Force
Defense Medical Research and Development Program
Fort Detrick, MD

Brian D. Johnson, PhD, MDiv, PMHNP-BC, DABPS
University of San Diego
San Diego, CA

Meggan Jordan, PhD
Health Science Specialist
Center of Innovation for Disability and Rehabilitation Research
Veterans Health Administration
North Florida/South Georgia Veterans Health System
Gainesville, FL

John F. Kalinich, PhD
Armed Forces Radiobiology Research Institute
Uniformed Services University of the Health Sciences
Bethesda, MD

Christine E. Kasper, PhD, RN, FAAN, FACSM
Department of Veterans Affairs, Office of Nursing Services
Washington, DC
Daniel K. Inouye Graduate School of Nursing
Uniformed Services University of the Health Sciences
Bethesda, MD

Paul C. Lewis PhD, RN, FNP-BC
Col. U.S. Army
Assistant Professor
Daniel K. Inouye Graduate School of Nursing
Uniformed Services University of the Health Sciences
Bethesda, MD

Elizabeth A. Mann-Salinas, PhD, RN
LTC U.S. Army
U.S. Army Institute of Surgical Research
San Antonio, TX

Melissa A. McDiarmid, MD, PhD, DABT
Department of Veterans Affairs
VA Medical Center
Department of Medicine Occupational Health Program
University of Maryland School of Medicine
Baltimore, MD

Diane L. Padden, PhD, CRNP, FAANP
Vice President of Research, Education and Professional Practice
American Association of Nurse Practitioners
Austin, TX

Susan M. Perry, PhD, CRNA
Col. U.S. Air Force
Senior Air Force Faculty
Assistant Professor, Daniel K. Inouye Graduate School of Nursing
Uniformed Services University of the Health Sciences
Bethesda, MD

Patricia Schmidt, MSN, RN
LTC U.S. Army
Daniel K. Inouye Graduate School of Nursing
Uniformed Services University of the Health Sciences
Bethesda, MD

Katherine S. Squibb, PhD
Department of Veterans Affairs
VA Medical Center
Department of Medicine Occupational Health Program
University of Maryland School of Medicine
Baltimore, MD

J. Frank Titch, DNP, CRNA, RN
School of Nursing, Nurse Anesthesia Program
Duke University School of Nursing
Durham, NC

Constance R. Uphold, PhD, ARNP, FAAN
Research Health Scientist
Center of Innovation for Disability and Rehabilitation Research
Associate Director of Implementation & Outcomes Research
Geriatric Research Education
Clinical Center, Veterans Health Administration
North Florida/South Georgia Veterans Health System
Gainesville, FL

Charles A. Vacchiano, PhD, RN
CAPT (ret) U.S. Navy
School of Nursing, Nurse Anesthesia Program
Duke University School of Nursing
Durham, NC

Elizabeth A. Vane, MSN, RN
Col. U. S. Army
U.S. Army Medical Department Center of History and Heritage
Fort Sam Houston, TX

Sally Weinrich, PhD, RN, FAAN
University of San Diego
San Diego, CA

Kenneth A. Wofford, PhD, CRNA
CDR U.S. Navy
Daniel K. Inouye Graduate School of Nursing
Uniformed Services University of the Health Sciences
Bethesda, MD

Preface

This 32th volume in the *Annual Review of Nursing Research* series delves into the continually expanding area of research into military and Veterans health care. Dr. Patricia Watts Kelley, a well-known scholar and researcher in the field of military nursing, health care, and research, has served with distinction as the volume editor. Drawing from her career as a prominent and dedicated member of the United States Navy Nurse Corps, director of the TriService Nursing Research Program, and currently a member of the Department of Veterans Affairs, Office of Research and Development directing the Nursing Research Initiative, content for the chapters was carefully chosen and compiled into this review of nursing research in "Military and Veteran Innovations of Care." As series editor, it is my hope that these topically based chapters will be used not only by those conducting research studies, but also as texts and supplements to nursing curricula for both undergraduate and graduate students, as the advances in military health care during war has provided the innovations that move the conduct of clinical care in the civilian sector.

Since the start of the deep unrest in the Middle East, and terrorist attacks in the United States and throughout the world in 2001, nursing and other healthcare providers have been faced with caring for patients with a level of complexity of care and polytrauma previously unseen in either military or civilian hospitals. Recovery and rehabilitation is now central to continued quality of life as advanced emergency trauma interventions have succeeded in substantially increasing the magnitude of survival of the injured. It should be noted that despite the growing "firepower" and lethality of weapons, survival rates continue to increase. In the earliest of known wars detailed in Homer's *The Iliad,* overall mortality rates were 77%. During the Civil War of the United States these rates fell to 14%, and again declined to 4% during the Vietnam War (Allison, 2009; Gawande, 2004). While many areas of specialty saw improvement in care, the dramatic fall in mortality can be attributed to three broad areas: improvement in systems of care, wound management, and treatment of shock. The knowledge of these has formed the basis of much of modern medicine and health care.

While it is impossible to provide a detailed and comprehensive review of the vast outpouring of recent military and Veteran research related to nursing practice and research, this volume thoughtfully and clearly presents key areas of study, which lend themselves for translation to clinical settings or expansion into other related areas of research. It should also be noted that the complexity of the research has led to nurse scientists engaging with new and more expansive programs of interdisciplinary research. These interdisciplinary teams have aided in the movement of core nursing disciplinary thought into broader research thought and practice.

This volume is comprised of nine chapters. These begin with Charles A. Vacchiano, Kenneth A. Wofford, and J. Frank Titch addressing the effects of surgery on posttraumatic stress disorder (PTSD) in Chapter 1. In Chapter 2, Patricia Schmidt and Elizabeth A. Mann-Salinas review the advances and changes in the delivery of care to those with severe burns. Jennifer J. Hatzfeld, Susan Dukes, and Elizabeth Bridges discuss innovations of en route care and the transport of the severely injured in Chapter 3. John F. Kalinich and colleagues examine the pathophysiologic effects of military relevant and other embedded metals in Chapter 4.

The volume continues with an in-depth review by Jill E. Bormann, Sally Weinrich, Carolyn B. Allard, Danielle Beck, Brian D. Johnson, and Lindsay Cosco Holt on the novel and effective use of mantram repetition and complementary medicine practices to treat stress and PTSD in military and Veterans in Chapter 5. Janice Agazio, Petra Goodman, and Diane L. Padden tackle the important issue of the effects of deployment on military families in Chapter 6. In Chapter 7, Susan M. Perry reviews the impact of stress and the autonomic nervous system in the triggering of malignant hyperthermia events. In Chapter 8, Constance R. Uphold, Meggan Jordan, and Magaly Freytes and tackle the facilitation building of nursing capacity and research in the family caregivers of Veterans. In the final chapter, Paul C. Lewis investigates the history and future research in the use of prehospital tourniquet use.

It is easy to dismiss the body of work focusing on military and Veteran care as not applying to research and patient care in the civilian world; however, one would be remiss to do so, as much of the body of medical, nursing, and health-care science can be directly traced to wars and combat. It is hoped that this volume will inspire both researchers and clinicians in all sectors of health care to carefully consider the impact that service in the military has on their patients, and motivate the next generation of researchers to continue to pursue those avenues of inquiry which will better the lives of those who have "borne the battle," and their families (Lincoln, 1865).

Christine E. Kasper, PhD, RN, FAAN
Series Editor

REFERENCES

Allison, C. E., & Trunkey, D. D. (2009). Battlefield trauma, traumatic shock and consequences: War-related advances in critical care. *Critical Care Clinics, 25*(1), 31–45, vii. http://dx.doi.org/ 10.1016/j.ccc.2008.10.001

Gawande, A. (2004). Casualties of war: Military care for the wounded from Iraq and Afghanistan. *New England Journal of Medicine, 351*(24), 2471–2475. http://dx.doi.org/ 10.1056/NEJMp048317

Lincoln, A. (1865). *Second inaugural address* (Vol. Senate document [United States. Congress. Senate]; 101–10.). Washington, DC: U.S. G.P.O.

Acknowledgments

The editor would like to acknowledge the support of the Department of Defense, Uniformed Services University of the Health Sciences, the Department of Veterans Affairs, Office of Research and Development, and the Office of Nursing Services.

Patricia Watts Kelley

Dedication

This volume is dedicated to the Veterans of the United States of America and the service members of the U.S. military and their families, without whose honor, courage, commitment, and sacrifice, this work would not be possible. Thank you!

ANNUAL REVIEW OF NURSING RESEARCH

VOLUME 32, 2014

CHAPTER 1

Posttraumatic Stress Disorder

A View From the Operating Theater

Charles A. Vacchiano, Kenneth A. Wofford, and J. Frank Titch

ABSTRACT

Posttraumatic stress disorder (PTSD) is an anxiety disorder that develops following exposure to a traumatic event. The prevalence and symptom severity of PTSD is greater in military combat Veterans than the civilian population. Although PTSD is a psychiatric disorder, in Veterans, it is associated with several physical comorbidities, chronic pain, substance abuse, and worse self-reported health status which may predispose them to greater perioperative morbidity and mortality. At present, the effect of surgery on the severity of PTSD is largely unknown. However, the perioperative clinician should consider PTSD a chronic illness associated with the accumulation of risk factors across the life span.

POSTTRAUMATIC STRESS DISORDER

Posttraumatic stress disorder (PTSD) is an anxiety disorder characterized by unwanted recurrent memories, avoidant behavior, physiological reactivity, emotional numbing, and intrusive thoughts that develop after exposure to a traumatic event and persist for at least 1 month (American Psychiatric Association, 2000). The lifetime prevalence of PTSD in the United States is estimated to be 6.8% (Kessler et al., 2005). The prevalence is greater in military Veterans, with 9%–43% demonstrating the disorder depending on the method used to diagnose

http://dx.doi.org/10.1891/0739-6686.32.1

PTSD and the Veteran's era of service (Blake, Keane, et al., 1990; Dohrenwend et al., 2006; Hoge & Castro, 2006; Hoge et al., 2004; Vasterling et al., 2010).

There are 20 recognized symptoms of PTSD, divided into four clusters (Table 1.1; American Psychiatric Association, 2013). In order for a patient to be diagnosed with PTSD, he or she must (a) have been exposed to a traumatic event which evoked intense feelings of fear, hopelessness, or horror; (b) demonstrate at least one clinically significant symptom of intrusion, one clinically significant symptom of avoidance, two clinically significant symptoms of negative

TABLE 1.1

Symptoms of Posttraumatic Stress Disorder

Cluster	Symptom
Intrusion	Intrusive memories of traumatic event(s)
	Nightmares involving traumatic event(s)
	Dissociative reactions
	Psychological distress after exposure to reminders of traumatic event(s)
	Physiologic reactivity after exposure to reminders of traumatic event(s)
Avoidance	Persistent efforts to avoid thoughts or feelings related to the traumatic event(s)
	Persistent efforts to avoid external reminders of the traumatic event(s)
Negative alterations in mood and/or cognition	Inability to recall important features of the traumatic event(s)
	Negative beliefs about oneself and the world
	Distorted blame of self and/or others for the traumatic event(s) and sequelae
	Negative emotions related to the traumatic event(s)
	Diminished interest in activities
	Sense of alienation from others
	Inability to experience positive emotions
Hyperarousal/hyperreactivity	Irritability or aggressive behavior
	Self-destructive or reckless behavior
	Hypervigilance
	Exaggerated startle response
	Difficulty concentrating
	Disturbances of sleep

Note. From *Diagnostic and Statistical Manual of Mental Disorders*, 5th ed., by the American Psychiatric Association, 2013, Washington, DC. Copyright 2013 by the American Psychiatric Association.

alterations in mood and/or cognition, and two clinically significant symptoms of hyperarousal/hyperreactivity which persisted for at least 1 month; (c) have symptoms that adversely impacted functioning or resulted in significant distress; and (d) lack an alternative organic cause (e.g., substance use, medications, illness) for symptoms (American Psychiatric Association, 2013).

Dual representation is a predominant theory of how a patient develops and maintains PTSD after exposure to a traumatic event (Brewin, Dalgleish, & Joseph, 1996). Dual representation theory posits that memories of a traumatic event exist in the form of verbally and/or situationally accessible memories. Verbally accessible memories are voluntarily accessible and have manageable emotional impact when recalled. In contrast, situationally accessible memories are accessed involuntarily in response to reminders of the trauma or during states of intense arousal and are accompanied by an emotional state similar to that experienced during the traumatic event.

PTSD develops when situationally accessible memories of a traumatic event are accompanied by incomplete verbally accessible memories of that event. When triggered by reminders of the trauma or heightened states of emotional arousal, unopposed situationally accessible memories produce intense emotional and somatic states similar to those experienced during the trauma, resulting in an overgeneralized fear response. Cognitive and exposure therapies for PTSD assist the person to form verbally accessible memories of the information held in situationally accessible memories by talking about, imagining, or actually being exposed to trauma-related cues (Brewin, 2001).

Although cognitive and exposure therapies are the mainstays of treatment, many patients with PTSD will receive some form of pharmacotherapy (Foa, Keane, & Friedman, 2000). The first-line medications for the treatment of PTSD are the selective serotonin reuptake inhibitors (SSRIs; Foa et al., 2000). When SSRIs and time are ineffective in decreasing the severity of posttraumatic symptoms, additional medications may be added (Foa et al., 2000).

PTSD as a Chronic Illness

Despite the availability of evidence-based treatment, there is evidence that many Veterans may develop chronic PTSD. For example, a sample (Solomon & Mikulincer, 2006) of Israeli combat Veterans who participated in the 1984 Lebanon conflict demonstrated a 39% incidence of PTSD 1 year after exposure and 19% incidence of PTSD 20 years after exposure to combat. This finding suggests that only half of those Veterans who developed PTSD went on to experience complete and sustained resolution of symptoms. Similar results have been reported in U.S. Veterans: Perconte, Griger, and Bellucci (1989) reported that 55% of Vietnam Veterans who demonstrated significant posttraumatic symptom improvement after 4 weeks of inpatient treatment were rehospitalized for posttraumatic symptom recurrence within 2 years. Aging and cognitive decline may also affect PTSD severity because several case reports describe sudden onset or relapse of previously well-controlled posttraumatic symptoms in older Veterans with new-onset cognitive impairment (Hamilton & Workman, 1998; Mittal, Torres, Abashidze, & Jimerson, 2001). Therefore, data suggests that some Veterans with a history of PTSD may never be completely free of the disorder (Foa, Keane, Friedman, & Cohen, 2009). The chronicity of PTSD in some Veterans means that posttraumatic symptoms may still affect that patient's care decades after the traumatic event.

POSTTRAUMATIC STRESS DISORDER IN THE SURGICAL PATIENT

Considerable effort has been devoted to defining patients at risk for morbidity and mortality after surgery and establishing evidence-based recommendations for their perioperative care. As a result, evidence-based practice guidelines exist for the preoperative preparation, intraoperative management, and postoperative care of patients with cardiac, pulmonary, and neurological illnesses. In contrast, few studies have examined the effect of mental illnesses such as PTSD on risk of morbidity and mortality after surgery and little evidence exists to guide the perioperative care of such patients (Copeland et al., 2008).

Prevalence and Severity of PTSD in Veterans Undergoing Surgery

The prevalence of PTSD in Veterans undergoing surgery differs depending on the surgical diagnosis. In Veterans presenting for elective noncardiac surgery, approximately 8% were previously diagnosed with PTSD (Brzezinski, Marmar, Cason, Au, & Wallace, 2009a, 2009b), suggesting prevalence similar to the 6.8% estimated in the general populace of Americans (Kessler et al., 2005). However, approximately 35% of a sample of military Veterans undergoing cardiac surgery had been previously diagnosed with PTSD (Hudetz et al., 2010). The greater prevalence of PTSD in Veterans undergoing cardiac surgery may represent a selection effect in which the cardiovascular risk factors, depression, and health risk behaviors such as substance abuse associated with PTSD predispose Veterans with the disorder to develop coronary artery disease necessitating surgical intervention (Brzezinski et al., 2009b; Buckley, Mozley, Bedard, Dewulf, & Greif, 2004; Hudetz et al., 2010).

The validity of using a previous diagnosis to identify patients with PTSD has been challenged based on that diagnostic criteria change over time and are inconsistent across screening instruments (Tully, 2010). In a sample of Veterans previously diagnosed with PTSD (*N* = 29) and administered the Clinician-Administered PTSD Scale (CAPS) before undergoing elective outpatient surgery, 83% met criteria for PTSD 1 week preoperatively (when scored using the "symptom frequency ≥ 1, intensity ≥ 2" rule proposed by Blake, Weathers, et al., 1990; Wofford, 2012). In this sample, the mean preoperative posttraumatic symptom severity score was 69.6 (*SE* = 5.0), indicating severe clinical posttraumatic symptoms (Weathers, Keane, & Davidson, 2001), with a mean symptom duration of 24.8 years (*SE* = 3.1; Wofford, Hertzberg, Silva, & Vacchiano, in press). These findings indicate that Veterans with a previous diagnosis of PTSD who were awaiting surgery were at increased risk of meeting criteria for the disorder at clinically relevant levels of severity, even decades after being exposed to a traumatic event.

At present, the effect of surgery on severity of posttraumatic symptoms is largely unknown. Veterans with preexisting PTSD did not report significant increases in posttraumatic symptom severity after elective outpatient surgery (Wofford et al., in press). After gastric bypass surgery, outpatient medical records indicated that mental health clinicians' global impressions were that posttraumatic symptom severity had improved in 41%, worsened in 8.3%, and remained unchanged in 50% of Veterans with preexisting PTSD (Ikossi, Maldonado, Hernandez-Boussard, & Eisenberg, 2010). Therefore, there is a lack of evidence at present that surgery is associated with increases in posttraumatic symptom severity.

Depression

Several studies have noted an association between PTSD and depression. Among Veterans who underwent major noncardiac surgery, the prevalence of depression was 36% in Veterans with PTSD versus 3.5% in Veterans without PTSD (Brzezinski et al., 2009b). In a sample of Veterans with PTSD undergoing outpatient elective surgery, the prevalence of lifetime depression was 62% with a mean preoperative Geriatric Depression Scale severity score of 18.3 (*N* = 29, *SD* = 1.7), indicating mild to moderate depressive symptom severity (Wofford et al., in press). Among Veterans who underwent coronary artery bypass graft (CABG) surgery, the prevalence of depression was 53% in Veterans with PTSD versus 9% in Veterans without PTSD (Hudetz et al., 2010). When compared with the 16.6% lifetime prevalence of depression reported in the National Comorbidity Study, these findings indicate that patients presenting for surgery with PTSD were more likely to have a lifetime diagnosis of depression than the average American (Kessler et al., 2005).

A portion of this relationship can be attributed to the similarity of posttraumatic and depressive symptoms. Depression and PTSD share the symptoms of loss of interest in significant activities, insomnia, and difficulty concentrating (American Psychiatric Association, 2000) and items assessing these symptoms appear on measures of both depression and PTSD. However, studies on pairs of twins who served in the military during the Vietnam era have shown that PTSD and depression may share a common genetic liability. Pairs of monozygous twins were more likely than pairs of dizygous twins to develop comorbid PTSD and depression when controlling for various life experiences, including exposure to traumatic events (Koenen et al., 2008). Therefore, depressive symptoms and post-traumatic symptoms correlate, and this correlation may arise from a genetic basis.

Although the association between PTSD and depression is well-described, there is no evidence at present that surgery adversely affects depressive symptoms in Veterans with PTSD. Depressive symptom severity was unchanged in a sample of Veterans with preexisting PTSD from before to 3 months after elective outpatient surgery (Wofford et al., in press). These findings suggest that Veterans with preexisting PTSD can undergo relatively minor procedures without experiencing depressive symptom exacerbation, but the findings cannot be applied to Veterans undergoing more extensive or debilitating procedures.

Substance Use

Veterans presenting for surgery with PTSD demonstrated greater prevalence of alcohol, tobacco, and other drug abuse than Veterans without PTSD. Before major elective surgery, Veterans with PTSD demonstrated three times greater prevalence of smoking (37.1% vs. 11.6%), five times greater prevalence of alcohol abuse (25.8% vs. 4.4%), and more than three times greater prevalence of other drug abuse (57.7% vs. 14.6%) compared to Veterans without PTSD (Brzezinski et al., 2009b). Before CABG, Veterans with PTSD demonstrated more than two times greater prevalence of alcohol dependence (50% vs. 20%) than Veterans without PTSD (Hudetz et al., 2010). These findings are consistent with studies of outpatient Veterans with PTSD. Outpatient Veterans with PTSD reported approximately twice the national average prevalence of tobacco, alcohol, and drug use (Buckley et al., 2004). The prevalence of concurrent substance abuse disorders and PTSD may represent self-medication of PTSD symptoms or a vulnerability of the Veteran that facilitates the development of both substance use disorder and PTSD (Brown & Wolfe, 1994). Therefore, Veterans with PTSD are more likely to be engaged in some form of substance use regardless of the setting in which they are encountered.

Cognitive Function

In addition to greater prevalence of cardiovascular risk factors and depression, Veterans with PTSD also demonstrate worse preoperative cognitive function.

Before CABG, Veterans with PTSD demonstrated worse cognitive functioning on measures of verbal memory in comparison to both Veterans without PTSD and nonsurgical Veterans of similar age (Hudetz et al., 2010). This finding was consistent with previous research regarding the relationship between PTSD and cognitive functioning in nonsurgical populations that suggest that cognitive capability was inversely related to posttraumatic symptoms (Macklin et al., 1998; McNally & Shin, 1995; Vasterling & Brailey, 2005). In particular, Veterans with PTSD performed worse than Veterans without PTSD on tasks that required the respondent to immediately learn and retain new information for a short time, manipulate that information in a meaningful way, and produce a response based on the manipulated information—a set of tasks collectively known as *executive function* (Beckham, Crawford, & Feldman, 1998; Gilbertson, Gurvits, Lasko, Orr, & Pitman, 2001; Hart et al., 2008). These findings suggest that the cognitive deficits associated with PTSD are concentrated in specific domains rather than affecting overall intelligence and result in the patient having decreased cognitive reserve (Beckham et al., 1998; Gilbertson et al., 2001; Hart et al., 2008).

Cognitive reserve refers to the hypothesis that premorbid cognitive abilities create a buffer against the sequelae of degenerative neurological processes such as Alzheimer's disease, allowing cognition to undergo a process of graceful degradation as damage or disruption progresses. When less cognitive reserve is present, less damage or disruption is required to produce overt clinical signs of brain dysfunction such as dementia or delirium. Cognitive reserve has been estimated with proxies such as performance during neuropsychological testing and educational level, and those proxies of cognitive reserve have demonstrated predictive value for delirium and cognitive decline after surgery (Greene et al., 2009; Moller et al., 1998; Monk et al., 2008).

To date, only one study has investigated PTSD as a predictor of cognitive decline after surgery. One week after CABG, subjects with preexisting PTSD were more likely to demonstrate a significant decline in nonverbal memory, verbal memory, and executive function than subjects without PTSD (Hudetz et al., 2010). This finding suggests that Veterans with preexisting PTSD may be more vulnerable to cognitive decline after surgery but cannot clarify whether the greater risk of cognitive decline after surgery was attributable to PTSD or to associated factors such as comorbid depression or a history of alcohol abuse.

Emergence Delirium

Emergence delirium (ED) is a self-limiting syndrome that occurs immediately or shortly after emergence from general anesthesia and is characterized by psychomotor agitation ranging from frequent, nonpurposeful movement to overt physical aggressiveness (Smessaert, Schehr, & Artusio, 1960; Radtke et al., 2010;

Lepouse, Lautner, Liu, Gomis, & Leon, 2006). The etiology of ED is unknown. One current hypothesis for the occurrence of ED is that brain regions recover at different rates from general anesthesia and that this differential recovery rate can result in disinhibition and disorientation immediately after surgery. When the disinhibited and disoriented patient is exposed to a noxious stimulus, he or she responds with psychomotor agitation (Yu et al., 2010). ED in adult patients is relatively uncommon with an incidence estimated at 5% in the civilian surgical population (Lepouse et al., 2006). However, military anesthesia providers and postanesthesia care unit (PACU) nurses have observed an increasing number of patients with combat exposure emerging from general anesthesia confused, agitated, angry, verbal, combative, and violent with thrashing behaviors (McGuire & Burkard, 2010). The incidence and severity of ED is suspected to be greater in the wounded warrior population as compared to civilian patients (McGuire, 2012; Wilson & Pokorny, 2012). McGuire and Burkard (2010) surveyed 72 military certified registered nurse anesthetists and reported a 27% incidence of ED behaviors either in the operating room (OR), the PACU, or both.

Mental health issues such as PTSD, anxiety, and depression are common following military deployment (Hoge et al., 2008). Military combat Veterans experience more severe PTSD symptomatology, especially dissociative experiences, when compared to civilian noncombat victims (Naifeh et al., 2008). McGuire (2012) have noted that PTSD, anxiety, and depression in wounded warriors are risk factors for developing ED. Radtke and colleagues (2010) have reported that premedication with benzodiazepines was a risk factor for ED in civilian patients. He suggested that patients with psychological disturbances more frequently request preoperative sedation, and therefore, the increased risk of ED may be associated with these disturbances. Likewise, Burns (2003) noted in a case report that the interaction of anesthetic medications with antidepressants along with the patient's baseline psychosocial dysfunctional issues markedly increased the likelihood of ED.

Little has been published regarding ED in the nongeriatric population in the peer-reviewed literature in the last decade likely because of its low incidence and limited impact in civilian anesthesia practice. The sum of this body of work amounts to four peer-reviewed studies and a similar number of reviews or commentaries regarding ED including one in military patients (Hudek, 2009; Lepouse et al., 2006; McGuire & Burkard, 2010; O'Brien, 2002; Radtke et al., 2008, 2010; Yu et al., 2010). A growing number of wounded warrior surgical patients develop severe ED in the OR which may continue for several hours in the PACU. This form of ED presents fundamentally different from ED observed in the civilian population. The wounded warrior patient appears to experience a flashback of the combat environment which manifest as aggressive disoriented behavior expressed by intense fear and active resistance to being physically touched or confined in any way (McGuire, 2012). These behaviors can result in the removal of intravenous, arterial, or central lines and damage to the surgical repair; are a direct and significant threat to the health and safety of the patient and his or her caregivers; and are a growing concern in the OR and PACU (Hudek, 2009; O'Brien, 2002). The fact that many of these wounded warriors are exposed to multiple anesthetics and surgical procedures makes the potential for ED an even greater concern. There are presently no evidence-based strategies to prevent or treat ED in adult civilian patients or wounded warriors. Anecdotal recommendations from studies of ED include avoiding preoperative benzodiazepines; ruling out potential physiological causes such as airway obstruction or hypoxemia; identifying and eliminating noxious stimuli such as urinary retention, bright lights, and environmental noise; treating pain; and removing tubes and catheters as early as possible. If these strategies are unsuccessful, then a small amount of a rapid-acting sedative such as propofol or midazolam is recommended to keep the patient from injuring themselves or others (Lepouse et al., 2006; Radtke et al., 2010; Yu et al., 2010).

Although anecdotal reports from the military anesthesia community suggest that the incidence of ED in the wounded warrior patient population is increasing, no multiservice, systematic prospective research has been implemented to confirm this observation. Understanding ED in the military patient is problematic because no standardized validated instrument exists to identify ED or quantify its severity. Determining the true incidence and severity as well as identifying strategies to reduce and prevent ED in the wounded warrior population are important objectives. The first steps to achieve these objectives are to identify behaviors associated with ED in this population, to determine the relevance of existing instruments with respect to these behaviors, and to examine the feasibility of using such an instrument to measure ED in military ORs and PACUs. The ability to ascertain the risk for and quantify the incidence and severity of ED in the wounded warrior population as a first step toward developing clinical interventions is hampered by the lack of a military-specific measurement tool.

Cardiovascular Risk Factors

Although PTSD is a psychiatric disorder, it is associated with physical comorbidity. Veterans diagnosed with PTSD prior to surgery demonstrate greater prevalence of cardiovascular risk factors, and this finding is most likely attributable to lifestyle. In Veterans presenting for major elective surgery, patients with PTSD had greater prevalence of hypertension, diabetes, and hypercholesterolemia than patients without PTSD despite being an average of 6 years of age younger

(Brzezinski et al., 2009b). Veterans with PTSD presenting for major elective surgery also had greater prevalence of health risk behaviors including smoking, drug abuse, and alcohol abuse than Veterans without PTSD (Brzezinski et al., 2009b).

Subjective Health Status

Subjective health status is the patient's assessment of his or her own health status and is a holistic concept that includes aspects of physical and mental well-being (Covinsky et al., 1999; Smith, Avis, & Assmann, 1999). Before undergoing outpatient elective surgery, a sample of Veterans with preexisting PTSD reported mean physical subjective health status an average of 1.3 standard deviations below population norms. After elective outpatient surgery, Veterans reported a 0.4 standard deviations decline in physical subjective health status but recovered to baseline by 1 month after surgery. Similar patterns were observed for mental subjective health status. Before undergoing outpatient elective surgery, a sample of Veterans with preexisting PTSD reported mean mental subjective health status an average of 1.4 standard deviations below population norms. After elective outpatient surgery, Veterans reported a 0.3 standard deviations decline in mental subjective health status but recovered to baseline by 1 month after surgery.

The poor baseline physical health status in Veterans with PTSD is consistent with findings in outpatient Veterans. In outpatient Veterans, PTSD was associated with worse subjective health status, including greater pain, greater impairment of role performance, worse perceived physical functioning, and worse perceived overall physical health (Buckley et al., 2004). These findings may be the result of information processing biases in PTSD that cause the patient to negatively interpret ambiguous health cues (Constans, 2005). The poor subjective health status of Veterans with PTSD is concerning because subjective physical or mental health status more than 1 standard deviation below population normative values has been associated with increased risk of 1 year mortality (Fan, Au, McDonell, & Fihn, 2004).

Postoperative Mortality

In large datasets, preexisting PTSD was associated with greater risk of short- and long-term postoperative mortality (Brzezinski et al., 2009a). In a retrospective study of Veterans undergoing major elective surgery, Veterans with PTSD were approximately three times more likely to die within 1 or 5 years of undergoing major elective surgery than Veterans without PTSD, even after controlling for other predictors of mortality such as age, hypertension, diabetes, hypercholesterolemia, depression, and tobacco use (Brzezinski et al., 2009a). However, the investigators did not report on the statistical effect of interactions among predictors of mortality; that is, they did not report whether greater mortality was related to specific combinations of mortality predictors in a given patient (Brzezinski et al., 2009b). Therefore, data suggests that there was an association between preexisting PTSD and postoperative mortality but does not elucidate whether this greater mortality was related to the presence of specific combinations of comorbid cardiovascular risk factors, to the severity of comorbid illness that was not captured by the databases, or to an effect of PTSD which was independent of surgery.

The greater risk of postoperative mortality in Veterans with PTSD may be an epiphenomenon unrelated to surgery. Studies of Vietnam-era Veterans have demonstrated that since the war, those with PTSD were more likely to die from cardiovascular and external causes, including suicide, homicide, and accidents, than those without PTSD (Boscarino, 2006a, 2006b, 2008a, 2008b). As noted, this greater mortality is likely mediated by lifestyle (Boscarino, 2006b). Therefore, studies that estimate the risk of postoperative mortality in Veterans with PTSD in comparison to Veterans without PTSD may be confounding maturation and history; that is, studies may confound the natural maturation of mortality in Veterans with PTSD with the historical effect of having surgery. Such a comparison may lead to data that suggests that Veterans with PTSD are exposed to greater risk of mortality by undergoing surgery when actually, they are at greater risk of mortality than their peers without PTSD, but the magnitude of risk is relatively unaffected by surgery.

Other Outcomes

Despite its association with postoperative mortality, the presence of PTSD or severity of posttraumatic symptoms was unrelated to many other common metrics of postoperative outcome. Hudetz et al. (2010) reported that a previous diagnosis of PTSD was unrelated to length of intensive care unit (ICU) stay and 6-month incidence of hospital readmission after cardiac surgery. In addition, Oxlad, Stubberfield, Stuklis, Edwards, & Wade (2006a, 2006b) found that posttraumatic symptom severity was inversely related to length of ICU stay and unrelated to risk of rehospitalization within 6 months of surgery. After gastric bypass surgery, a previous diagnosis of PTSD was unrelated to length of hospital stay, incidence of postoperative complications, and 1-year weight loss (Ikossi et al., 2010). Therefore, PTSD has not been demonstrated to be a predictor of hospital length of stay, readmission rate, or certain surgery-specific outcomes after cardiac or gastric bypass surgery.

A Novel Approach to Treatment of PTSD

Although several interventions are available to treat PTSD ranging from yoga to psychotherapeutic approaches with or without various combinations of pharmacotherapeutics, not all patients respond to initial treatment, and many patients remain resistant to long-term therapies. At present, most therapies rely heavily on the use of SSRIs (Ipser & Stein, 2012). Yet only 50%–60% of patients treated with SSRIs obtain an appreciable reduction in PTSD symptoms (Institute of Medicine, 2012). The Assistant Secretary of Defense for Health Affairs has noted (U.S. Department of Defense, 2012), "PTSD and mild traumatic brain injury (mTBI) are two of the most prevalent injuries suffered by our warfighters in Iraq and Afghanistan, and identifying better treatments for those impacted is critical. Therefore, we must seek interventions with the greatest potential for improving care." An innovative therapeutic intervention using local anesthetic blockade of the stellate ganglion as reported by Lipov, Joshi, Lipov, Sanders, & Siroko (2008) may prove beneficial in the management of PTSD.

Historically, injection of local anesthetic around the stellate ganglion (stellate ganglion blockade [SGB]) was used to treat conditions ranging from severe hot flashes associated with menopause to mental depression (Karnosh & Gardner, 1947; Lipov, Lipov, & Stark, 2005). In 2008, Lipov and colleagues published a case report describing a previously diagnosed patient with PTSD suffering from profound anxiety and other related symptoms. Following injection of local anesthetic into the region of the right stellate ganglion 55 days posttrauma, the patient immediately reported that his anxiety had subsided. Three months following the procedure, he continued to report improved relief of his PTSD symptoms.

The stellate ganglion is located in the neck at the level of the seventh cervical and first thoracic vertebrae (Raj, 1996). Injection of local anesthetic in the area of the stellate ganglion is classically performed using an anterior approach at the level of the sixth cervical vertebrae. The goal of SGB is the interruption of sympathetic innervation to the head. Block of the stellate ganglion following local anesthetic injection is confirmed by a transient increase in blood flow and the development of Horner's syndrome (miosis, ptosis, and enophthalmos; Raj, 1996).

Although dual representation is a predominant theory of how an individual develops PTSD, the origin of PTSD is poorly understood, and the palliative effects of SGB are most likely more complicated than a transient increase in blood flow. Westerhaus and Loewy established stellate ganglion neural connections to the hypothalamus and amygdala in a rat model in 2001. Lipov, Joshi, Sanders, and Slavin (2009) postulated that the pathological state of PTSD results from increased levels of nerve growth factor producing elevated levels of brain norepinephrine. Indeed, infusing nerve growth factor into the brains of rats elicited sprouting of sympathetic axons and increased norepinephrine levels (Isaacson & Billieu, 1996). Previous studies also validated the release of norepinephrine in the amygdala along with noradrenergic activation as necessary for memory consolidation (McGaugh, 2013). Ferry and Quirarte (2012) have noted the role of norepinephrine modulation and its influence on inhibitory avoidance memory storage in the basolateral amygdala. Furthermore, Takatori, Kuroda, and Hirose (2006) found that local anesthetics suppress nerve growth factor–mediated neurite outgrowth which may then suppress sympathetic sprouting thus decreasing norepinephrine levels. Lipov and colleagues (2009) have therefore concluded that local anesthetic injection of the stellate ganglion reduces nerve growth factor, which reduces brain norepinephrine, thus deactivating the chronically active state of the sympathetic nervous system associated with PTSD.

Following Lipov and colleagues' (2008) report of a significant reduction in PTSD symptoms following a right-sided SGB in a 48-year-old male patient diagnosed with PTSD, Mulvaney, McLean, and de Leeuw (2010) described the successful use of a right-sided SGB to treat two soldiers diagnosed with chronic, combat-related PTSD. They also assessed the degree of symptom improvement using the Posttraumatic Stress Disorder Checklist (PCL). Both patients experienced immediate and sustained relief as measured by the PCL tool and eventually discontinued all antipsychotic and antidepressant medications. Recently, Hicky, Hanling, Pevney, Allen, and McLay (2012) reported a series of nine military patients with PTSD treated with SGB. The patients were evaluated before and after SGB using the CAPS, which is considered the gold standard for PTSD assessment. CAPS scores were tracked after a single injection of local anesthetic in seven patients, and a second treatment was performed 4–6 weeks later in two patients. Five patients reported a clinically significant reduction in PTSD symptoms as measured by the CAPS (>30% reduction) 1 week after the procedure. Two patients reported a noticeable reduction in symptoms, whereas the other two reported essentially no change in PTSD symptoms.

Given the prevalence of PTSD in the active duty and Veteran populations, the debilitating nature of this condition, the lack of a definitive treatment, and the potential value of local anesthetic blockade of the stellate ganglion in treating this malady, further study examining the safety and efficacy of SGB is warranted.

Cognitive Reserve Theory, PTSD, and Mild Traumatic Brain Injury

Military members deployed to Iraq and Afghanistan and exposed to blast from various improvised explosive devices often have minor or even no physical injuries but suffer a mild traumatic brain injury (mTBI). This injury is often associated with headaches; fatigue; and cognitive deficits including memory, attention, and comprehension; and emotional disturbances and depression (Hoge, Auchterlonie, & Milliken, 2006). However, these symptoms may not be apparent immediately following the traumatic event, which has led to this insult being referred to as a "silent injury." Approximately 20% of combat personnel returning from the Afghanistan and Iraq conflicts have experienced a traumatic brain injury (TBI) in theater (Jagoda et al., 2008). In addition, it has not gone unnoticed that the symptoms of mTBI and PTSD have significant overlap, and this complicates diagnosis and treatment. The initial evaluation of mTBI is a particular diagnostic and management challenge because the absence of clinical evidence of focal neurological findings does not exclude intracranial pathology.

It has become increasingly evident that neurocognitive abnormalities are common after brain trauma in patients with mTBI. These neurocognitive abnormalities may include deficits in several cognitive domains including attention, concentration, memory, executive function, and processing speed. Moreover, persistent postconcussive symptoms, including headache, irritability, photophobia, and sleep disturbance, are also common in this clinical population. Although these deficits are often subtle and do not result in obvious motor disability, they may seriously impair cognitive function and quality of life. Dikmen, Machamer, Winn, Anderson, and Temkin (2000) reported specific neurocognitive deficits that interfere with quality of life may persist for 6 months following mTBI. Kneafsey and Gawthorpe (2004) reviewed a large number of quantitative and qualitative studies exploring the impact of TBI and reported that even patients with mTBI may experience a range of physical, emotional, cognitive, and social and behavioral problems, and these problems will also have significant impact on the lives of their families. Vanderploeg, Curtiss, Luis, and Salazar (2007) examined the long-term neuropsychological outcomes in a large sample of nonreferred, nonlitigating community-dwelling male Veterans with an mTBI of on average 8 years duration. They compared this group to demographically similar normal controls and controls in motor vehicle accidents without head injury. The results of this study suggest that mTBI can have adverse long-term neuropsychological outcomes on subtle aspects of working memory and complex attention task. These findings provide clear evidence of some long-term neurobehavioral sequelae associated with mTBI.

The identification of postconcussive symptoms and cognitive abnormalities that persist following mTBI has been the subject of increased inquiry across several neurological disciplines. Unfortunately, the optimum management of patients presenting with mTBI remains poorly defined, and patients often do not receive adequate follow-up after discharge from the acute care setting. The identification of patients who may be at risk for residual neurocognitive sequelae remains difficult based on clinical examination even though it is widely accepted that TBI may affect several cognitive domains. Despite the lack of coordinated follow-up care and disagreement about which tests are capable of identifying specific immediate or delayed cognitive deficits, cognitive testing is commonly used to measure changes in cognitive performance over time in individuals who have suffered a brain injury. These cognitive tests are typically administered with the individual in a resting state without the intentional imposition of any physiological stressors. Although convenient to the examiner and the patient, this methodology may fail to reveal some cognitive deficits during testing because of a significant cognitive reserve present in many individuals.

The concept of cognitive reserve arose from the observation that different individuals exhibit variable thresholds for the presentation of symptoms after similar neurological insults. This threshold model suggests that there is a critical threshold of "brain reserve capacity" (BRC) such that specific clinical or functional deficits emerge once BRC is depleted past this threshold (Satz, 1993). This model begins to account for the disjunction between the extent of pathology and the extent of clinical change. For example, if two patients have differing amounts of BRC, a brain lesion of identical size may deplete BRC past the threshold where deficits are apparent in one patient but not in the other. In a healthy brain, cognitive reserve confers superior mental capability; in a damaged brain, cognitive reserve provides a means to compensate when repair cannot be achieved (Stern, 2009). A greater cognitive reserve is generally correlated with younger chronological age, a greater number of functioning neurons, and higher educational level (Stern, 2003). This suggests that the anatomic correlates to BRC might include the number of functioning neurons or the ability of a particular individual to recruit and use alternate information pathways to accomplish a cognitive task. From a clinical evaluation standpoint, the implication is that cognitive reserve can mask residual cognitive deficits and reduce the sensitivity of cognitive tests when administered in the traditional manner. This suggests the possibility of modifying the manner in which cognitive testing is performed by adding an intentional physiological stressor, with the goal of limiting the influence of cognitive reserve on the test results and discovering the true extent of potential cognitive deficits.

The idea of using a physiological stressor to unmask cognitive deficits was suggested by Ewing, McCarthy, Gronwall, and Wrightson's 1980 report in the clinical neuropsychology literature. The physiological stressor chosen by these investigators was hypoxic stress imposed by exposure to simulated altitude in a hypobaric chamber. Ewing and colleagues demonstrated that it was possible to detect latent cognitive deficits in subjects with a history of head injury (each who had an apparent full recovery) only when exposed to this hypoxic environment. Therefore, hypoxic stress produced the desirable effect of reducing the degree of cognitive reserve and served to increase the sensitivity of the cognitive test being used. This suggests the possible use of using this approach for the detection of cognitive deficits in patients with an mTBI and forms the basis for the creation of a "cognitive stress test." A cognitive stress test is based on a similar assumption to that of the much used cardiac stress test, which is to expose subtle deficits that are not apparent under conditions of physiological homeostasis by imposing a controlled stressor. In the case of the cardiac stress test, the stressor is typically aerobic or pharmacologically induced cardiac work that produces an imbalance between oxygen consumption and oxygen delivery capability in a diseased heart. This imbalance is assessed by monitoring electrocardiographic changes with the goal of exposing latent coronary artery disease. For the cognitive stress test, the stressor is exposure to a hypoxic environment combined with cognitive performance testing with the goal of exposing subtle cognitive deficits.

Despite Ewing and colleagues (1980) initial compelling results, there are no other reports in the literature of the use of hypoxic stress to unmask latent cognitive deficits in patients with TBI. Further investigation of this phenomenon has been impractical for several reasons. First, there is the extreme logistical difficulty faced by investigators in obtaining routine access to a hypobaric chamber necessary to produce the hypoxic environment. Second, use of a hypobaric chamber to produce a hypoxic environment has the attendant risk of barotraumas and decompression sickness. Third, there is a lack of normative data in the current scientific literature for cognitive performance under conditions of hypoxic stress. Detection of subtle deficits in patients with mTBI will require data that predict the expected performance reduction with hypoxic stress in the absence of cognitive deficits. If these barriers can be overcome, use of mild hypoxia in conjunction with existing cognitive testing may be a viable methodology to uncover latent cognitive dysfunction in patients with an mTBI who appear to have made an initial recovery.

DISCUSSIONS AND RESEARCH RECOMMENDATIONS/IMPLICATIONS

There are many unanswered questions about the effect of surgery on Veterans with PTSD. Accurate estimation of risk of postoperative morbidity and mortality in this population is further confounded by the patterns of risk factors associated with PTSD, and at present, there are no good theories in the literature that explicate a causal process between preexisting PTSD and greater risk of long-term mortality after surgery. Therefore, future research should aim to better define the contribution of PTSD to postoperative morbidity and mortality and to identify the unique perioperative needs of patients with PTSD.

Recent case reports indicate that local anesthetic block of the stellate ganglion may be a useful modality for treatment of PTSD; however, randomized controlled trials need to be undertaken before this treatment can be recommended. Finally, the ever increasing number of cases of mTBI demand further study to define the relationship and overlap between mTBI and PTSD and to discover better methods to evaluate those with mTBI for long-term cognitive deficits.

CONCLUSIONS

Veterans with preexisting PTSD present for surgery with risk factors which predispose them to greater postoperative morbidity and mortality, including greater prevalence of cardiovascular risk factors, depression, substance abuse, and chronic pain than Veterans without PTSD. Veterans with PTSD also perform worse on preoperative measures of cognitive function and may be at greater risk of cognitive decline after surgery, but this finding has only been investigated in patients undergoing cardiac surgery. Anecdotal and survey evidence suggest that recent Veterans of the Iraq and Afghanistan wars have a higher incidence of ED following general anesthesia than their civilian counterparts and its expression is fundamentally different from the ED observed in the civilian population. Veterans with PTSD demonstrate greater risk of long-term mortality after noncardiac surgery in large studies, but the mechanism by which PTSD influences risk of mortality after surgery is unclear. At present, there is no evidence to suggest that surgery systematically exacerbates posttraumatic or depressive symptoms in Veterans with PTSD, but this effect has only been studied after relatively minor surgeries.

The perioperative clinician should consider PTSD as a chronic illness associated with the accumulation of risk factors across the life span. Patients at high risk of exposure to traumatic events (e.g., Veterans) should be asked if they have PTSD. If a patient has PTSD, then the perioperative care should focus on identifying and managing comorbidities, including cardiac disease, substance use, mild cognitive impairment, and chronic pain, and discussions of perioperative risk should focus on the contribution of the specific risk factors present in that patient. Perioperative clinicians should inquire about potential PTSD symptom triggers (e.g., "Now that I have told you what we are going to do for you, is there anything about the process that makes you really nervous?") but should not engage the patient in an extensive discussion about his or her symptoms because discussion of traumatic events and posttraumatic symptoms can exacerbate anxiety (Foa et al., 2000) and are unlikely to help plan the patient's care.

After surgery, every effort should be made to ensure that the patient remains oriented to place and time. Benzodiazepines should be used judiciously because of their potential to disorient the patient and their association with emergence agitation (Lepouse et al., 2006; Radtke et al., 2010). If the patient with PTSD also has chronic pain, he or she may be opiate-tolerant, and multimodal pain management techniques should be incorporated into the plan of care because postoperative pain has been associated with emergence agitation as well (Lepouse et al., 2006; Radtke et al., 2010; Yu et al., 2010). If possible, trusted friends or family members should be available because their presence can help maintain or restore the patient's orientation to place and time in case of acute anxiety or flashbacks (Crosby, Mashour, Grodin, Jiang, & Osterman, 2007).

ACKNOWLEDGMENTS

The authors wish to thank the men and women of the Armed Forces for their willingness to put themselves in harm's way for the cause of liberty and the defense of their comrades in arms, especially those who have been injured physically or mentally, and the military and Veterans administration nurses who endeavor to make them whole again.

DISCLAIMER

The views expressed in this work are those of the authors and do not reflect the official policy or position of the U.S. government, Department of Defense, or Uniformed Services University of the Health Sciences.

REFERENCES

American Psychiatric Association. (2000). *Diagnostic criteria from DSM-IV-TR*. Washington, DC: Author.

American Psychiatric Association. (2013). *Diagnostic and statistical manual of mental disorders* (5th ed.). Washington, DC: Author.

Beckham, J. C., Crawford, A. L., & Feldman, M. E. (1998). Trail making test performance in Vietnam combat Veterans with and without posttraumatic stress disorder. *Journal of Traumatic Stress*, *11*(4), 811–819. http:dx.doi.org/10.1023/A:1024409903617

Blake, D. D., Keane, T. M., Wine, P. R., Mora, C., Taylor, K. L., & Lyons, J. A. (1990). Prevalence of PTSD symptoms in combat Veterans seeking medical treatment. *Journal of Traumatic Stress*, *3*(1), 15–27.

Blake, D. D., Weathers, F. W., Nagy, L. M., Kaloupek, D. G., Klauminzer, G., Charney, D. S., & Keane, T. M. (1990). A clinician rating scale for assessing current and lifetime PTSD: The CAPS-1. *Behavior Therapist*, (13), 187–188.

Boscarino, J. A. (2006a). External-cause mortality after psychologic trauma: The effects of stress exposure and predisposition. *Comprehensive Psychiatry*, *47*(6), 503–514. http://dx.doi.org/10.1016/j.comppsych.2006.02.006

Boscarino, J. A. (2006b). Posttraumatic stress disorder and mortality among U.S. Army Veterans 30 years after military service. *Annals of Epidemiology*, *16*(4), 248–256. http://dx.doi.org/10.1016/j.annepidem.2005.03.009

Boscarino, J. A. (2008a). A prospective study of PTSD and early-age heart disease mortality among Vietnam Veterans: Implications for surveillance and prevention. *Psychosomatic Medicine*, *70*(6), 668–676. http:dx.doi.org/10.1097/PSY.0b013e31817bccaf

Boscarino, J. A. (2008b). Psychobiologic predictors of disease mortality after psychological trauma: Implications for research and clinical surveillance. *Journal of Nervous and Mental Disease*, *196*(2), 100–107. http://dx.doi.org/10.1097/NMD.0b013e318162a9f5

Brewin, C. R. (2001). A cognitive neuroscience account of posttraumatic stress disorder and its treatment. *Behaviour Research and Therapy*, *39*(4), 373–393. http://dx.doi.org/10.1016/S0005-7967(00)00087-5

Brewin, C. R., Dalgleish, T., & Joseph, S. (1996). A dual representation theory of posttraumatic stress disorder. *Psychological Review*, *103*(4), 670–686.

Brown, P. J., & Wolfe, J. (1994). Substance abuse and post-traumatic stress disorder comorbidity. *Drug and Alcohol Dependence*, *35*(1), 51–59.

Brzezinski, M., Marmar, C., Cason, B., Au, S., & Wallace, A. (2009a, October). *Diagnosis of PTSD is associated with 1- and 5-year mortality*. Paper presented at the Annual Meeting of the American Society of Anesthesiologists, New Orleans, LA.

Brzezinski, M., Marmar, C., Cason, B., Au, S., & Wallace, A. (2009b, March). *Preoperative diagnosis of PTSD is associated with increased prevalence of cardiac risk factors*. Paper presented at the Annual Meeting of the American Society of Anesthesiologists, New Orleans, LA.

Buckley, T. C., Mozley, S. L., Bedard, M. A., Dewulf, A. C., & Greif, J. (2004). Preventive health behaviors, health-risk behaviors, physical morbidity, and health-related role functioning impairment in Veterans with post-traumatic stress disorder. *Military Medicine*, *169*(7), 536–540.

Burns, S. M. (2003). Delirium during emergence from anesthesia: A case study. *Critical Care Nurse*, *23*(1), 66–69.

Constans, J. (2005). Information-processing biases in PTSD. In J. J. Vasterling & C. R. Brewin (Eds.), *Neuropsychology of PTSD* (pp. 105–130). New York, NY: Guilford Press.

Copeland, L. A., Zeber, J. E., Pugh, M. J., Mortensen, E. M., Restrepo, M. I., & Lawrence, V. A. (2008). Postoperative complications in the seriously mentally ill: A systematic review of the literature. *Annals of Surgery*, *248*(1), 31–38. http://dx.doi.org/10.1097/SLA.0b013e3181724f25

Covinsky, K. E., Wu, A. W., Landefeld, C. S., Connors, A. F., Jr., Phillips, R. S., Tsevat, J., . . . Fortinsky, R. H. (1999). Health status versus quality of life in older patients: Does the distinction matter? *American Journal of Medicine*, *106*(4), 435–440. http://dx.doi.org/10.1016/S0002-9343(99)00052-2

Crosby, S. S., Mashour, G. A., Grodin, M. A., Jiang, Y., & Osterman, J. (2007). Emergence flashback in a patient with posttraumatic stress disorder. *General Hospital Psychiatry*, *29*(2), 169–171. http://dx.doi.org/10.1016/S0163-8343(06)00218-0

Dikmen, S. S., Machamer, J. E., Winn, H. R., Anderson, J. D., & Temkin, N. R. (2000). Neuropsychological effects of valproate in traumatic brain injury. *Neurology, 54,* 895–902.

Dohrenwend, B. P., Turner, J. B., Turse, N. A., Adams, B. G., Koenen, K. C., & Marshall, R. (2006). The psychological risks of Vietnam for US Veterans: A revisit with new data and methods. *Science*, *313*(5789), 979–982. http://dx.doi.org/10.1126/Science.1128944

Ewing, R., McCarthy, D., Gronwall, D., & Wrightson, P. (1980). Persisting effects of minor head injury observable during hypoxic stress. *Journal of Clinical Neuropsychology, 2*(2), 147–55.

Fan, V. S., Au, D. H., McDonell, M. B., & Fihn, S. D. (2004). Intraindividual change in SF-36 in ambulatory clinic primary care patients predicted mortality and hospitalizations. *Journal of Clinical Epidemiology*, *57*(3), 277–283. http://dx.doi.org/10.1016/j.jclinepi.2003.08.004

Ferry, B., & Quirarte, G. L. (2012). Role of norepinephrine in modulating inhibitory avoidance memory storage: Critical involvement of the basolateral amygdala. In B. Ferry (Ed.), *The amygdala: A discrete multitasking manager.* Rijeka, Croatia: InTech.

Foa, E. B., Keane, T. M., & Friedman, M. J. (2000). Guidelines for treatment of PTSD. *Journal of Traumatic Stress*, *13*(4), 539–588.

Foa, E. B., Keane, T. M., Friedman, M. J., & Cohen, J. A. (2009). *Effective treatments for PTSD: Guidelines from the International Society for Traumatic Stress Studies*. New York, NY: Guilford Press.

Gilbertson, M. W., Gurvits, T. V., Lasko, N. B., Orr, S. P., & Pitman, R. K. (2001). Multivariate assessment of explicit memory function in combat Veterans with posttraumatic stress disorder. *Journal of Traumatic Stress*, *14*(2), 413–432. http://dx.doi.org/10.1023/A:1011181305501

Greene, N. H., Attix, D. K., Weldon, B. C., Smith, P. J., McDonagh, D. L., & Monk, T. G. (2009). Measures of executive function and depression identify patients at risk for postoperative delirium. *Anesthesiology*, *110*(4), 788–795.

Hamilton, J. D., & Workman, R. H., Jr. (1998). Persistence of combat-related posttraumatic stress symptoms for 75 years. *Journal of Traumatic Stress, 11*(4), 763–768. http://dx.doi.org/10.1023/A:1024449517730

Hart, J., Jr., Kimbrell, T., Fauver, P., Cherry, B. J., Pitcock, J., Booe, L. Q., . . . Freeman, T. W. (2008). Cognitive dysfunctions associated with PTSD: Evidence from World War II prisoners of war. *Journal of Neuropsychiatry and Clinical Neurosciences, 20*(3), 309–316. http://dx.doi.org/10.1176/appi.neuropsych.20.3.309

Hicky, A., Hanling, S., Pevney, E., Allen, R., & McLay, R. N. (2012). Stellate ganglion block for PTSD. *The American Journal of Psychiatry, 169*(7), 760. http://dx.doi.org/10.1176/appi.ajp.2012.11111729

Hoge, C. W., Auchterlonie, J. L., Milliken, C. S. (2006). Mental health problems, use of mental health services, and attrition from military service after returning from deployment to Iraq or Afghanistan. *Journal of the American Medical Association, 295,* 1023–1032).

Hoge, C. W., Castro, C. A., Messer, S. C., McGurk, D., Cotting, D. I., & Koffman, R. L. (2008). Combat duty in Iraq and Afghanistan, mental health problems and barriers to care. *US Army Medical Department Journal,* 7–17.

Hoge, C. W., & Castro, C. A. (2006). Post-traumatic stress disorder in UK and US forces deployed to Iraq. *Lancet, 368*(9538), 837. http://dx.doi.org/10.1016/S0140-6736(06)69315-X

Hoge, C. W., Castro, C. A., Messer, S. C., McGurk, D., Cotting, D. I., & Koffman, R. L. (2004). Combat duty in Iraq and Afghanistan, mental health problems, and barriers to care. *New England Journal of Medicine, 351*(1), 13–22. http://dx.doi.org/10.1056/NEJMoa040603

Hudek, K. (2009). Emergence delirium: A nursing perspective. *AORN Journal, 17*(2), 384–392.

Hudetz, J. A., Gandhi, S. D., Iqbal, Z., Patterson, K. M., Byrne, A. J., Warltier, D. C., & Pagel, P. S. (2010). History of post-traumatic stress disorder is associated with impaired neuropsychometric performance after coronary artery surgery. *Journal of Cardiothoracic and Vascular Anesthesia, 24*(6), 964–968. http://dx.doi.org/10.1053/j.jvca.2010.02.019

Ikossi, D. G., Maldonado, J. R., Hernandez-Boussard, T., & Eisenberg, D. (2010). Post-traumatic stress disorder (PTSD) is not a contraindication to gastric bypass in Veterans with morbid obesity. *Surgical Endoscopy, 24*(8), 1892–1897. http://dx.doi.org/10.1007/s00464-009-0866-8

Institute of Medicine (U.S.). (2012). *Treatment for posttraumatic stress disorder in military and Veteran populations: Initial assessment.* Retrieved from http://www.iom.edu/Reports/2012/Treatment-for-Posttraumatic-Stress-Disorder-in-Military-and-Veteran-Populations-Initial-Assessment.aspx

Ipser, J. C., & Stein, D. J. (2012). Evidence-based pharmacotherapy of post-traumatic stress disorder (PTSD). *The International Journal of Neuropsychopharmacology, 15*(6), 825–840. http://dx.doi.org/10.1017/S1461145711001209

Isaacson, L. G., & Billieu, S. C. (1996). Increased perivascular norepinephrine following intracerebroventricular infusion of NGF into adult rats. *Experimental Neurology, 139*(1), 54–60. http://dx.doi.org/10.1006/exnr.1996.0080

Jagoda, A. S., Bazarian, J. J., Bruns, J. J., Cantrill, S. V., Gean, A. D., Howard, P. K., . . . Whitson, R. R. (2008). Clinical policy: Neuroimaging and decision making in adult mild traumatic brain injury in the acute setting. *Annals of Emergency Medicine, 52*(6), 714–748.

Karnosh, L. J., & Gardner, W. J. (1947). The effects of bilateral stellate ganglion block on mental depression; report of 3 cases. *Cleveland Clinic Quarterly, 14*(3), 133–138.

Kessler, R. C., Berglund, P., Demler, O., Jin, R., Merikangas, K. R., & Walters, E. E. (2005). Lifetime prevalence and age-of-onset distributions of DSM-IV disorders in the National Comorbidity Survey Replication. *Archives of General Psychiatry, 62*(6), 593–602. http://dx.doi.org/10.1001/archpsyc.62.6.593

Kneafsey, R., & Gawthorpe, D. (2004). Head injury: Long-term consequences for patients and families and implications for nurses. *Journal of Clinical Nursing, 13,* 601–608.

Koenen, K. C., Fu, Q. J., Ertel, K., Lyons, M. J., Eisen, S. A., True, W. R., . . . Tsuang, M. T. (2008). Common genetic liability to major depression and posttraumatic stress disorder in men. *Journal of Affective Disorders, 105*(1–3), 109–115. http://dx.doi.org/10.1016/j.jad.2007.04.021

Lepouse, C., Lautner, C. A., Liu, L., Gomis, P., & Leon, A. (2006). Emergence delirium in adults in the post-anaesthesia care unit. *British Journal of Anaesthesia, 96*(6), 747–753. http://dx.doi.org/10.1093/bja/ael094

Lipov, E. G., Joshi, J. R., Lipov, S., Sanders, S. E., & Siroko, M. K. (2008). Cervical sympathetic blockade in a patient with post-traumatic stress disorder: A case report. *Annals of Clinical Psychiatry, 20*(4), 227–228. http://dx.doi.org/10.1080/10401230802435518

Lipov, E. G., Joshi, J. R., Sanders, S., & Slavin, K. V. (2009). A unifying theory linking the prolonged efficacy of the stellate ganglion block for the treatment of chronic regional pain syndrome (CRPS), hot flashes, and posttraumatic stress disorder (PTSD). *Medical Hypotheses, 72*(6), 657–661. http://dx.doi.org/10.1016/j.mehy.2009.01.009

Lipov, E., Lipov, S., & Stark, J. T. (2005). Stellate ganglion blockade provides relief from menopausal hot flashes: A case report series. *Journal of Women's Health* (2002), *14*(8), 737–741. http://dx.doi.org/10.1089/jwh.2005.14.737

Macklin, M. L., Metzger, L. J., Litz, B. T., McNally, R. J., Lasko, N. B., Orr, S. P., & Pitman, R. K. (1998). Lower precombat intelligence is a risk factor for posttraumatic stress disorder. *Journal of Consulting and Clinical Psychology, 66*(2), 323–326.

McGaugh, J. L. (2013). Making lasting memories: Remembering the significant. *Proceedings of the National Academy of Sciences of the United States of America, 110*(Suppl 2), 10402–10407. http://dx.doi.org/10.1073/pnas.1301209110

McGuire, J. M., & Burkard, J. F. (2010). Risk factors for emergence delirium in U.S. military members. *Journal of PeriAnesthesia Nursing, 25*(6), 392–401. Retrieved from http://dx.doi.org/10.1016/j.jopan.2010.07.012

McGuire, J. M. (2012). The incidence of and risk factors for emergence deliriumin U.S. military combat Veterans. *Journal of PeriAnesthesia Nursing, 27*(4), 236–245.

McNally, R. J., & Shin, L. M. (1995). Association of intelligence with severity of posttraumatic stress disorder symptoms in Vietnam combat Veterans. *American Journal of Psychiatry, 152*(6), 936–938.

Mittal, D., Torres, R., Abashidze, A., & Jimerson, N. (2001). Worsening of post-traumatic stress disorder symptoms with cognitive decline: Case series. *Journal of Geriatric Psychiatry and Neurology, 14*(1), 17–20.

Moller, J. T., Cluitmans, P., Rasmussen, L. S., Houx, P., Rasmussen, H., Canet, J., . . . Gravenstein, J. S. (1998). Long-term postoperative cognitive dysfunction in the elderly ISPOCD1 study. ISPOCD investigators. International Study of Post-Operative Cognitive Dysfunction. *Lancet, 351*(9106), 857–861. http://dx.doi.org/10.1016/S0140-6736(97)07382-0

Monk, T. G., Weldon, B. C., Garvan, C. W., Dede, D. E., van der Aa, M. T., Heilman, K. M., & Gravenstein J. S. (2008). Predictors of cognitive dysfunction after major noncardiac surgery. *Anesthesiology, 108*(1), 18–30. http://dx.doi.org/10.1097/01.anes.0000296071.19434.1e

Mulvaney, S. W., McLean, B., & de Leeuw, J. (2010). The use of stellate ganglion block in the treatment of panic/anxiety symptoms with combat-related post-traumatic stress disorder; Preliminary results of long-term follow-up: A case series. *Pain Practice, 10*(4), 359–365. http://dx.doi.org/10.1111/j.1533-2500.2010.00373.x

Naifeh, J. A., North, T. C., Davis, J. L., Reyes, G., Logan, C. A., & Elhai, J. D. (2008). Clinical profile differences between PTSD-diagnosed military Veterans and crime vicitims. *Journal of Trauma and Dissociation,* 321–334.

O'Brien, D. (2002). Acute postoperative delirium: Definitions, incidence, recognition, and interventions. *Journal of PeriAnestheisa Nursing 17*(6), 384–392.

Oxlad, M., Stubberfield, J., Stuklis, R., Edwards, J., & Wade, T. D. (2006a). Psychological risk factors for cardiac-related hospital readmission within 6 months of coronary artery bypass graft surgery. *Journal of Psychosomatic Research, 61*(6), 775–781. http://dx.doi.org/1016/j.jpsychores.2006.09.008

Oxlad, M., Stubberfield, J., Stuklis, R., Edwards, J., & Wade, T. D. (2006b). Psychological risk factors for increased post-operative length of hospital stay following coronary artery bypass graft surgery. *Journal of Behavioral Medicine, 29*(2), 179–190. http://dx.doi.org/10.1007/s10865-005-9043-2

Perconte, S. T., Griger, M. L., & Bellucci, G. (1989). Relapse and rehospitalization of Veterans two years after treatment for PTSD. *Hospital and Community Psychiatry, 40*(10), 1072–1073.

Radtke, F. M., Franck, M., Schneider, M., Luetz, A., Seeling, M., Heinz, A., & Wernecke, K. D. (2008). Comparison of three scores to screen for delirium in the recovery room. *British Journal Anaesthesia, 101*(3), 338–343.

Radtke, F. M., Franck, M., Hagemann, L., Seeling, M., Wernecke, K. D., & Spies, C. D. (2010). Risk factors for inadequate emergence after anesthesia: Emergence delirium and hypoactive emergence. *Minerva Anestesiologica, 76*(6), 394–403.

Raj, P. P. (1996). Stellate Ganglion Block. In S. Waldman & A. Winnie (Eds.), Interventional Pain Management (pp. 267–274). Philadelphia: W. B. Saunders Co.

Satz, P. (1993). Brain reserve capacity and symptom onset after brain injury: A formulation and review of evidence for threshold theory. *Neuropsychology, 7,* 273–295.

Smessaert, A., Schehr, C. A., & Artusio, J. F., Jr. (1960, April). Observations in the immediate post-anaesthesia period, II: Mode of recovery. *British Journal of Anaesthesia, 32,* 181–185.

Smith, K. W., Avis, N. E., & Assmann, S. F. (1999). Distinguishing between quality of life and health status in quality of life research: A meta-analysis. *Quality of Life Research, 8*(5), 447–459.

Solomon, Z., & Mikulincer, M. (2006). Trajectories of PTSD: A 20-year longitudinal study. *American Journal of Psychiatry, 163*(4), 659–666. http://dx.doi.org/10.1176/appi.ajp.163.4.659

Stern, Y. (2003). The concept of cognitive reserve: A catalyst for research. *Journal of Clinical Experimental Neuropsychology, 25*(5), 589–593.

Stern, Y. (2009). Cognitive reserve. *Neuropsychologia, 47*(10), 2015–2028.

Takatori, M., Kuroda, Y., & Hirose, M. (2006). Local anesthetics suppress nerve growth factor-mediated neurite outgrowth by inhibition of tyrosine kinase activity of TrkA. *Anesthesia and Analgesia, 102*(2), 462–467. http://dx.doi.org/10.1213/01.ane.0000194334.69103.50

Tully, P. J. (2010). Post-traumatic stress disorder and neuropsychologic impairment among cardiac surgery patients. *Journal of Cardiothoracic and Vascular Anesthesia, 25*(2), e8–e9. http://dx.doi.org/10.1053/j.jvca.2010.06.007

U.S. Department of Defense. (2012). VA, DOD to Fund $100 Million PTSD and TBI Study. Retrieved from http://www.defense.gov/news/newsarticle.aspx?id=117933

Vanderploeg, R. D., Curtiss, G., Luis, C. A. & Salazar, A. M. (2007). Long-term morbidities following self-reported mild traumatic brain injury. *Journal of Clinical & Experimental Neuropyschology, 29,* 585–598.

Vasterling, J. J., & Brailey, K. (2005). Neuropsychological findings in adults with PTSD. In J. J. Vasterling & C. R. Brewin (Eds.), *Neuropsychology of PTSD* (pp. 178–207). New York, NY: Guilford Press.

Vasterling, J. J., Proctor, S. P., Friedman, M. J., Hoge, C. W., Heeren, T., King, L. A., & King, D. W. (2010). PTSD symptom increases in Iraq-deployed soldiers: Comparison with nondeployed soldiers and associations with baseline symptoms, deployment experiences, and postdeployment stress. *Journal of Traumatic Stress*, *23*(1), 41–51. http://dx.doi.org/10.1002/jts.20487

Weathers, F. W., Keane, T. M., & Davidson, J. R. T. (2001). Clinician-administered PTSD Scale: A review of the first ten years of research. *Depression and Anxiety, 13*, 132–156.

Westerhaus, M. J., & Loewy, A. D. (2001). Central representation of the sympathetic nervous system in the cerebral cortex. *Brain Research, 903*(1–2), 117–127.

Wilson, J. T., & Pokorny, M. E. (2012). The experiences of military CRNAs with service pesonnel who are emerging from general anesthesia. *AANA Journal, 80*(4), 260–265

Wofford, K. (2012). *The influence of elective surgery on functional health in Veterans with chronic posttraumatic stress disorder* (Unpublished doctoral dissertation). PhD, Duke University, Durham. Retrieved from http://dukespace.lib.duke.edu/dspace/bitstream/handle/10161/6179/Wofford_duke_0066D_11719.pdf?sequence=1

Wofford, K., Hertzberg, M., Silva, S., & Vacchiano, C. (in press). A quasi-experimental study of the effect of elective surgery on subjective health in Veterans with chronic PTSD. *AANA Journal.*

Yu, D., Chai, W., Sun, X., & Yao, L. (2010). Emergence agitation in adults: Risk factors in 2,000 patients. *Canadian Journal of Anaesthesia.* Retrieved from http://dx.doi.org/10.1007/s12630-010-9338-9.

CHAPTER 2

Evolution of Burn Management in the U.S. Military

Impact on Nursing

Patricia Schmidt and Elizabeth A. Mann-Salinas

ABSTRACT

As the only burn center in the Department of Defense, the U.S. Army Institute of Surgical Research is the primary location for care of service members with burn injuries. The combat operations in Iraq and Afghanistan during the past decade have caused an increase in burn patients. As a result of this increased need, advancements in care were developed. The speed and precision of transporting patients from the battlefield to the burn center has improved over previous conflicts. Technological advancements to support treating complications of burn wound healing were leveraged and are now integrated into daily practice. Clinical decision support systems were developed and deployed at the burn center as well as to combat support hospitals in combat zones. Technology advancements in rehabilitation have allowed more service members to return to active duty or live productive civilian lives. All of these advancements were developed in a patient-centered, interdisciplinary environment where the nurses are integrated throughout the research process and clinical practice with the end goal of healing combat burns in mind.

http://dx.doi.org/10.1891/0739-6686.32.25

INTRODUCTION

The adage that the only winner in war is medicine holds true for the lengthy military conflicts coalition forces have engaged in since the devastating events of September 11, 2001. The last decade of war has led to major advancements in caring for burn victims as a direct result of innovations in the transport and management of our combat wounded.

Unique combination of both thermal and traumatic injury makes the military burned patient arguably one of the most complex trauma patients to care for (Wolf et al., 2006). Transporting such a patient around the world through a chain of evacuation composed of at least 11 independent care teams en route to the U.S. Army Burn Center in San Antonio, Texas, is a significant accomplishment. Approximately 2,250 U.S. service members have been burned while serving in Iraq or Afghanistan since 2003; approximately 1,000 of them were transported to the Army Burn Center (Cancio, Schmidt, Moore, & Feider, 2014). The service members with injuries severe enough to require treatment at the burn center showed no demonstrable difference in outcomes from civilians cared for in the same center, transported from the local area (Wolf et al., 2006).

Care of the burn patient has evolved into a comprehensive multidisciplinary team effort where the nurse is an integral member. Military burn nursing practice has been revolutionized from point of injury through the rehabilitation of burn patients (Olson et al., 2013). Significant discoveries that address multiple aspects of comprehensive burn care which have been driven by advances in military health care will be discussed.

EN ROUTE CARE

The combat casualty burn patient from the wars in Iraq and Afghanistan are rapidly evacuated to the U.S. Army Institute of Surgical Research (USAISR) Burn Center in San Antonio, Texas. Their average time from injury in theater to arrival in San Antonio is 48–72 hr. Previously, burn evacuation occurred at a much slower rate. During the Vietnam conflict, burn patients were not evacuated from theater until Day 14 postinjury (White, Chubb, Rossing, & Murphy, 1971).

The USAISR Burn Flight Team (BFT) and Air Force Critical Care Air Transport Teams (CCATT) are integral to the rapid evacuation of combat casualties to the continental United States (Renz et al., 2008). CCATT transport burn patients from combat hospitals to the military hospitals in the United States. From the start of major combat operations in 2003, the BFT mission has been to transport combat burned patients from Landstuhl Regional Medical Center in Germany to the Army Burn Center in San Antonio, Texas, for definitive care. Flight nurses from the USAISR meet the patients in Germany and assume care of the patient from the CCATT teams for transport to the Army Burn Center. The goal of the flight teams is to provide expert burn care in flight to the severely wounded. Stabilizing the patient prior to his or her arrival at the burn center allows for early excision of the burn wounds and grafting to occur (Renz et al., 2008).

The decline in worldwide military operations stimulates the need for creative solutions to sustain skills and readiness for multifaceted en route burn care. Incorporating essential elements of complex patient care into checklists and clinical guidelines and sustaining group training preserve these skills and knowledge. Such techniques can support all transport teams responsible for burn care and provide support for civilian mass casualty scenarios (Barillo et al., 2010; Bruce, Bridges, & Holcomb, 2003).

Missions not related to the combat operations have required the capability of the BFT. The BFT's capability to establish a satellite burn intensive care unit (BICU) at Tripler Army Medical Center and stabilize patients before transporting them to the burn center in San Antonio, Texas, demonstrates the flexibility necessary when caring for burn patients (Barillo et al., 2010). Without the continued focus on mission readiness, even during a time of declining mission needs, the BFT would not have been prepared to care for this group of critically burned service members.

Research comparing the outcomes for patients evacuated from long distances and the local patients treated at the USAISR Burn Center found no difference in outcomes (Wolf et al., 2006). Future research regarding patient care during the evacuation process could include evaluation of the documentation process. Currently, fluid resuscitation is documented both on paper and electronically during evacuation. Consolidation and evaluation of accuracy and outcomes from the fluid resuscitation documentation may provide insights for further streamlining of the process.

COMBAT BURN NURSING

Local national patients with burn injuries are cared for in U.S. Combat Support Hospitals (CSHs) within Iraq and Afghanistan. A local national is defined as a patient who is classified as a refugee, non-NATO (North American Treaty Organization) coalition force, non-NATO military, or local civilian. Local national patients include Afghan and Iraqi civilians (adults and children), military, police, and National Guard. Through the summer of 2013, the total number of local national burn patients treated in CSHs is approximately 1,800 patients; of which, approximately 10% were children (Cancio et al., 2014). Local national patients are treated at CSHs because the health care within their respective countries lack the means to treat these complex patients. The deployed military nurse is expected to provide comprehensive care that in the United States would be supported by an interdisciplinary care team of nurses, physical and occupational therapists, social workers, dieticians, respiratory therapists, and behavioral health providers (Smith, 2008). Burn care training for nurses prior to deployment is limited and generally focuses on the resuscitation process (first 48 hr; Barillo et al., 2005; Greenfield & Winfree, 2005). NATO military casualties are rapidly evacuated from combat hospitals to definitive care in their home countries. Local national patients stay through the entire healing process, and deployed nurses provide comprehensive care generally until discharge to home. On the job training is the primary modality for learning to care for those with burn injuries. The Army Burn Center has one deployed surgeon at a time; severely burned individuals are sent to the CSH where the surgeon is located. Frequently, the burn surgeon is the only person with prior experience caring for burns. There is no mechanism for placing experienced burn nurses in combat hospitals.

As a way to provide the best possible care to the patients and prepare nursing staff to care for the burns, the surgeons teach a group of nurses to be burn "experts" for wound care. These nurses work as a team to bathe the patients and conduct wound care. They attended mini-lectures on the burn healing process and wound care best practices. Other topics also included are those related to nutritional needs of the burn patient, pain management, and rehabilitation therapy. These areas are all managed by nursing staff because in deployed units, nutritional and rehabilitation staff and resources are limited (Stout et al., 2007).

To compensate for the limited resources available, nurses develop creative solutions. At the burn center, there are various types of equipment that are used to splint, protect, and elevate patients' limbs. In Iraq and Afghanistan, this equipment is not available so adaptations are made with resources which are available. An example of this type of ingenuity is using a wrist restraint tied with a quick-release knot attached to an intravenous pole to keep an arm elevated and prevent contractures in lieu of custom splints fabricated by occupational therapists.

Although in previous military conflicts, some care was provided to the local people; this has never been conducted on the scale in Iraq and Afghanistan. With little prior training in caring for burn patients, deployed nurses take on the responsibility of caring for these complex and what some would consider burdensome patients. The mortality rates for burn patients cared for exclusively in CSHs was 11.45% (Cancio et al., 2014). Assignment of personnel with experience caring for burns with the deployed burn surgeon may improve combat burn care (Stout et al., 2007).

With such a substantial number of burn patients receiving definitive care in the combat zone, comparison of outcomes between CSHs with deployed burn center physicians and those caring for burn patients without a physician from the burn center could confirm a gap in the training for deployed health care professionals. Standardized burn wound care practices and predeployment preparation could be developed based on the outcomes from this study.

WOUND CARE ADVANCES

Decreasing the time it takes for burn wounds to heal is a continuous challenge. The longer wounds remain without definitive closure with permanent skin grafts, the more potential exists for developing infection and increased mortality. Care for wounds of those burned in combat zones requires additional vigilance to prevent infections (Brown, Walker, Cortez, Murray, & Wenke, 2010). Burn wounds are already extremely susceptible to infection because the bodies' first defense, the skin, is compromised. The burn injury creates opportunity for infection to enter the body. Combat wounds are especially susceptible to wound infections related to the environment and common mechanisms of injury in combat (Kauvar et al., 2006). Burns that occur in a combat zone are exposed to dirt from explosions; antibiotic-resistant bacteria become an increased concern when caring for patients with exposure to unknown substances (Brown et al., 2010; Kauvar et al., 2006).

Nurses are primarily responsible for daily showers and wound care. While working in teams of two or three, burn nursing staff maintain sterile technique to shower and redress the burn wounds. This process can occur as frequently as twice daily or as infrequently as every 5 days depending on the type of dressings and size of the patient's burns (Moore & Schmidt, 2012; Serio-Melvin, Yoder, & Gaylord, 2010). In the last decade, several wound dressings have helped to promote wound healing and reduce infection among burn patients.

Silver sponge, negative-pressure wound dressings decrease infection rates in burn wounds (Lalliss et al., 2010; Stinner, Waterman, & Wenke, 2011). The mechanisms within the dressing are particularly useful when wound beds are from blast injuries and considered dirty (Lalliss et al., 2010). Not only does the silver prevent infections but also the vacuum mechanism of the dressing removes unwanted material from the wound bed and provides a slight negative pressure to promote wound bed growth (Stinner et al., 2011).

Studies regarding methods to heal graft donor sites have been done to develop methods to reduce pain and healing time of donor sites. The Army Burn Center conducted three such studies during the past decade. Silverlon dressings decrease pain and healing time for donor sites compared to Xeroform gauze dressings but are cost-prohibitive (Albrecht et al., 2013). The silver-coated nylon with DC microcurrent applied to donor sites did not improve the healing time or reduce the pain associated with donor site healing (Malin et al., 2013). Oxygen diffusion dressing applied to donor sites were found to decrease healing time by 3 days as well as decrease the pain associated with donor sites (Lairet, Baer, Leas, Renz, & Cancio, 2013).

EXTRACORPOREAL LIFE SUPPORT

Despite recent advances in burn care, the diagnosis of renal failure is associated with increased morbidity and mortality. Much controversy exists regarding the mode, timing, dose, and frequency of renal replacement therapy (Bellomo & Ronco, 1999; Buchari, 1998; Kellum et al., 2002; Swartz, Messana, Orzol, & Port, 1999). In our BICU prior to 2005, intensive care unit (ICU) patients with acute renal failure were treated conservatively, with care driven by nephrology consultants. When patients met criteria for dialysis based on traditional indications, they were placed on intermittent hemodialysis. Not all patients were dialyzed. In fact, for many critically ill patients, dialysis was considered contraindicated because of hemodynamic instability. Continuous renal replacement therapy (CRRT) is a general term that describes an extracorporeal renal support therapy that is continuous. Continuous venovenous hemofiltration (CVVH), continuous venovenous hemodialysis, and continuous venovenous hemodiafiltration all come under the CRRT umbrella.

CRRT has been rapidly introduced to worldwide BICUs, yet program management has traditionally been the responsibility of nephrology services. CRRT has become a standard of care in the U.S. Army Burn Center since its introduction in 2005 (Chung et al., 2008; Chung et al., 2009). This therapy is fully supported by the organic burn center nursing staff and overseen by the burn medical intensivist. Development of a comprehensive nursing-managed program required significant coordination between nursing, logistics, pharmacy, and medical staff. The initial 5-day nurse training was provided by the device vendor for 10 "superusers," who were responsible for then training additional staff nurses. By the start of bedside CRRT delivery in November 2005, 15 nurses were certified as competent out of 97 total BICU staff nurses (15%). Ongoing competency evaluation was conducted annually, with one-on-one evaluation, and biannual skills fairs incorporated refresher training; on-the-spot feedback and hand-on refreshers were provided by the program coordinator and superusers. In July 2012, we had 70 CRRT certified nurses (85% of 82 staff).

From November 2005 to July 2012, 199 burn patients (194 with thermal injury) were treated for 4,753 therapy days. CVVH was the most common modality for 4,690 therapy days (98%). Renal support was the identified intervention for 86% of the documented indications for therapy in the physician daily notes (1,832/2,320), acute kidney injury (AKI) 1,750 notes (95.5%), rhabdomyolysis 44 notes (2.4%), and end-stage renal disease for 38 documented notes (2%). Nonrenal indications accounted for 14% (296) of the physician daily notes. Treatment for sepsis was the most common nonrenal indication for CRRT (58%, 173 notes), followed by circulatory shock (15%, 46 notes), "other" (16%, 47), during burn resuscitation (2%, 6 notes), and electrical injury (2%, 6 notes). Death occurred in 65% (129/199) patients treated with CRRT.

Because use of CRRT in the burn population is limited, the Army Burn Center is currently participating in a multicenter clinical trial to identify the optimal flow rate of CRRT to treat burn patients suspected of severe sepsis. Results of this study will inform best practice for the use of CRRT in the burn population.

The future use of extracorporeal support moves the technology forward to the battle field and incorporates other body systems. CRRT has been successfully executed in the combat zone on a small number of patients ($N = 9$) with AKI (Zonies et al., 2013). Other forms of extracorporeal support are on the technology horizon. Extracorporeal membrane oxygenation (ECMO) provides cardiopulmonary support to patients and is being used in the burn center for patients with adult respiratory distress syndrome (Neff et al., 2013). Although still novel and used prudently, burn nurses must have a familiarity and thorough understanding of extracorporeal support equipment to use it in practice. Continued success with CRRT and ECMO programs will foster their transition to mainstream practice and prepare nursing staff for a future where extracorporeal support is the standard of care for critically ill burn patients.

DECISION SUPPORT SYSTEMS

The Army Burn Center has been at the forefront of development and adoption of technological solutions to address gaps and variability in burn management. Computer decision support systems (CDSS) facilitate expanding the expertise of the burn specialist to users of software designed to assist clinical decision making. The Burn Navigator (Arcos Medical, Houston, TX) is the flagship CDSS device for the initial fluid management of burn shock. Recently approved for clinical use by the Federal Drug Administration, the Burn Navigator is a standalone device that guides hourly crystalloid fluid administration tailored to an individual patient's urinary output. Developed for en route burn management of combat casualties, this system is in the final process of deployment to the battlefield. The same software is integrated with the hospital electronic medical record and is currently in use at the Army Burn Center. This system has been demonstrated to outperform clinical judgment, with improved mortality, length of ICU stay, and ventilator days (Salinas et al., 2011).

A similar commercially available CDSS software system to manage serum glucose was introduced to the Army Burn Center and evaluated for safety in the burn population. EndoTool (EndoTool, LLC, Charlotte, NC) software provides the nurse recommendations for insulin titration each hour based on the changes in the patients' serum glucose. A prospective randomized crossover study was conducted in the 16-bed BICU (Mann, Jones, Wolf, & Wade, 2011). Adult patients were initially randomized to receive glucose management using a paper-based protocol (PP) or computer protocol (CP) for 72 hr then crossed over to the alternate method for an additional 72 hr. Time in target glucose range (80–110 mg/dl; $N = 18$) was higher in the CP group ($47 \pm 17.0\%$ vs. $41 \pm 16.6\%$; $p \leq .05$) with no difference in values less than 60 mg/dl ($p = .65$) and less than 40 mg/dl ($p = 1.0$). Mean glucose for the CP arm was significantly lower than the PP arm (113 ± 10.2 mg/dl vs. 119 ± 14.0 mg/dl, $p = .02$). More glucose measurements were performed in the CP group ($p = .0003$), and nursing staff compliance with CP recommendations was greater ($p < .0001$). The conclusions from this study were that glycemic control using CDSS is safe and efficacious for critically burned patients; time in target range improved with no increase in hypoglycemic events. Consistency in practice is enhanced using CDSS, providing standardization among various levels of nursing education and experience.

Evaluation of user satisfaction ($N = 40$) with the Burn Resuscitation and EndoTool CDSS platforms among physicians (MDs), registered nurses (RNs), and licensed vocational nurses (LVNs) revealed that staff members do not appreciate the benefits of the CDSS technology regarding positive impact on patient outcomes; improvement should be communicated clearly to staff to ensure ongoing compliance with CDSS (Mann, Allen, Serio-Melvin, Wolf, & Salinas, 2012). Such data may improve perception of interference and trust in recommendations of Burn decision support system (DSS). Training for EndoTool was perceived to be better than that provided for the Burn DSS, and trust in recommendations by nursing staff was greater. This may be because nurses titrate insulin infusion hourly on most critically burned patients, compared to the infrequent admission of a severely burned patient who required fluid resuscitation. Familiarity in the underlying process may influence comfort with computer recommendations in the nursing staff. Overall satisfaction was no different from neutral for both systems for both nurses and physicians.

An electronic wound mapping system (Wound Flow) was developed at the Army Burn Center to display the pattern of burn injury and the results of surgical intervention. Graphical displays of wound healing progression over time are a useful tool to direct the attention of the interdisciplinary team to patients who may require addition interventions to optimize wound healing. Wound Flow has been used daily at the bedside by the interdisciplinary burn care team to include physicians, physician assistants, nurses, dieticians, physical therapists, wound care coordinators, and clinical nurse specialists. Wound Flow allows for incorporation of wound photographs into the medical record and animation of wound progression during the course of hospitalization (Williams et al., 2013).

To evaluate the use of the wound mapping system in the burn center, a retrospective review of the Wound Flow database was performed (Shingleton et al., 2012). The use of Wound Flow during interdisciplinary rounds resulted in improved communication within the team regarding wound assessment and healing, triggering earlier recognition of setbacks initiating aggressive efforts toward resolution. The rate of wound healing can now be tracked more precisely and may provide diagnostic potential should a patient fail to meet expected healing goals.

The burn patient's caloric needs are increased related to the healing process. Burn-induced hypermetabolism is a result of an increased heart rate and respiratory rate, oxygen consumption, carbon dioxide production, glucose use, glycogenolysis, lipolysis, and proteolysis (Herndon, 2007; Shields et al., 2013; Wolf, 2007). Nurses caring for burn patients must be vigilant to ensure that the patients are receiving the necessary calories to maintain a healthy weight, participate in rehabilitation activities, prevent skin breakdown, and have continued wound healing (Shields et al., 2013). Ensuring that nursing staff understands the importance of patient nutrition is integral to this piece of the healing process. Not only do nurses need to understand the safety practices involved with using tube feedings, but they must also understand the importance of accurately documenting when tube feedings are on or off. If tube feedings are stopped for wound care, turning, or surgery, vigilance is necessary to remember to restart them so the patient gets as many calories as possible (Moore & Schmidt, 2012; Serio-Melvin et al., 2010). A decision support program is currently in development to facilitate the bedside nurse to meet daily caloric goals (Shields et al., 2013).

REHABILITATION AND REINTEGRATION

The goal of rehabilitation practices of combat-wounded is to return them to the highest functioning state possible postinjury. During the past decade, this capability has evolved and many combat-wounded who previously were unable to return to duty are now able to continue a military career. This ability to rehabilitate the wounded service member is because of the collaboration, diligence, and hard work of the patients, rehabilitation staff, and nurses.

The rehabilitation process can be broken into three phases: acute, intermediate, and long-term. Nursing staff are primarily involved with the first two phases because long-term rehabilitation takes place in the outpatient setting. During the acute phase, the nurse works closely with rehabilitation staff members to ensure splinting, range of motion, and skin breakdown measures are completed. The splinting and range of motion activities prevent scar contractures as early wound healing occurs (Dewey, Richard, & Parry, 2011). Prevention of pressure points and adequate air circulation are essential for burn patients who are at high risk of further skin breakdown. Equipment to facilitate skin protection prevents skin breakdown; examples of equipment commonly used include protective cups for the ears and mesh netting placed on a metal frame to elevate limbs while promoting airflow (Hedman et al., 2007). The acute patients' rehabilitation needs primarily focus on the promotion of wound healing in a manner which will prevent loss of function in the future. The acute phase is especially important for the wounded service members because it sets them up for their future rehabilitation needs. When skin breakdown and contractures are prevented before they occur, length of stay and outpatient rehabilitation needs are decreased (Hedman et al., 2009).

During the intermediate phase, restoring function is the focus of rehabilitation (Dewey et al., 2011; Hedman et al., 2009). The nurses and rehabilitation staff work together to promote independence for activities of daily living and mobility (Hedman et al., 2009). Adaptive equipment such as large foam handles on utensils and tooth brushes facilitate the patients' feeding of themselves and brushing their own teeth. Splinting and range of motion continue to be emphasized as the patients' skin heals (Dewey et al., 2011). The scars that form with the new skin put the patient at risk of losing functionality without continued vigilance.

Although the acute and intermediate phases have had little advancements, the long-term phase has grown exponentially. Through the technology advances which have occurred related to prosthetic limbs and rehabilitation therapy, combat-wounded burn patients have been able to return to active duty military service or lead active lives as medically retired service members (Hedman et al., 2009). Once discharged to outpatient status, the wounded service member spends up to 1 year participating in outpatient rehabilitation, after the year a medical board consisting of three physicians evaluates that service member's ability to continue to serve in the military. If unable to serve in the military, the wounded service member receives a medical retirement from service (Hedman, et al., 2009). The determination of the patients combined with the anything-is-possible attitude of the staff has facilitated patients with three missing limbs to return to activity duty and innumerous patients to flourish within military and civilian communities.

As a manner of determining whether combat-injured burn patients' needs are being met, long-term, follow-up as outpatients is ongoing. A longitudinal study of burn center patients using the burn specific health scale is providing information about the scale's efficacy within the combat-wounded population. Preliminary data from the research suggests that clarification is necessary because there are multiple versions of the scale (Yoder, Nayback, & Gaylord, 2010). Results from this study should be informative of the long-term capabilities of combat Veterans with burn injuries.

APPLICATION TO CLINICAL PRACTICE

The advancements to burn care discussed have already been implemented within the military health system. These advancements are also applicable to the civilian population. Combat burn nursing practices, although uncommon in the civilian sector, can be applied to natural disasters as well as acts of terror, both circumstances in which a proportion of the injured population will suffer burn injuries which may have to be initially treated by nurses with limited burn care experience. Products that facilitate wound healing which were novel at the beginning of the conflicts are now commonplace not only in burn centers but also for general wound healing as well. The success of extracorporeal life support measures in BICU patients has also shown favorable outcomes in other ICU patients with renal failure. The practices categorized as CRRT are becoming commonplace in BICUs across the country as well as transitioning to other critical care environments. The use of clinical decision support programs is also becoming integrated into everyday nursing practice. Whether using programs to assist with appropriate medication titration, fluid resuscitation, or early detection of potential complications, the integration of these programs assists the nurse's decision making and helps them to provide state of the art timely care to patients. Because large burn injuries are frequently survived today, rehabilitation and reintegration become a priority once the original burn injuries are healed. Vigilance of the nursing staff and use of appropriate equipment to prevent newly grown skin from shearing or breaking down is a primary focus. Through collaboration with physical and occupational therapy, nursing staff is able to provide an environment that promotes the rehabilitation process and promotes wounds to continue to heal. Long-term survival of patients with large burns was previously uncommon. It is unknown what future challenges these survivors may face as they age. Follow-up in the outpatient setting will be important for longitudinal understanding of the challenges faced and how nursing care can facilitate facing such challenges. Many of the advancements in burn care that have occurred during the Iraq and Afghanistan conflicts have been implemented in the clinical practice setting and are already assisting nurses to provide even better care to burn patients across the country.

POLICY IMPLICATIONS

Policy implications from the advancements in burn care directly relate to the prevention of burn injuries as well as burn care delivered in theater and during en route care. The wear of protective equipment and proper procedures for dangerous tasks such as refueling and trash burning could reduce the number of non–combat-related burn injuries. Review of these policies across the Department of Defense to ensure they are up-to-date and accurate will facilitate the prevention of burn injuries in future deployments. Standardizing burn care in theaters of operation through predeployment training and complete integration of decision support tools is a must. Currently, burn clinical practice guidelines in the deployed setting are vague and insufficient for long-term care of a burn patient. Burn care is frequently provided by nurses with little or no knowledge of burn patients and the complexities of the disease process. A standardized predeployment program would ensure that the care received by all patients in a deployed setting was conducted by nurses with the appropriate knowledge. Policies implemented need to reflect the advances made in caring for burn patients as well as consideration for the ever-evolving combat theater, influencing the types and severity of burn injuries sustained.

FUTURE RESEARCH

Because of the military conflicts in Iraq and Afghanistan, advancements in burn care have occurred in all phases of the healing process. The areas of research have primarily focused on the burn care of patients who can be evacuated to the burn center. An understanding of definitive burn care delivered in the combat zone and outcomes of that care is limited. Future research should continue to harness technology to improve care for all burn patients as well as investigate the definitive care provided in the combat zone. Development of clinical practice guidelines for care of burn patient in a combat zone could be based on the results of this research. Furthermore, considerations for methods to provide burn care training to nurses prior to deployment needs to be assessed. Finally, an assessment of the effectiveness of noncombat burn prevention policies is needed to determine their effectiveness and where improvements can be made to prevent unnecessary injuries from occurring. With the continued advancements in burn care, adaptation to meet the needs of a combat environment should also be reflected. Burn injuries continue to be a common, complex injury related to military conflict. Understanding the care of burn patients during the last 13 years will provide the knowledge to improve the care of burn patients in the future.

CONCLUSION

It is unfortunate that a decade of war led to the advances made to burn care; one would hope these advances would have occurred regardless. But the burn care provided to wounded service members has made advancements which decreased the mortality rates of severely burned patients. The research conducted to improve burn care has been multidisciplinary, with a common thread throughout: the incorporation of the bedside nurse. Nurses who care for burn patients must be continuously learning. Dynamic advancements in their daily routines have occurred over the last decade. Leveraging technology capabilities will continue to improve care for the burn patient. The ability to detect and monitor minute changes early and provide intervention continues to improve care. Although technology advancements continue to improve patient care, the laborious care of dressing wounds and bathing burn patients will continue. The intrepid spirit of the nursing staff at the USAISR Burn Center is only shadowed by that of their patients. Their hard work and diligence has helped advance the field of burn nursing on a global scale.

DISCLAIMER

The opinions or assertions contained herein are the private views of the authors and are not to be construed as official or as reflecting the views of the Department of the Army or the Department of Defense.

REFERENCES

Albrecht, M., Renz, E., Cancio, L., White, C., Blackborne, L., Chung, K., . . . Holcomb, J. (2013). *Comparison of Silverlon dressing to Xeroform gauze in the treatment of skin graft donor site wounds.* Retrieved from silverlon.com/wp-content/.../Silverlon_Xeroform_Burn_Comparision.ppt

Barillo, D., Cancio, L., Hutton, B., Mittelsteadt, P., Gueller, G., & Holcomb, J. (2005). Combat burn life support: A military burn-education program. *Journal of Burn Care & Rehabilitation, 26*(2), 162–165.

Barillo, D., Cancio, L., Stack, R., Carr, S., Broger, K., Crews, D., . . . Blackbourne, L. (2010). Deployment and operation of a transportable burn intensive care unit in response to a burn multiple casualty incident. *American Journal of Disaster Medicine, 5*(1), 5–13.

Bellomo, R., & Ronco, C. (1999). Continuous renal replacement therapy in the intensive care unit. *Intensive Care Medicine, 25*(8), 781–789.

Brown, K., Walker, J., Cortez, D., Murray, C., & Wenke, J. (2010). Earlier debridement and antibiotic administration decrease infection. *Journal of Surgical Orthopaedic Advances, 19*(1), 18–22.

Bruce, S., Bridges, E., & Holcomb, J. (2003). Preparing to respond: Joint Trauma Training Center and USAF Nusing Warskills Simulation Laboratory. *Critical Care Nursing Clinics of North America*, *15*(2), 149–162.

Buchari, H. (1998). History and development of continuous renal replacement techniques. *Kidney International Supplement*, *54*, S120–S124.

Cancio, L. C., Schmidt, P. M., Moore, C. L., & Feider, L. L. (2014). *Burns on the battlefields of Iraq and Afghanistan*. Unpublished manuscript.

Chung, K., Juncos, L., Wolf, S., Mann, E., Renz, E., White, C., . . . Holcomb, J. (2008). Continuous renal replacement therapy improves survival in severely burned military casualties with acute kidney injury. *Journal of Trauma*, *64*, S179–S185.

Chung, K., Lundy, J., Matson, J., Renz, E., White, C., King, B., . . . Wolf, S. (2009). Continuous venovenous hemofiltration in severely burned patients with acute kidney injury: A cohort study. *Critical Care*, *13*(3), R62.

Dewey, W., Richard, R., & Parry, I. (2011). Positioning, splinting, and contracture management. *Physical Medicine and Rehabilitation Clinics of North America*, *22*(2), 229–247.

Greenfield, E., & Winfree, J. (2005). Nursing's role in planning, preparation, and response to burn disaster or mass casualty events. *Journal of Burn Care & Rehabilitation*, *26*(2), 166–169.

Hedman, T. L., Chapman, T. T., Dewey, W. S., Quick, C. D., Wolf, S., & Holcomb, J. (2007). Two simple leg net devices designed to protect lower-extremity skin grafts and donor sites and prevent decubitus ulcer. *Journal of Burn Care & Research*, *28*(1), 115–119.

Hedman, T., Quick, C., Richard, R., Renz, E., Fisher, S., Rivers, E., . . . Young, A. (2009). Rehabilitation of burn casualties. In M. D. Army (Ed.), *Care of the combat amputee* (pp. 277–380). Fort Sam Houston, TX: Office of the Surgeon General and the U.S Army Medical Department Center and School.

Herndon, D. (2007). *Total burn care*. Philadelphia, PA: Saunders/Elsevier.

Kauvar, D., Wolf, S., Wade, C., Cancio, L., Renz, E., & Holcomb, J. (2006). Burns sustained in combat explosions in Operations Iraqi and Enduring Freedom (OIF/OEF explosion burns). *Burns*, *32*(7), 853–857.

Kellum, J., Angus, D., Johnson, J., Leblanc, M., Griffin, M., Ramakrishnan, N., & Linde-Zwirble, W. (2002). Continuous versus intermittent renal replacement therapy: A meta-analysis. *Intensive Care Medicine*, *28*(1), 29–37.

Lairet, K., Baer, D., Leas, M., Renz, E., & Cancio, L. (2014). Evaluation of an oxygen-diffusion dressing for accelerated healing of donor-site wounds. *Journal of Burn Care & Rehabilitation*, *35*(3), 214–218.

Lalliss, S., Stinner, D., Waterman, S., Branstetter, J., Masini, B., & Wenke, J. (2010). Negative pressure wound therapy reduces pseudomonas wound contamination more than *Staphylococcus aureus*. *Journal of Orthopaedic Trauma*, *24*(9), 598–602.

Malin, E., Galin, C., Lairet, K., Huzar, T., Williams, J., Renz, E., . . . Cancio, L. (2013). Silver-coated nylon dressing plus active DC microcurrent for healing of autogenous skin donor sites. *Annals of Plastic Surgery*, *71*(5), 481–484.

Mann, E., Allen, D., Serio-Melvin, M., Wolf, S., & Salinas, J. (2012). Clinician satisfaction with computer decision support in the intensive care unit. *Dimensions of Critical Care Nursing*, *31*(1), 31–36.

Mann, E., Jones, J., Wolf, S., & Wade, C. (2011). Computer decision support software safely improves glycemic control in the burn intensive care unit: A randomized controlled clinical study. *Journal of Burn Care & Research*, *32*(2), 246–255.

Moore, C., & Schmidt, P. (2012). A burn progressive care unit: Customized care from admission through discharge. *Perioperative Nursing Clinics*, *7*(1), 99–105.

Neff, L., Cannon, J., Stewart, I., Batchinsky, A., Zonies, D., Pamplin, J., & Chung, K. (2013). Extracorporeal organ support following trauma: The dawn of a new era in combat casualty critical care. *Journal of Trauma and Acute Care Surgery*, *75*(2 Suppl. 2), S120–S128; discussion S128–S129.

Olson, C., Bailey, J., Mabry, R., Rush, S., Morrison, J., & Kuncir, E. (2013). Forward aeromedical evacuation: A brief history, lessons learned from the Global War on Terror, and the way forward for US policy. *Journal of Trauma and Acute Care Surgery*, *75*(2 Suppl. 2), S130–S136.

Renz, E., Cancio, L., Barillo, D., White, C., Albrecht, M., Thompson, C., . . . Holcomb, J. (2008). Long range transport of war-related burn casualties. *Journal of Trauma*, *64*(2 Suppl.), S136–S144.

Salinas, J., Chung, K., Mann, E., Cancio, L., Kramer, G., Serio-Melvin, M., . . . Wolf, S. (2011). Computerized decision support system improves fluid resuscitation following severe burns: An original study. *Critical Care Medicine*, *39*(9), 2031–2038.

Serio-Melvin, M., Yoder, L., & Gaylord, K. (2010). Caring for burn patients at the United States Institute of Surgical Research: The nurses' multifaceted roles. *The Nursing Clinics of North America*, *45*(2), 233–248.

Shields, B., Doty, K., Chung, K., Wade, C., Aden, J., & Wolf, S. (2013). Determination of resting energy expenditure after severe burn. *Journal of Burn Care & Research*, *34*(1), e22–e28.

Shingleton, S., Serio-Melvin, M., Salinas, J., Fenrich, C., Mann-Salinas, E., Peterson, C., . . . Chung, K. (2012). Experience of using an electronic wound mapping system in a burn center. *Journal of Burn Care & Research*, *28*(2), S92.

Smith, K. (2008). Critical care nursing in an austere environment. *Critical Care Medicine*, *36*, S297–S303.

Stinner, D., Waterman, S. M., & Wenke, J. (2011). Silver dressings augment the ability of negative pressure wound therapy to reduce bacteria in a contaminated open fracture model. *Journal of Trauma*, *71*, S147–S150.

Stout, L., Jezior, J., Melton, L., Walker, J., Brengman, M., Neumeier, S., . . . Cancio, L. C.. (2007). Wartime burn care in Iraq: 28th Combat Support Hospital, 2003. *Military Medicine*, *172*(11), 1148–1153.

Swartz, R. D., Messana, J. M., Orzol, S., & Port, F. (1999). Comparing continuous hemofiltration with hemodialysis in patients with severe acute renal failure. *American Journal of Kidney Diseases*, *34*(3), 424–432.

White, M., Chubb, R., Rossing, R., & Murphy, J. (1971). Results of early aeromedical evacuation of Vietnam casualties. *Aerospace Medicine*, *42*(7), 780–784.

Williams, J., King, B., Aden, J., Serio-Melvin, M. C., Salinas, J., Renz, E., . . . Cancio, L. (2013). Comparison of traditional burn wound mapping with a computerized program. *Journal of Burn Care & Research*, *34*(1), e29–e35.

Wolf, S. (2007). Nutrition and metabolism in burns: State of the science, 2007. *Journal of Burn Care & Research*, *28*(4), 572–576.

Wolf, S. E., Kauvar, D. S., Wade, C. E., Cancio, L. C., Renz, E. P., Horvath, E. E., . . . Holcomb, J. B. (2006). Comparison between civilian burns and combat burns from Operation Iraqi Freedom and Operation Enduring Freedom. *Annals of Surgery*, *243*(6), 786–792; discussion 792–795.

Yoder, L., Nayback, A., & Gaylord, K. (2010). The evolution and utility of the burn specific health scale: A systematic review. *Burns*, *36*(8), 1143–1156.

Zonies, D., DuBose, J. E., Bruno, T., Benjamin, C., Cannon, J., & Chung, K. (2013). Early implementation of continuous renal replacement therapy optimizes casualty evacuation for combat-related acute kidney injury. *Journal of Trauma and Acute Care Surgery*, *75*(2 Suppl. 2), S210–S214.

CHAPTER 3

Innovations in the En Route Care of Combat Casualties

Jennifer J. Hatzfeld, Susan Dukes, and Elizabeth Bridges

ABSTRACT

The en route care environment is dynamic and requires constant innovation to ensure appropriate nursing care for combat casualties. Building on experiences in Iraq and Afghanistan, there have been tremendous innovations in the process of transporting patients, including the movement of patients with spinal injuries. Advances have also been made in pain management and noninvasive monitoring, particularly for trauma and surgical patients requiring close monitoring of their hemodynamic and perfusion status. In addition to institutionalizing these innovations, future efforts are needed to eliminate secondary insults to patients with traumatic brain injuries and technologies to provide closed-loop sedation and ventilation.

INTRODUCTION

The importance of quickly transporting combat casualties to medical care has been attributed to a French military surgeon during the Napoleonic Wars between 1792 and 1815 (Manring, Hawk, Calhoun, & Andersen, 2009). In fact, it is asserted that the improved patient outcomes noted from the organized evacuation process used by the French during the Crimean War from 1854 to 1855

http://dx.doi.org/10.1891/0739-6686.32.41

were directly responsible for the assignment of Florence Nightingale to Istanbul, Turkey, to improve the care provided to British combat casualties (Manring et al., 2009). After the development of modern aircraft, casualties began to be transported back to the United States via transport planes by the Army Air Corps in World War II, and beginning in the Korean War, the helicopter was used to transport patients from the point of injury to initial medical care, particularly when the patient's location was remote (Carter, Couch, & O'Brien, 1988). Today, combat casualties are transported in many different types of aircraft, but generally follow this same rapid evacuation approach, using helicopters at the point of injury and transport aircraft to return patients to the United States.

Advances in combat casualty care over the last several years have been consistent, determined, and truly remarkable. Perhaps, a single graph published in the *Journal of Trauma and Acute Care Surgery* (Rasmussen, Gross, & Baer, 2013) reflects this most succinctly. In the figure, the case fatality rate (CFR), which is the percentage of deaths among all combat injuries in Afghanistan, decreases steadily from 17% in late 2005 (when reliable data were available) down to 8% in 2013. Between 2007 and 2013, while the CFR continued to fall, the mean injury severity score (ISS) increased from less than 12 to greater than 14. To put this in context, an ISS from 9 to 15 is considered a "moderate" injury and associated with higher mortality rates when compared to "mild" injuries, with ISS less than 9 (Bolorunduro et al., 2011). Together, these results confirm that the decreasing CFR is not because of a larger proportion of minor injuries but because of improved survival rates for combat casualties with increasingly severe injuries. Caring for these more severely injured patients has been attributed to a "revolution" within the military medical system (Blackbourne, Baer, Eastridge, Butler, et al., 2012). But the transport of these patients within the combat zone and ultimately back to the United States, called the "en route care" system, has also required significant innovation to ensure optimal outcomes for these wounded warriors.

CURRENT EN ROUTE CARE SYSTEM

According to military doctrine (Chairman of the Joint Chiefs of Staff [CJCS], 2012), medical care within the combat casualty care system begins with first responder care where a field medic provides lifesaving interventions and calls for transport to initial medical treatment. This initial treatment is considered forward resuscitative care, which is usually provided in a temporary structure (such as a tent) and begins with damage-control surgery for traumatic injuries (Blackbourne, Baer, Eastridge, Butler, et al., 2012). From here, patients are transferred to a theater hospital, which has additional surgical and specialty capabilities, where the casualty is either returned to duty or further stabilized before being transported to definitive care outside of the operational area (CJCS, 2012).

The en route care (ERC) system ensures that all patients are safely transported between these levels of care, while maintaining the patient's clinical condition (CJCS, 2012). As seen in Figure 3.1, casualty evacuation and medical evacuation can use multiple vehicle types, including rotary wing aircraft (helicopters), smaller fixed-wing aircraft (airplanes), boats, ships, or ground vehicles. Aeromedical evacuation (AE), or strategic evacuation, is a regulated movement that focuses on moving patients between military medical facilities using larger fixed-wing aircraft, usually from the theater hospital to definitive care (CJCS, 2012). In the most recent conflicts in Iraq and Afghanistan, this definitive care has been provided either at Landstuhl Regional Medical Center (LRMC) in Germany or one of several medical centers in the United States.

Depending on the mode of transportation, there are multiple stressors that can negatively impact the patient, including vibration, movement, and noise. However, because patients evacuated on fixed-wing aircraft are at a much higher altitude, this introduces additional physiological stressors on the injured patient. There are eight classic stresses of flight in fixed-wing aircraft, including decreased partial pressure of oxygen, barometric pressure changes, thermal changes, decreased humidity, and gravitational forces, in addition to vibration, noise, and fatigue. The combination of these physiological stresses encountered at altitude acts in a cumulative manner, and although fatigue is identified as a

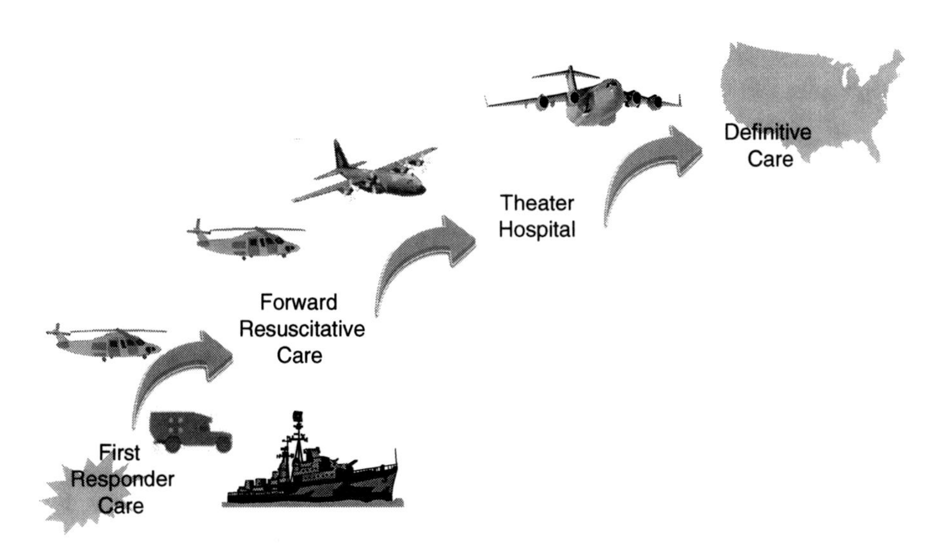

FIGURE 3.1 En route care system (CJCS, 2012).

separate stress of flight, it also is the end product of the other seven (Hickman & Mehrer, 2001).

From October 2001 until December 2011, 19,437 military personnel were medically evacuated from Afghanistan with at least one medical encounter in a fixed medical facility outside the operational theater (Armed Forces Health Surveillance Center [AFHSC], 2012b). From January 2003 until December 2011, 50,634 military personnel were also medically evacuated from Iraq followed by at least one medical encounter in a fixed medical facility outside the operational theater (AFHSC, 2012a). An analysis of the diagnoses for these military members medically evacuated from Iraq demonstrates that 17.7% (n = 8,944) were battle injury–related, with nonbattle musculoskeletal injuries a close second at 16.3% (n = 8,257). Mental disorders, including adjustment reactions, mood disorders, anxiety, and posttraumatic stress disorder (PTSD), reflected 11.6% (n = 5,892) of military members transported (AFHSC, 2012a).

Although not reflecting the military "surge" in Afghanistan in 2010, an analysis of 34,006 military personnel aeromedically evacuated from both Iraq and Afghanistan between January 2004 and December 2007 found that the most common reason for medical evacuation was musculoskeletal and connective tissue disorders (n = 8,104, 24%), followed by combat injuries (n = 4,713, 14%), neurological disorders (n = 3,502, 10%), psychiatric diagnoses (n = 3,108, 9%), and spinal pain (n = 2,445, 7%; Cohen et al., 2010). Among this group of military members, more than 22% (n = 7,675) returned to duty within 2 weeks after their evacuation (Cohen et al., 2010).

In an analysis of all patients transported by a Critical Care Air Transport Team (CCATT), which is a specialized team that provides critical care capability within AE, 2,439 patients (with 3,492 patient moves) were transported from October 2001 to May 2006 in support of military operations in Iraq and Afghanistan (Bridges & Evers, 2009). Among the 1,995 patients transported out of the operational area, battle injuries accounted for 64% of these patients (n = 1,280) and 25% (n = 504) with a noninjury, or disease, diagnosis (Bridges & Evers, 2009). Trauma patients (either because of battle injuries or nonbattle injuries) most commonly had soft tissue trauma (64%, n = 948), and 43% (n = 636) had an orthopedic injury; 69% (n = 1,034) had polytrauma, defined as having two or more areas of the body injured (Bridges & Evers, 2009).

A more in-depth analysis of 133 patients transported by CCATT from Iraq identified that 59% (n = 78) were combat trauma patients; lower extremity trauma, to include amputations, fractures, vascular injuries, and soft tissue injuries, was the most prevalent (Mason, Eadie, & Holder, 2008). The mean ISS for these CCATT patients with combat trauma was 20, with 60% of these patients having an ISS of more than 15, which is considered "severe" injury (Mason et al., 2008). Despite the critical care capability of CCATT, some patients exceed that level of care in the ERC setting, particularly because of lung injuries and inadequate ventilation. To meet this need, an Acute Lung Rescue Team was developed and transported 24 critically ill patients out of the operational area (Fang et al., 2011).

From these descriptive studies, it becomes clear that the transport of combat casualties and the ERC system are dynamic. The patients transported reflect a wide variety of acuity levels from the most stable patients who are able to return to duty within 2 weeks to those most critically injured who require a specialized critical care team. The necessity to transport these types of patients thousands of miles around the world is itself unique and innovative. However, the dramatic changes to combat casualty care and the large proportion of patients with musculoskeletal injuries have required innovations to the nursing care provided within the ERC system to ensure the appropriate level of care is provided.

INNOVATIONS

System-Level Innovations

The development of CCATT and Acute Lung Rescue Teams, as well as a Burn Flight Team which is dedicated to transporting burn casualties, has been important to expand the level of care provided within the ERC system and decrease the amount of time it takes to move the combat casualties out of the operational area—from 21 days during the Vietnam War to an average of 28 hr during the conflict in Iraq and Afghanistan (Blackbourne, Baer, Eastridge, Renz, et al., 2012). In addition, it has been identified that the need for a higher level of nursing care during transport within the combat zone has become increasingly necessary, particularly when transporting critically injured patients on rotary-wing transport (Nagra, 2011). This need for a higher level of far forward care led to the development of the en route critical care nurse role, after it was shown that 40%–80% of flights required nurse or medical intervention during transport (Nagra, 2011). The need for flight medics with paramedic training was also established when it was identified that there were lower mortality rates for critically injured patients (ISS >15) transported by a deployed National Guard medical evacuation unit staffed by critical care-trained flight paramedics (Blackbourne, Baer, Eastridge, Renz, et al., 2012; Holland, Apodaca, & Mabry, 2013).

A physician-led medical emergency response team was developed within the British military medical system and used in southern Afghanistan, with lower mortality rates among critically injured patients compared to the traditional casualty evacuation system led by either a basic emergency medical technician or paramedic (Apodaca et al., 2013). Although it is unclear why there is a benefit to the physician-led medical emergency response team response, it is hypothesized that earlier advanced interventions may be partially responsible for the improved survival rates, particularly among patients with ISS scores from 16 to 50 (Morrison et al., 2013). Acknowledging the need for earlier blood administration, one medical evacuation unit developed a process improvement study to evaluate the impact of providing blood products in the prehospital setting (Malsby et al., 2013). Preliminary findings suggest that this innovative approach is safe, but specific mortality outcomes have not yet been determined.

The U.S. Air Force has also developed a three-person Tactical Critical Care Evacuation Team (also referred to as "TCCET") consisting of a physician, a certified nurse anesthetist, and an emergency department or intensive care unit (ICU) nurse intended to provide critical care at the point of injury (Ricks, 2012). The current doctrine has been changed to support TCCET capability to transport patients from forward resuscitative care to theater hospitals (Vice Chairman of the Joint Chiefs of Staff, 2012), with TCCET clinicians already deployed to the combat zone who have provided critical care to these patients during transport.

Each of these innovative changes to the ERC system is dynamic and, as new evidence is identified, continues to evolve. These rapid changes, although necessary and groundbreaking, will require additional work to integrate with existing structure and clinical practices. However, these innovative practices can also be used as a model to consider in civilian trauma systems, particularly in rural areas (Bailey, Morrison, & Rasmussen, 2013).

Innovations in Spinal Immobilization

Between 2001 and 2009, among the 10,979 individuals with trauma evacuated from Iraq or Afghanistan, there were 502 individuals with spine injuries. These injuries were complex; each patient had an average of 3.7 spine injuries in addition to at least one other injury (Blair et al., 2012; Patzkowski, Blair, Schoenfeld, Lehman, & Hsu, 2012). A unique challenge in ERC is the need to safely transport patients with suspected unstable thoracolumbar spinal fractures. Although the standard of care in the United States is to secure the patients on a backboard during short transport from the site of injury to the hospital, this would not be feasible for the 8- to 10-hr transport from the theater to the U.S. military hospital in Germany. Previously, patients with unstable spinal fractures were transported on a North Atlantic Treaty Organization (NATO) litter with a 5-in. foam pad. To add rigidity, a piece of plywood was placed under the foam pad and the patients were log-rolled for pressure reduction. An innovation in the care of these patients was the introduction of the vacuum spine board (VSB) in 2009 (Mok, Jackson, Fang, & Freedman, 2013). The VSB is a bead-filled bag, which is molded around the patient. Air is then evacuated from the bag to create a hard shell, which immobilizes the patient. During initial evaluation, which was conducted by a team of Air Force nurse scientists and clinicians, the skin interface pressure was evaluated under conditions experienced in AE, including ascent and descent from 10,000-ft cabin altitude. A unique interface between the environment and the VSB was noted. With ascent to altitude, barometric pressure decreases. To maintain the rigidity of the VSB, additional air must be removed from the device upon ascent. With descent, the vacuum pressure may need to be adjusted to account for increased barometric pressure. A concern with the use of the VSB is the increased risk for pressure ulcers because the VSB creates a rigid surface that directly molds to the body. In ground-based care, patients with spinal precautions are log-rolled to decrease sacral pressure. Although lateral rotation in the VSB is possible because of the rigid nature of the VSB, there is no reduction in skin interface pressure. This finding led to the recommendation that the VSB be released upon ascent to altitude and that the patient be log-rolled as usual. Additional padding of the heels and occiput is also recommended; however, no padding interventions were feasible for the sacrum. These guidelines were disseminated as a part of the Joint Theater Trauma System (JTTS) Clinical Practice Guideline (CPG): Cervical and Thoracolumbar Spine Injury (JTTS, 2012). To evaluate the safety of the VSB, a study was conducted to compare the incidence of pressure ulcers in 60 patients transported on the VSB compared to 30 historical controls. In the VSB group, pressure ulcers occurred in 13% of cases. There were five Stage I and three Stage II pressure ulcers, with all the Stage II ulcers on the buttocks or sacrum. This incidence was not significantly different from the 10% rate observed in the control group. In addition, there were no cases of neurological deterioration in any of the patients. In both groups, patients requiring mechanical ventilation had the highest incidence of pressure ulcers. These results demonstrate the equivalence of the VSB with the previous immobilization method on the NATO litter. Further research is needed to decrease the risk of pressure ulcers on the sacrum and buttocks while maintaining spinal immobilization and to consider other options for spinal immobilization because the VSB restricts the nursing care which can be provided for these unique patients. Research is currently ongoing to characterize risk factors for pressure ulcers among all critically ill and injured patients undergoing long-distance AE.

Innovations in Pain Management

Pain has been a significant and frequently reported symptom in Veterans of Operations Enduring Freedom and Iraqi Freedom (Gironda, Clark, Massengale, & Walker, 2006). Adverse outcomes associated with poor pain control include the development of chronic pain and PTSD. Early identification and treatment of pain are known to reduce the incidence and severity of chronic pain conditions

(Gironda et al., 2006). Effective pain management serves to decrease or modulate the potent inflammatory response resulting in hypercoagulability, multiorgan dysfunction, systemic inflammatory response, acute lung injury, traumatic brain injury (TBI), depression, and PTSD (Malchow & Black, 2008).

The Air Force mission to evacuate casualties from theater to Germany and Germany to the United States in military transport aircraft provides a unique environment in which patient pain management is crucial. Patients enter into the AE system early in the course of illness and injury treatment and recovery. During strategic fixed-wing patient transport, the stresses of flight undoubtedly contribute to pain and difficulty in communicating pain to the AE crew.

Patients evacuated back to the United Kingdom were questioned about severity of pain from point of injury back through the chain of evacuation. Two-thirds of the patients rated the pain as either moderate or severe, with the severe score indicated by 53% of those who could remember (Aldington, McQuay, & Moore, 2011). Fast and Newton (2008) reviewed the literature for pain assessment in the civilian transport environment and found little empirically based information. In a 2008 study of pain during AE from LRMC to the United States, in 120 medical and surgical/trauma patients, 27% of patients reported moderate pain (pain score 4–7 out of 10) and 11% reported severe pain (pain score 8–10 out of 10; Pfennig & Bridges, 2008). Among the subset of trauma/surgical patients (n = 65), 51% reported moderate pain and 9% reported severe pain. Similarly, in a study of 41 combat trauma patients being evacuated from Afghanistan to LRMC, upon arrival to the aircraft from the hospital, 33% had moderate pain and 22% had severe pain (Gentry et al., 2010). The most severe pain (8.7 ± 1.1) was in patients with orthopedic injuries with external fixators. In addition, a study conducted by Buckenmaier and colleagues (2009) of pain during AE transport used an exploratory mixed methods design which included a survey and semistructured interviews. In this study, in which patients were surveyed after being transported to LRMC in Germany, 65% reported 50% or less pain relief during transport (Buckenmaier et al., 2009). Ground transport, often a bumpy ride to and from the aircraft and medical facilities, also contributes to pain experienced by ill and injured patients.

Anesthesiologists in the military have met to institute changes to address pain needs of trauma patients (Carter, 2010). Innovative pain care strategies have been instituted during all phases of casualty care, but there are limited data on the use and impact of these strategies in the short- and long-term outcomes of patients (Clark, Bair, Buckenmaier, Gironda, & Walker, 2007). Pain management with regional anesthesia techniques has been studied at Walter Reed Army Medical Center and has been found to be safe and effective (Stojadinovic et al., 2006). Organized in 2002, the Military Advanced Regional Anesthesia and Analgesia (MARAA) Committee is a triservice group that had a mission to develop, recommend, and implement advanced pain initiatives to be placed in the ERC environment. This group advocated for the use of continuous peripheral nerve blocks, which have been used extensively to treat isolated extremity injuries in civilian trauma. The group also advocated for use of patient-controlled analgesia and epidurals (Carter, 2010). The first successful application of a continuous peripheral nerve block on the battlefield, as described by MARAA, provided pain relief during a soldier's entire evacuation to include initial surgery and four subsequent surgeries. A peripheral nerve catheter remained in place for 16 days with no complications (Buckenmaier & Bleckner, 2008).

One of the primary advantages of preoperative regional anesthesia is the reduction of required intravenous opioid to relieve pain (Wu, Lollo, & Grabinsky, 2011). Recent research has found opioids to have some deleterious effects. The distribution of opioid receptors outside the central nervous system, such as the cells of the immune system (T cells, B cells, macrophages, etc.), indicates that opioids are capable of exerting immunomodulation (Ninković & Roy, 2013). Studies have shown that chronic opioid use can directly and indirectly suppress the immune system (Ninković & Roy, 2013). This immunomodulation could play a role in the frequency of posttrauma and postsurgical infection.

The JTTS Management of Pain, Anxiety, and Delirium in Injured Warfighters CPG (JTTS, 2013) advocates for a multimodality approach to pain therapy for injured combat casualties. Included with the more traditional intravenous narcotic pain control treatment options are epidural and peripheral nerve blocks and ketamine infusions. Low-dose ketamine infusions have been found to have a profound analgesic effect with minimal side effects. Ketamine binds the *N*-methyl-D-aspartate receptor and decreases the total dose of narcotics needed to treat a patient (JTTS, 2013).

Beginning in 2011, the U.S. Air Force Air Mobility Command initiated a policy establishing guidelines which allow patients with epidural analgesia and peripheral nerve blocks to move through the ERC system under the management of AE crew members and aeromedical staging facility personnel. Although pain management in the AE environment has received the attention of the military medical community and advancements have been made in management, the characterization of pain assessment, management, effectiveness, and outcomes have not been studied. Accurate pain assessment is a necessary precursor to effective pain management. However, pain assessment can be challenging in polytrauma patients, especially in those with severe head injury, cognitive impairment, and multiple wounds (Clark, Scholten, Walker, & Gironda, 2009). The environment of the aircraft adds additional difficulties to the assessment and documentation of pain.

Recently, a prospective assessment of real-time ratings of pain acceptability, intensity, and satisfaction of patients was conducted on AE missions from Ramstein Air Field, Germany, to Andrews Air Force Base (AFB), Maryland (Dukes, Bridges, McNeill, et al., 2013). A sample of 114 U.S. military personnel with injuries transported by AE on flights between December 2012 and May 2013 participated. Acceptable pain intensity was a median of 6/10 (range 2–9), with 76% of patients indicating an acceptable pain intensity greater than 4. During AE transport, 75% of patients reported at least one pain score of 4 or more, with the highest pain scores occurring upon arrival at the aircraft (4.3 ± 2.3), suggesting the need for interventions to safely optimize pain management during this handoff period.

In an effort to capture the environmental factors and social context impacting pain management in AE, an ethnographic study was also conducted onboard AE missions from Ramstein, Germany, to Andrews AFB, Maryland (Hatzfeld, Serres, & Dukes, 2013). Data collection was conducted during eight missions throughout 2013. The results of this study highlighted the need to have a coordinated effort through the ERC system, recognizing the need for preparatory guidance on pain management given to patients while they are still in the aeromedical staging facilities. This study also confirmed the commitment of both AE crew members and aeromedical staging facility personnel to helping patients manage pain. One particular area for interventions to further improve en route pain management is to overcome barriers to communication during transport.

Systems and human factors engineering approaches are also being used to document and assess pain management in the AE system. Human factors engineering considers the interactions of the environment, people, technologies, processes, information, and flow to improve system processes, performance, and safety. Preliminary results suggest pain management might be improved by implementing enhanced information sharing practices and enhanced system monitoring and feedback loops, streamlining and redesigning documentation, and expanding and supplementing procedures for patient flight preparation.

As we explore pain in the ERC system from various disciplines and begin to understand the AE patient's pain experience, innovative nonpharmacological means to treat pain in the ERC environment are also being pursued. Battlefield acupuncture is one such intervention that has been evaluated in the ERC environment. Battlefield acupuncture, which consists of acupuncture to the ear, was shown to be a feasible technique to be performed within the ERC system. Patients reported an average pain rating of 4.07 before battlefield acupuncture and pain scores 1-hr posttreatment and postflight of 2.17 and 2.76, respectively ($p < 000.1$; Burns et al., 2013).

Innovations in Monitoring

In the study of 2,439 casualties evacuated by CCATT in support of Operation Enduring Freedom and Operation Iraqi Freedom between 2001 and 2006, 69% of the casualties suffered polytrauma (Bridges & Evers, 2009). The complexity of these injuries is further highlighted in an analysis of 1,151 combat casualties, who had 3,500 surface wounds and 12,889 injuries, with an average of 11.2 injuries per casualty (Champion et al., 2010). Recently, there has been an increased incidence of complex dismounted blast injuries, where the casualty has suffered traumatic amputations of at least two extremities with or without pelvic and perineal blast involvement. In 63 combat casualties with complex blast injuries (137 amputations), the casualties received an average of 19.5 ± 18.2 (range 0–104) units of packed red blood cells (PRBCs; Fleming, Waterman, Dunne, D'Alleyrand, & Andersen, 2012). The ability to care for these complex patients in the austere and demanding ERC environment is challenging, particularly for those casualties who are stabilizing but may not be stable. Because of these complex injuries, there is a need for innovative use of technologies to enhance the ability to detect occult hemorrhage and the onset of hypoperfusion, guide therapies such as fluid volume resuscitation, and evaluate the patient's response because these critically injured casualties move across the care continuum.

Monitoring a patient's physiological status, detection of deterioration, and the response to therapies is based traditionally on standard vital signs (heart rate, blood pressure, oxygen saturation). A series of studies conducted by the U.S. Army Combat Casualty Research Program found that standard vital signs may remain unchanged in the face of impending cardiovascular collapse (Convertino & Ryan, 2007), and they failed to identify patients who required lifesaving interventions or to differentiate between patients with severe trauma who survived or died (Convertino et al., 2008). In contrast to vital signs, less invasive or noninvasive physiological parameters have been found to be potentially useful in monitoring and guiding therapy for patients at high risk for hemodynamic compromise.

Noninvasive Monitoring

Functional hemodynamic indicators, which include ventilator-induced variations in the amplitude of the arterial blood pressure or pulse oximeter waveform (pleth variability index [PVI]), are accurate indicators of a patient's ability to respond to a fluid bolus with an increase in stroke volume (Bridges, 2013; Marik, Cavallazzi, Vasu, & Hirani, 2009; Sandroni et al., 2012). However, the use of arterial-based measurements in ERC may be limited because not all patients have invasive monitoring. The Masimo Rainbow SET/Radical-7 Pulse Co-Oximeter, which is a noninvasive pulse oximeter, provides a continuous functional hemodynamic indicator (PVI) and total hemoglobin (SpHb). However, no studies had used this noninvasive monitoring method to describe the physiological status of severely injured combat casualties undergoing resuscitation. As an example of an innovation in care, a study of 24 critically injured combat casualties (ISS; 21 ± 10) who were admitted to two U.S. Military Role III trauma hospitals in Afghanistan was conducted to describe their physiological status during resuscitation across the emergency room, operating room, and ICU continuum. The patients' physiological status was described using standard vital signs, invasive and noninvasive functional hemodynamic indicators, and continuous hemoglobin (Bridges, 2011, 2012).

In a subset of 15 patients who had greater than 60 min of monitoring in the ICU, the PVI was significantly correlated with arterial-based functional hemodynamic indicators, and it was a sensitive and specific indicator of fluid responsiveness. The PVI was significantly higher in fluid responders versus nonresponders (23.0 ± 9.0 vs. 11.6 ± 2.8; $p < .001$), and a PVI threshold of 16 or more had a sensitivity of 86%, specificity of 94%, and an area under the curve of 0.93 (95% confidence interval [0.87–1.00]) to predict fluid responsiveness. These findings are important because they may aid in tailoring resuscitation to avoid the administration of fluids to a patient who is a nonresponder. In this case, if the patient is hypoperfused, alternative therapy such as a vasoactive medication may be needed. An important finding in this study was that changes in the PVI preceded clinical deterioration (Figure 3.2), which may provide an early warning sign of impending compromise. Although the PVI was an accurate predictor in the ICU setting, it was not useful in the operating room because of the frequent administration of vasoactive medications, continuous transfusions, and surgical stimulation.

Trending of SpHb has also been found to be useful in monitoring physiological status in trauma and surgical patients (Applegate et al., 2013; Baulig et al., 2013; Berkow, Rotolo, & Mirski, 2011; Miller, Ward, Shiboski, & Cohen, 2011). In the same study of the 24 combat casualties, the SpHb was not precise enough to replace the laboratory hemoglobin value (SpHb-Coulter Hb bias 0.3 ± 1.6 g/dl; 95% limits of agreement −2.8, 3.4 g/dl); however, continuous SpHb accurately detected acute changes in hemoglobin and identified critical decreases which were not detected by intermittent laboratory measurements. In 14 cases, one or more clinical events (systolic blood pressure [SBP] <90 mmHg, mean arterial pressure <60 mmHg, PRBC given) occurred, and in 6 out of 14 cases, the SpHb decreased >10% or 1 g/dl before the clinical event. In the case presented in Figure 3.2, the SpHb did not increase despite the administration of three units of PRBCs, suggesting that the transfusions were likely replacing ongoing blood losses. In addition, the increase in the PVI (suggesting a decrease in preload

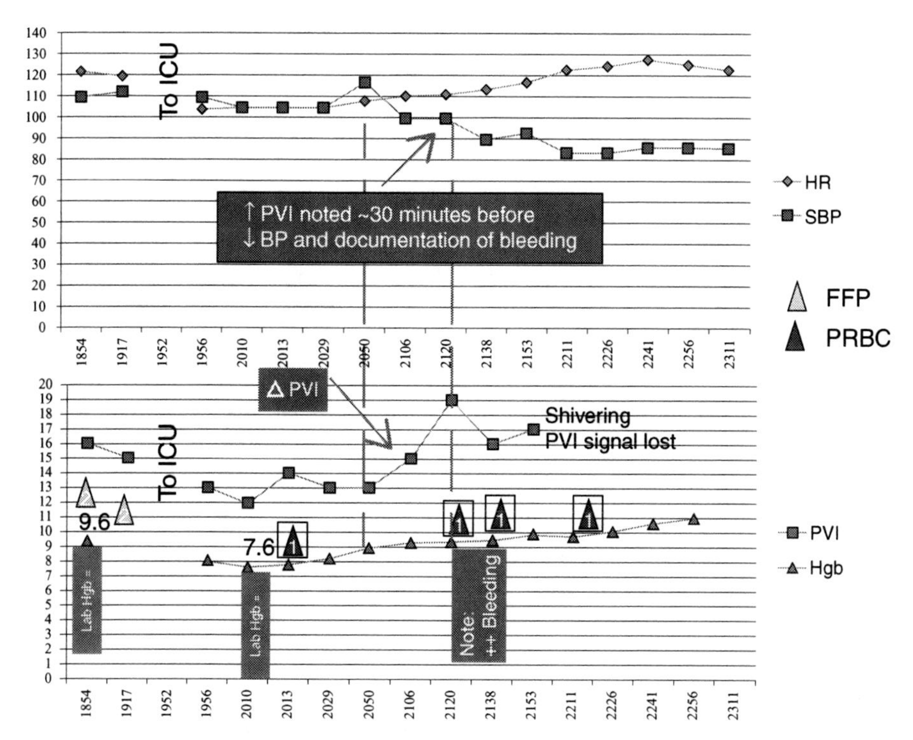

FIGURE 3.2 Physiological status of a combat casualty with injuries caused by an improvised explosive device. Injuries include a right leg below the knee amputation, left leg above the knee amputation, right arm fracture, puncture wounds on the buttocks and perineum, a scrotal injury, and right femoral neck fracture. The patient was admitted to the emergency department in a coagulopathic state. In the emergency department, the patient received four units of FFP. The decision was made to resuscitate the patient in the ICU with a surgical procedure to follow. In the ICU, the patient received one unit of PRBCs at 2,010 for a hemoglobin of 7.6 g/dl. The SpHb increased to approximately 9 g/dl after the transfusion. At 2,120, the patient was noted to be exsanguinating from his left leg amputation (HR = 110 bpm; SBP = 100 mmHg). The patient received three units of PRBCs over a 60-min period without a significant change in the SpHb (note that no laboratory hemoglobin was obtained). Also of note, the PVI started to increase at 2,050, which was approximately 30 min before a change in vital signs or blood loss was noted. (Abbreviations: ICU = intensive care unit; PVI = pleth variability index; BP = blood pressure; HR = heart rate; SBP = systolic blood pressure; FFP = fresh frozen plasma; PRBC = packed red blood cell; Hgb = hemoglobin)

because of hemorrhage) occurred approximately 30 min before the documentation of the blood loss and almost 1 hr before significant changes were noted in the vital signs. Together, these additional parameters may provide earlier identification of occult deterioration. Although this study describes the patients' physiological status while they move across the resuscitation continuum in a fixed facility, there have not been any published studies describing continuous SpHb monitoring or noninvasive functional hemodynamic monitoring to further characterize the patients' physiological status as they move across the medical evacuation or AE phases of the ERC continuum.

Monitoring Perfusion Status

The ability to monitor a patient's perfusion status to detect hypoperfusion and evaluate the response to therapy is integral to shock resuscitation. However, perfusion indicators that are available and feasible in the operational environment, such as base deficit (BD) or lactate, are intermittent. Skeletal tissue oxygen saturation (StO_2 <75%), which is obtained using noninvasive near-infrared spectroscopy, has been found to predict the development of organ dysfunction and outcomes in severely injured trauma victims (Cohn et al., 2007; Moore et al., 2008). The StO_2 measurement is obtained using a probe placed on the thenar eminence or forearm. A pilot study in 13 trauma patients demonstrated the feasibility of StO_2 monitoring in the prehospital setting, even when other vital signs could not be obtained (Lyon, Thompson, & Lockey, 2013). In 150 civilian trauma patients, although the absolute prehospital StO_2 did not predict the need for life-saving interventions, changes in the StO_2 in response to a vascular occlusion test were associated with severity of injury and mortality (Guyette et al., 2012). In a laboratory study involving the creation of central hypovolemia using lower body negative pressure, skeletal muscle oxygen saturation decreased during the first stage of the creation of central hypovolemia, in contrast to vital signs, which were late indicators of impending cardiovascular collapse (Soller et al., 2012). The use of StO_2 has been described in the military setting. In severely injured combat casualties, the StO_2 tracked with resuscitation efforts (Beilman & Blondet, 2009) and predicted which patients would require a blood transfusion despite having "stable" vital signs (Beekley et al., 2010). All of these studies demonstrate the frequency of occult hypoperfusion in trauma patients and the potential benefit of additional perfusion monitoring to detect this occult state and to guide therapy. A limitation of these previous studies is that the measurements were obtained at a single fixed location.

Given the rapid transport and need to maintain the highest level of care across the care continuum, it is important to understand the incidence of occult hypoperfusion as the combat casualties move from point of injury through transport and resuscitation at forward resuscitative care and theater hospitals. In an ongoing study being conducted in Afghanistan, intermittent vital signs and indicators of perfusion status (BD, lactate, and StO_2) are being measured in seriously injured combat casualties at the forward resuscitative care setting immediately before and after transport to theater hospital (Bridges & Beilman,

2013). In preliminary analysis of these data, hypoperfusion was present in 13 of 24 patients, with 6 patients in a severe state of shock and 6 with occult hypoperfusion. In two cases, the StO_2 was also less than 75%, which is consistent with a state of hypoperfusion. The case in Table 3.1 provides an example of a critically injured patient with occult hypoperfusion (BD = −12, StO_2 73%) despite aggressive resuscitation. In addition, despite relatively "normal" vital signs, the patient's condition may have deteriorated during the transport phase, as indicated by the worsening of the StO_2 (BD = −11, StO_2 62%).

A unique finding in this study, which is exemplified in Table 3.2, is the presence of hypoperfusion in three casualties with normal vital signs but a markedly elevated StO_2 (>90%). The increased StO_2 may suggest a shunt state or failure of oxygen use at the level of the mitochondria. The implications of this abnormal perfusion state were described in a pilot study of 10 seriously injured trauma patients (Burggraf & Waydhas, 2009). In 3 patients who had an initial StO_2 level greater than 85%, two developed multisystem organ failure (MOF) and 1 died. In 3 patients with an StO_2 level less than 75% on admission, 1 patient developed MOF and subsequently died. In contrast, no patients with a normal StO_2 (75%–85%) developed MOF or died. Further data collection is ongoing, with analysis focusing on absolute StO_2 values, as well as changes in StO_2 values pre- and posttransport and the incidence of hypoperfusion in the presence of an abnormally elevated StO_2. These results may inform future

TABLE 3.1

Example of Hypoperfusion and an Abnormally Low StO_2 in a Casualty Who Suffered a Gunshot Wound to the Arm, Abdomen, and Thigh

Vital Sign	Forward Resuscitative Care (pretransport)	Theater Hospital (posttransport)
HR (bpm)	60	104
BP (mmHg)	178/103	188/88
SaO_2 (%)	99	99
StO_2 (%)	73	62
Hgb (g/dl)	18	19
BD	−12	−11

Note. The patient underwent emergent damage control surgery (splenectomy, nephrectomy, and repair of soft tissue injuries) and received 12 units of packed red blood cells, 8 units of fresh frozen plasma, and 6 units of whole blood. The patient was hypothermic (93.3°F) despite warming. Pretransport vital signs were obtained 6.5 hr after injury and flight time was approximately 30 min. HR = heart rate; bpm = beats per minute; BP = blood pressure; SaO_2 = arterial oxygen saturation; StO_2 = skeletal tissue oxygen saturation; Hgb = hemoglobin; BD = base deficit.

TABLE 3.2

Casualty Who Fell Approximately 50 ft and Suffered a Mandibular Laceration, Bilateral Hemothorax/Pneumothorax, and an L1/L2 Vertebral Fracture

Vital Sign	Forward Resuscitative Care (pretransport)	Theater Hospital (posttransport)
HR (bpm)	102	93
BP (mmHg)	102/63	118/84
SaO_2 (%)	100	100
StO_2 (%)	100	58
Hgb (g/dl)	6	10
BD	−10	−5

Note. The casualty received 6 units of packed red blood cells (PRBCs) and 6 units of fresh frozen plasma (FFP) during the initial resuscitation. Preparation for transport from the Role II hospital was approximately 2 hr after the injury; 35 min elapsed between the pretransport and posttransport vital signs. During the transport, the patient received an additional 2 units of PRBCs and 2 units of FFP. HR = heart rate; bpm = beats per minute; BP = blood pressure; SaO_2 = arterial oxygen saturation; StO_2 = skeletal tissue oxygen saturation; Hgb = hemoglobin; BD = base deficit.

research integrating continuous StO_2 monitoring during transport and characterizing the microvascular perfusion state under cases where there is an abnormally increased StO_2.

IMPLICATIONS FOR FURTHER INNOVATION, RESEARCH, AND POLICY

In military operations in Iraq and Afghanistan, explosive blast has been, and continues to be, the most common wounding etiology, earning TBI the title of the "signature injury" of the conflict in Iraq (Hoge et al., 2008). TBI patients who survive the primary trauma are highly susceptible to secondary insults to the injured brain. These secondary insults are a delayed, physiological response to the primary injury and associated with worse outcomes (Chestnut et al., 1993). The austere ERC environment poses challenges to the monitoring and care of patients with TBI, and the stresses of flight can potentially contribute to secondary neurological insults (Fang, Dorlac, Allan, & Dorlac, 2010; Goodman et al., 2010). A study was conducted of secondary insults (e.g., hypotension, hypoxia, hyperthermia, hypothermia, hyperglycemia, and hypertension) which occurred in patients with severe TBI who were evacuated from Iraq or Afghanistan from 2003 to 2006 (Dukes, Bridges, & Johantgen, 2013). This study found that hyperthermia was the secondary insult documented most frequently, with 47%

of the patients suffering at least one episode of an increased temperature. In addition, 25% of the patients suffered from hypoxia at some point from the point of injury to arrival back in the United States. A study by O'Connell, Littleton-Kearney, Bridges, and Bibb (2012) identified that secondary insults of hypothermia and hypoxemia after TBI increased the odds of 24-hr mortality. These studies help provide a better understanding of secondary insults in patients with TBI in the unique ERC environment. Innovative preventive or protective measures are needed to contribute to improved outcomes for these combat casualties.

Closed-loop technology is another emerging capability within health care because it allows clinicians to focus on multiple priorities while patients are maintained at a safe equilibrium (Arney et al., 2010). This innovation may be particularly helpful in the transport environment, when clinicians may be unable to monitor and respond to patients at certain points during flight, such as takeoff and landing and during turbulence. The prospective study of pain during fixed-wing flight from LRMC to Andrews identified that the mean time from "wheels up" (or takeoff) to cruising altitude, when it is safe for crew members to remove their seatbelt and attend to a patient, was 39 ± 33 min, but this restricted period lasted as long as 131 min in at least one flight (Dukes, Bridges, McNeill, et al., 2013). This unique care environment demonstrates the necessity and potential value of closed-loop technology within the ERC system, especially for ventilation and sedation. Further research and regulatory approvals will be needed to establish the reliability of closed-loop technology in this dynamic setting, and policies will need to be changed to incorporate this future innovation.

CONCLUSION

The ERC setting is an essential part of combat casualty care, and providing nursing care in this unique environment is both challenging and dynamic. System innovations, as well as innovations to provide spinal immobilization, adequate pain management, and technology to monitor patient status, have demonstrated improved outcomes and continue to increase the survival rates for these wounded warriors. Further refinement of these innovations and additional analysis of clinical data are essential to capture the full benefits. However, continued innovations are needed in the future, particularly to understand the secondary insults for complex injuries such as TBI and closed-loop technology. With the termination of military operations in Iraq and the anticipated conclusion of military operations in Afghanistan, the numbers of combat injured are expected to diminish. The ERC clinicians, researchers, and leaders will need to ensure that these innovations are institutionalized and future innovations keep pace with the rapid pace of discovery.

DISCLAIMER

The views expressed in this chapter are those of the authors and do not necessarily represent the official position or policy of the Air Force, the Department of Defense, or the U.S. government.

REFERENCES

Aldington, D. J., McQuay, H. J., & Moore, R. A. (2011). End-to-end military pain management. *Philosophical Transactions of the Royal Society of London. Series B, Biological Sciences*, *366*(1562), 268–275.

Apodaca, A., Olson, C. M., Jr., Bailey, J., Butler, F., Eastridge, B. J., & Kuncir, E. (2013). Performance improvement evaluation of forward aeromedical evacuation platforms in Operation Enduring Freedom. *Journal of Trauma and Acute Care Surgery*, *75*(2 Suppl. 2), S157–S163.

Applegate, R., Collier, C., Mangus, D., Barr, S. J., Macknet, M., Hassanian, M., & Allard, M. (2013, May). *Evaluation of absolute and trend accuracy of Revision G noninvasive and continuous hemoglobin monitoring during major surgery*. Paper presented at the 2013 Annual Meeting of the International Anesthesia Research Society, San Diego, CA.

Armed Forces Health Surveillance Center. (2012a). Medical evacuations from Operation Iraqi Freedom/Operation New Dawn, active and reserve components, U.S. Armed Forces, 2003–2011. *Medical Surveillance Monthly Report*, *19*(2), 18–21.

Armed Forces Health Surveillance Center. (2012b). Surveillance snapshot: Medical evacuations from Operation Enduring Freedom (OEF), active and reserve components, U.S. Armed Forces, October 2001-December 2011. *Medical Surveillance Monthly Report*, *19*(2), 22.

Arney, D., Pajic, M., Goldman, J., Lee, I., Mangharam, R., & Sokolsky, O. (2010, April). *Toward patient safety in closed-loop medical device systems*. Paper presented at Cyber-Physical Systems (ICCPS 2010), Stockholm, Sweden.

Bailey, J. A., Morrison, J. J., & Rasmussen, T. E. (2013). Military trauma system in Afghanistan: Lessons for civil systems? *Current Opinion in Critical Care*, *19*(6), 569–577.

Baulig, W., Prassler, S., Sulser, S., Dambach, M., Biro, P., & Theusinger, O. (2013). Non-invasive detection of hemoglobin concentration by pulse co-oximetry in severely traumatized patients. *European Journal of Anaesthesiology*, *30*(Suppl. 51), 50.

Beekley, A. C., Martin, M. J., Nelson, T., Grathwohl, K. W., Griffith, M., Beilman, G., & Holcomb, J. B. (2010). Continuous noninvasive tissue oximetry in the early evaluation of the combat casualty: A prospective study. *Journal of Trauma*, *69*(Suppl. 1), S14–25.

Beilman, G. J., & Blondet, J. J. (2009). Near-infrared spectroscopy-derived tissue oxygen saturation in battlefield injuries: A case series report. *World Journal of Emergency Surgery*, *4*, 25.

Berkow, L., Rotolo, S., & Mirski, E. (2011). Continuous noninvasive hemoglobin monitoring during complex spine surgery. *Anesthesia and Analgesia*, *113*(6), 1396–1402.

Blackbourne, L. H., Baer, D. G., Eastridge, B. J., Butler, F. K., Wenke, J. C., Hale, R. G., . . . Holcomb, J. B. (2012). Military medical revolution: Military trauma system. *Journal of Trauma and Acute Care Surgery*, *73*(6 Suppl. 5), S388–S394.

Blackbourne, L. H., Baer, D. G., Eastridge, B. J., Renz, E. M., Chung, K. K., DuBose, J., . . . Holcomb, J. B. (2012). Military medical revolution: Deployed hospital and en route care. *Journal of Trauma and Acute Care Surgery*, *73*(6 Suppl. 5), S378–S387.

Blair, J. A., Patzkowski, J. C., Schoenfeld, A. J., Cross Rivera, J. D., Grenier, E. S., Lehman, R. A. (2012). Are spine injuries sustained in battle truly different? *Spine Journal*, *12*(9), 824–829.

Bolorunduro, O., B., Villegas, C., Oyetunji, T. A., Haut, E. R., Stevens, K. A., Chang, D. C., . . . Haider, A. H. (2011). Validating the Injury Severity Score (ISS) in different populations: ISS predicts mortality better among Hispanics and females. *Journal of Surgical Research*, *166*(1), 40–44.

Bridges, E. (2011). Noninvasive hemoglobin monitoring in seriously injured combat casualties. *Critical Care Medicine*, *39*(12 Suppl.), 111.

Bridges, E. (2012). Monitoring of pleth variability index in seriously injured combat casualties. *American Journal of Critical Care*, *21*(3), e84.

Bridges, E. (2013). Using functional hemodynamic indicators to guide fluid therapy. *American Journal of Nursing*, *113*(5), 42–50.

Bridges, E., & Beilman, G. (2013). Occult hypoperfusion in seriously injured combat casualties pre/post MEDEVAC transport. *Critical Care Medicine*, *41*(12 Suppl. 1), A67.

Bridges, E., & Evers, K. (2009). Wartime critical care air transport. *Military Medicine*, *174*(4), 370–375.

Buckenmaier, C., & Bleckner, L. (2008). *Military advanced regional anesthesia and analgesia handbook*. Washington, DC: Borden Institute.

Buckenmaier, C. C., III, Rupprecht, C., McKnight, G., McMillan, B., White, R. L., Gallagher, R. M., & Polomano, R. (2009). Pain following battlefield injury and evacuation: A survey of 110 casualties from the wars in Iraq and Afghanistan. *Pain Medicine*, *10*(8), 1487–1496.

Burggraf, M., & Waydhas, C. (2009, October). *StO_2 measurement in the early post-resuscitation period after traumatic hemorrhagic shock*. Paper presented at the StO_2 Shock Conference, Vienna, Austria.

Burns, S., York, A., Niemtzow, R. C., Garner, B. K., Steele, N., & Walter, J. A. (2013). Moving acupuncture to the frontline of military medical care: A feasibility study. *Medical Acupuncture*, *25*(1), 48–54.

Carter, G., Couch, R., & O'Brien, D. J. (1988). The evolution of air transport systems: A pictorial review. *Journal of Emergency Medicine*, *6*(6), 499–504.

Carter, T. E. (2010). The multifaceted role of today's military anesthesiologist: Perioperative and transport physicians. *International Anesthesiology Clinics*, *48*(2), 123–135.

Chairman of the Joint Chiefs of Staff. (2012). Health service support (Joint Publication 4-02). Retrieved from http://www.dtic.mil/doctrine/new_pubs/jp4_02.pdf

Carter, G., Couch, R., O'Brien, D. J. The evolution of air transport systems: a pictorial review. *Journal of Emergency Medicine*, *6*(6), 499–504.

Champion, H. R., Holcomb, J. B., Lawnick, M. M., Kelliher, T., Spott, M. A., Galarneau, M. R., . . . Shair, E. K. (2010). Improved characterization of combat injury. *Journal of Trauma*, *68*(5), 1139–1150.

Chestnut, R. M., Marshall, L. F., Klauber, M. R., Blunt, B. A., Baldwin, N., Eisenberg, H. M., . . . Foulkes, M. A. (1993). The role of secondary brain injury in determining outcome from severe head injury. *Journal of Trauma*, *34*(2), 216–222.

Clark, M. E., Bair, M. J., Buckenmaier, C. C., III, Gironda, R. J., & Walker, R. L. (2007). Pain and combat injuries in soldiers returning from Operations Enduring Freedom and Iraqi Freedom: Implications for research and practice. *Journal of Rehabilitation Research and Development*, *44*(2), 179–194.

Clark, M. E., Scholten, J. D., Walker, R. L., & Gironda, R. J. (2009). Assessment and treatment of pain associated with combat-related polytrauma. *Pain Medicine*, *10*(3), 456–469.

Cohen, S. P., Brown, C., Kurihara, C., Plunkett, A., Nguyen, C., & Strassels, S. A. (2010). Diagnoses and factors associated with medical evacuation and return to duty for service members participating in Operation Iraqi Freedom or Operation Enduring Freedom: A prospective cohort study. *Lancet*, *375*, 301–309.

Cohn, S. M., Nathens, A. B., Moore, F. A., Rhee, P., Puyana, J. C., Moore, E. E. (2007). Tissue oxygen saturation predicts the development of organ dysfunction during traumatic shock resuscitation. *Journal of Trauma*, *62*(1), 44–54.

Convertino, V. A., & Ryan, K. L. (2007). Identifying physiological measurements for medical monitoring: Implications for autonomous health care in austere environments. *Journal of Gravitational Physiology*, *14*(1), P39–P42.

Convertino, V. A., Ryan, K. L., Rickards, C. A., Salinas, J., McManus, J. G., Cooke, W. H., & Holcomb, J. B. (2008). Physiological and medical monitoring for en route care of combat casualties. *Journal of Trauma*, *64*(4 Suppl.), S342–S353.

Dukes, S. F., Bridges, E., & Johantgen, M. (2013). Occurrence of secondary insults of traumatic brain injury in patients transported by critical care air transport teams from Iraq/Afghanistan: 2003–2006. *Military Medicine*, *178*(1), 11–17.

Dukes, S., Bridges, E., McNeill, M., Serres, J., Thomas, M., & Sapp, T. (2013, August). Assessment of pain in aeromedical evacuation. Poster presented at Military Health System Research Symposium, Ft. Lauderdale, FL.

Fang, R., Allan, P. F., Womble, S. G., Porter, M. T., Sierra-Nunez, J., Russ, R. S., . . . Dorlac, W. C. (2011). Closing the "care in the air" capability gap for severe lung injury: The Landstuhl Acute Lung Rescue Team and extracorporeal lung support. *Journal of Trauma*, *71*(1 Suppl.), S91–S97.

Fang, R., Dorlac, G. R., Allan, P. F., & Dorlac, W. C. (2010). Intercontinental aeromedical evacuation of patients with traumatic brain injuries during Operations Iraqi Freedom and Enduring Freedom. *Neurosurgical Focus*, *28*(5), E11.

Fast, M., & Newton, S. (2008). Assessment of pain in the transport environment: A review of the literature. *Journal of Emergency Nursing*, *34*(4), 301–304.

Fleming, M., Waterman, S., Dunne, J., D'Alleyrand, J. C., & Andersen, R. C. (2012). Dismounted complex blast injuries: Patterns of injuries and resource utilization associated with the multiple extremity amputee. *Journal of Surgical Orthopaedic Advances*, *21*(1), 32–37.

Gentry, C., Frazier, L., Ketz, A., Abel, L., Castro, M., Steele, N., & Bridges, E. J. (2010, November). *Preflight/enroute pain management of trauma victims transported by USAF AE from Operation Enduring Freedom*. Poster presented at the 116th Annual Meeting of AMSUS, the Society of Federal Health Professionals, San Antonio, TX.

Gironda, R. J., Clark, M. E., Massengale, J. P., & Walker, R. L. (2006). Pain among Veterans of Operations Enduring Freedom and Iraqi Freedom. *Pain Medicine*, *7*(4), 339–343.

Goodman, M. D., Makley, A. T., Lentsch, A. B., Barnes, S. L., Dorlac, G. R., Dorlac, W. C., . . . Pritts, T. A. (2010). Traumatic brain injury and aeromedical evacuation: When is the brain fit to fly? *Journal of Surgical Research*, *164*(2), 286–293.

Guyette, F. X., Gomez, H., Suffoletto, B., Quintero, J., Mesquida, J., Kim, H. K., . . . Pinsky, M. R. (2012). Prehospital dynamic tissue oxygen saturation response predicts in-hospital lifesaving interventions in trauma patients. *Journal of Trauma and Acute Care Surgery*, *72*(4), 930–935.

Hatzfeld, J., Serres, J., & Dukes, S. (2013, November). *Understanding pain management in the aeromedical evacuation system*. Poster presented at the 118th Annual Meeting of AMSUS, the Society of Federal Health Professionals, Seattle, WA.

Hickman, B. J., & Mehrer, R. (2001). Stress and the effects of air transport on flight crews. *Journal of Air Medical Transport*, *20*(6), 6–9.

Hoge, C. W., McGurk, D., Thomas, J. L., Cox, A. L., Engel, C. C., & Castro, C. A. (2008). Mild traumatic brain injury in U.S. soldiers returning from Iraq. *New England Journal of Medicine*, *358*, 453–463.

Holland, S. R., Apodaca, A., & Mabry, R. L. (2013). MEDEVAC: Survival and physiological parameters improved with higher level of flight medic training. *Military Medicine*, *178*(5), 529–536.

Joint Theater Trauma System. (2012). *Cervical and thoracolumbar spine injury*. Retrieved from http://www.usaisr.amedd.army.mil/assets/cpgs/Cervical_and_Thoracolumbar_Spine_Injury_9_Mar_12.pdf

Joint Theater Trauma System. (2013). *Management of pain, anxiety and delirium in injured warfighters*. Retrieved from http://www.usaisr.amedd.army.mil/assets/cpgs/Management_of_Pain_Anxiety_and%20Delirium_5_Apr_2013.pdf

Lyon, R. M., Thompson, J., & Lockey, D. J. (2013). Tissue oxygen saturation measurement in prehospital trauma patients: A pilot, feasibility study. *Emergency Medicine Journal*, *30*(6), 506–508.

Malchow, R. J., & Black, I. H. (2008). The evolution of pain management in the critically ill trauma patient: Emerging concepts from the global war on terrorism. *Critical Care Medicine*, *36* (7 Suppl.), S346–S357.

Malsby, R. F., III, Quesada, J., Powell-Dunford, N., Kinoshita, R., Kurtz, J., Gehlen, W., . . . Shackelford, S. (2013). Prehospital blood product transfusion by U.S. Army MEDEVAC during combat operations in Afghanistan: A process improvement initiative. *Military Medicine*, *178*(7), 785–791.

Manring, M. M., Hawk, A., Calhoun, J. H., & Andersen, R. C. (2009). Treatment of war wounds: Historical review. *Clinical Orthopaedics and Related Research*, *467*(8), 2168–2191.

Marik, P. E., Cavallazzi, R., Vasu, T., & Hirani, A. (2009). Dynamic changes in arterial waveform derived variables and fluid responsiveness in mechanically ventilated patients: A systematic review of the literature. *Critical Care Medicine*, *37*(9), 2642–2647.

Mason, P. E., Eadie, J. S., & Holder, A. D. (2008). Prospective observational study of United States (US) Air Force Critical Care Air Transport team operations in Iraq. *Journal of Emergency Medicine*, *41*(1), 8–13.

Miller, R. D., Ward, T. A., Shiboski, S. C., & Cohen, N. H. (2011). A comparison of three methods of hemoglobin monitoring in patients undergoing spine surgery. *Anesthesia and Analgesia*, *112*(4), 858–863.

Mok, J. M., Jackson, K. L., Fang, R., & Freedman, B. A. (2013). Effect of vacuum spine board immobilization on incidence of pressure ulcers during evacuation of military casualties from theater. *Spine Journal*, *13*(12), 1801–1808.

Moore, F. A., Nelson, T., McKinley, B. A., Moore, E. E., Nathens, A. B., Rhee, P. (2008). Massive transfusion in trauma patients: Tissue hemoglobin oxygen saturation predicts poor outcome. *Journal of Trauma*, *64*(4), 1010–1023.

Morrison, J. J., Oh, J., Dubose, J. J., O'Reilly, D. J., Russell, R. J., Blackbourne, L. H., . . . Rasmussen, T. E. (2013). En-route care capability from point of injury impacts mortality after severe wartime injury. *Annals of Surgery*, *257*(2), 330–334.

Nagra, M. (2011). Optimizing wartime en route nursing care in Operation Iraqi Freedom. *US Army Medical Department Journal*, 51–58.

Ninković, J., & Roy, S. (2013). Role of the mu-opioid receptor in opioid modulation of immune function. *Amino Acids*, *45*(1), 9–24.

O'Connell, K. M., Littleton-Kearney, M. T., Bridges, E., & Bibb, S. C. (2012). Evaluating the Joint Theater Trauma Registry as a data source to benchmark casualty care. *Military Medicine*, *177*(5), 546–552.

Patzkowski, J. C., Blair, J. A., Schoenfeld, A. J., Lehman, R. A., & Hsu, J. R. (2012). Multiple associated injuries are common with spine fractures during war. *Spine Journal*, *12*(9), 791–797.

Pfennig, P., & Bridges, E. (2008, May). *Pain management in operational aeromedical evacuation*. Paper presented at the 79th Annual Scientific Meeting of the Aerospace Medical Association, Boston, MA.

Rasmussen, T. E., Gross, K. R., & Baer, D. G. (2013). Where do we go from here? Preface. US Military Health System Research Symposium, August 2013. *The Journal of Trauma and Acute Care Surgery*, *75*(2 Suppl. 2), S105–S106.

Ricks, M. (2012, June 2). New tactical care teams aim to save more lives. *Air Force Times*, Retrieved from http://www.airforcetimes.com/article/20120602/NEWS/206020301/New-tactical-care-teams-aim-save-more-lives.

Sandroni, C., Cavallaro, F., Marano, C., Falcone, C., De Santis, P., & Antonelli, M. (2012). Accuracy of plethysmographic indices as predictors of fluid responsiveness in mechanically ventilated adults: A systematic review and meta-analysis. *Intensive Care Medicine*, *38*(9), 1429–1437.

Soller, B. R., Zou, F., Ryan, K. L., Rickards, C. A., Ward, K., & Convertino, V. A. (2012). Lightweight noninvasive trauma monitor for early indication of central hypovolemia and tissue acidosis: A review. *Journal of Trauma and Acute Care Surgery*, *73*(2 Suppl. 1), S106–S111.

Stojadinovic, A., Auton, A., Peoples, G. E., McKnight, G. M., Shields, C., Croll, S. M., . . . Buckenmaier, C. C., III. (2006). Responding to challenges in modern combat casualty care: Innovative use of advanced regional anesthesia. *Pain Medicine*, *7*(4), 330–338.

Vice Chairman of the Joint Chiefs of Staff. (2012). *Tactical critical care transport DOTMLPF change recommendation* (Joint Requirements Oversight Council Memorandum 026-12). Washington, DC: Joint Chiefs of Staff.

Wu, J. J., Lollo, L., & Grabinsky, A. (2011). Regional anesthesia in trauma medicine. *Anesthesiology Research and Practice*, 713281. http://dx.doi.org/10.1155/2011/713281

CHAPTER 4

Embedded Metal Fragments

John F. Kalinich, Elizabeth A. Vane, Jose A. Centeno, Joanna M. Gaitens, Katherine S. Squibb, Melissa A. McDiarmid, and Christine E. Kasper

ABSTRACT

The continued evolution of military munitions and armor on the battlefield, as well as the insurgent use of improvised explosive devices, has led to embedded fragment wounds containing metal and metal mixtures whose long-term toxicologic and carcinogenic properties are not as yet known. Advances in medical care have greatly increased the survival from these types of injuries. Standard surgical guidelines suggest leaving embedded fragments in place, thus individuals may carry these retained metal fragments for the rest of their lives. Nursing professionals will be at the forefront in caring for these wounded individuals, both immediately after the trauma and during the healing and rehabilitation process. Therefore, an understanding of the potential health effects of embedded metal fragment wounds is essential. This review will explore the history of embedded fragment wounds, current research in the field, and Department of Defense and Department of Veterans Affairs guidelines for the identification and long-term monitoring of individuals with embedded fragments.

By the late 17th century, when it was realized that the ball was not poisonous, surgeons were urged not to probe too deeply, but rather to let the ball remain if it could not be located easily.

—Mary Gillett, The Army Medical Department, 1775–1818, p. 18

http://dx.doi.org/10.1891/0739-6686.32.63

INTRODUCTION

It is estimated that close to 40,000 U.S. personnel injured in the conflicts in Iraq and Afghanistan may have embedded metal fragments in their bodies (Department of Defense [DOD], 2013). Standard surgical guidelines suggest leaving embedded fragments in place except for certain circumstances. These recommendations attempt to balance the potential long-term health risk of the embedded fragment with the risk of morbidity which extensive surgery brings. Adding to this dilemma is the fact that as a result of advances in vehicle armor and weapons design and the insurgent use of improvised explosive devices (IEDs), the list of metals and metal mixtures which may be found as embedded fragments is practically endless. Furthermore, little if anything is known about the toxicologic and carcinogenic effect of these materials when found as embedded fragment wounds. As a result, the issue of embedded metal fragments has become a primary concern both within the DOD and the Department of Veterans Affairs (DVA). This chapter will review some of the experimental data on embedded metal fragments, current DOD and DVA policy for long-term monitoring of personnel with these injuries, and critical shortcomings in our knowledge on the effects of embedded metal fragments.

HEALTH EFFECTS OF EMBEDDED FRAGMENTS: ANIMAL STUDIES

Laboratory investigations into the health effects of embedded metals have been ongoing for many decades. Primarily, these investigations have focused on the safety of implanted medical devices (International Agency for Research on Cancer [IARC], 1999) and the development of "nontoxic" hunting ammunition (Brewer, Fairbrother, Clark, & Amick, 2003; Kelly et al., 1998; Kraabel, Miller, Getzy, & Ringelman, 1996; Mitchell et al., 2001a; Mitchell et al., 2001b; Mitchell et al., 2001c). Little has been done throughout the years to assess the long-term health effects of military-relevant metals and metal mixtures (Kane, Kasper, & Kalinich, 2009). However, that changed after the First Persian Gulf War (Gulf War I) in 1991 when depleted uranium (DU) munitions were first used in combat. Natural uranium consists primarily of three isotopes: ^{234}U, ^{235}U, and ^{238}U. DU is the by-product of the enrichment process to extract the high-specific activity uranium isotopes (e.g., ^{234}U and ^{235}U) from natural uranium for nuclear weapon and power plant use. As a result of this process, a uranium fraction is generated that has a lower (or "depleted") ratio of ^{234}U and ^{235}U with respect to ^{238}U than that found in natural uranium. From a chemical perspective, DU is identical to natural uranium, but because of the lower percentage of ^{234}U and ^{235}U in DU as compared to natural uranium, it is approximately 40% less radioactive and is primarily an alpha and weak gamma emitter (Parkhurst et al., 2005). Because of the density of DU (about 1.7 times greater than lead), it is used in the armor of battle tanks, including the Abrams Main Battle Tank and the Bradley Fighting Vehicle. Along with its density, DU has two additional properties that make it ideal for use in kinetic energy penetrators. First, DU penetrators are "self-sharpening." Briefly, when a DU penetrator impacts a target, microscopic particles of DU are sheared off as a result. This process of adiabatic shear allows the DU penetrator to retain a sharp point as it perforates the target. Second, the DU particles resulting from the shearing effect are pyrophoric and can ignite under the proper conditions, causing further damage.

As a result of friendly-fire incidents in the First Persian Gulf War, several U.S. military personnel were wounded by DU fragments. Standard surgical guidelines suggested leaving embedded fragments in place. However, because of the unique chemical and radiological properties of DU, questions were raised over the wisdom of leaving these fragments in place for the life of the individual. Because of the lack of available information on the long-term effects of embedded DU, the Armed Forces Radiobiology Research Institute (AFRRI; Bethesda, Maryland) and the Inhalation Toxicology Research Institute (now Lovelace Respiratory Research Institute, Albuquerque, New Mexico) were tasked with investigating the biokinetics and toxicology of embedded DU fragments. A laboratory rodent model to study the health effects of embedded fragments was developed and validated at AFRRI (Castro et al., 1996) using military-grade metals manufactured into cylinders 1 mm in diameter by 2 mm in length. Embedded DU fragments were found to rapidly solubilize, releasing uranium into the body, with detectable levels of DU found in the urine of the fragment-implanted rodents within 2 days postimplantation (Pellmar et al., 1999). Although histopathology examination of the tissue surrounding the embedded fragment showed microscopic particulate debris identified as DU, no adverse tissue effects were observed, unless much larger fragments of DU were implanted, in which case, metal-associated sarcomas were found at the implantation site (Hahn, Guilmette, & Hoover, 2002). These findings led to a reassessment of the DOD fragment removal policy, as it related to embedded DU, with the recommendation that larger fragments (>1 cm in diameter) be more aggressively excised and patients followed for any long-term adverse health effects (Office of the Surgeon General [OTSG]/MEDCOM, 2011).

These initial studies paved the way for additional research on the biokinetics, neurotoxicity, mutagenicity, and reproductive toxicity of embedded DU. In a rat model system, uranium solubilized from embedded fragments was found to cross the blood–brain barrier and accumulate preferentially in specific areas of the brain including the cortex, midbrain, and cerebellum (Fitsanakis et al., 2006). However, this accumulation did not appear to affect any behavioral parameters (Arfsten et al., 2007; Pellmar et al., 1999). Other studies suggested that DU is mutagenic and that the genetic damage can be transferred to offspring from DU-implanted fathers in a laboratory mouse model (Miller, Stewart, & Rivas, 2010). However, other studies using embedded DU and a rat model system showed that embedded DU did not affect reproductive ability or the health of offspring when fathers were implanted with DU pellets (Arfsten et al., 2005; Arfsten et al., 2006; Arfsten et al., 2009).

Because of continuing concerns over the health and environmental effects of DU munitions, replacement materials were sought and several tungsten-based compositions appeared promising. However, when one of these compositions (tungsten/nickel/cobalt) was tested using the AFRRI embedded fragment model system, it was discovered that this composition induced malignant, highly aggressive rhabdomyosarcomas at the implantation sites (Kalinich et al., 2005). These tumors were clearly evident as early as 4 months after implantation. Conversely, a material composed of tungsten/nickel/iron did not result in any tumor formation (Schuster et al., 2012). These findings reinforced the primary caveat when designing studies with embedded fragments: The material under investigation must be identical, in terms of composition and manufacturing processes, to that found in the field. For example, tungsten-containing hunting ammunition was found to have no adverse health effects when surgically implanted into the muscles of mallards (Kraabel et al., 1996); however, military-grade tungsten alloy compositions induced rhabdomyosarcomas when implanted into the leg muscles of laboratory rodents. Although both these compositions contained primarily tungsten with smaller concentrations of transition metals, they were not manufactured using similar procedures. These findings highlight the danger of attempting to extrapolate health risks from similar but not identical compounds.

Several factors come into play when attempting to judge the risk from embedded metal fragments. Most obvious is the identity of the metal or metals themselves. Related to this is the bioavailability of the components of the fragments (Yokel, Lasley, & Dorman, 2006). Highly soluble metals have the potential to produce systemic toxicity as well as induce organ-specific effects, whereas this is not a primary issue with insoluble metals (Emond & Kalinich, 2012). In many cases, the solubilized metals are excreted in the urine, making urinary metal analysis an important tool in identifying embedded metal fragments (Kalinich, Vergara, & Emond, 2008). Reactions at the surface of the embedded fragment can produce reactive oxygen or nitrogen species, resulting in local tissue damage and potentially initiating cell transformation pathways leading to carcinogenesis (Thomsen & Gretzer, 2001). In other cases, this damage remains localized and a fibrous capsule forms around the fragment.

HEALTH EFFECTS OF EMBEDDED FRAGMENTS: THE HUMAN EXPERIENCE

Embedded metal fragment injuries are not a new phenomenon. They have been a potential battlefield injury since the invention of gunpowder. However, because of the ballistic properties of the ammunition used in early weapons, most injuries resulted in death or traumatic amputation (Manring, Hawk, Calhoun, & Andersen, 2009). It was not until the development of the full metal–jacketed bullet around the time of the Spanish–American War that the survivability from battle wounds improved and the probability of embedded metal fragments increased (Dougherty & Eidt, 2009). The health risk of embedded fragments was considered low because they were considered to be inert once in the body. However, there began appearing in the scientific literature occasional reports on medical issues associated with embedded fragment wounds (Eylon et al., 2005; Knox & Wilkinson, 1981; Ligtenstein, Krijnen, Jansen, & Eulderink, 1994; Lindeman, McKay, Taubman, & Bilous, 1990; Schenck & Kronman, 1977; Symonds, Mackay, & Morley, 1985). In most cases, these wounds were suffered during wartime many years prior to the manifestation of the adverse health effect and, in all cases, the fragment was not characterized. However, other reports describing health problems associated with retained metal fragments did analyze the excised fragment, and in most cases, it was identified as lead (Akhtar, Funnye, & Akanno, 2003; Coon, Miller, Shirazi, & Sullivan, 2006; Farrell, Vandevander, Schoffstall, & Lee, 1999; John & Boatright, 1999; McQuirter et al., 2004; McQuirter et al., 2001; Nguyen et al., 2005; Rehani & Wissman, 2011). In addition, in many of these cases, a viscous lead-containing liquid was found around the embedded fragment suggesting that, once in the body, many metals can solubilize and become systemic. Health issues with embedded fragments are not limited to lead bullets. Two recent reports describe granuloma formation resulting from embedded fragments of a chainsaw and lawnmower blade, respectively (Osawa et al., 2006; Saruwatari et al., 2009). Various metals comprised both the chain saw and lawnmower blades, but the primary component was tungsten. Even surgically implanted metal-containing medical devices can result in adverse health effects as was seen recently with cobalt and chromium release from metal-on-metal hip replacements (Keegan, Learmonth, & Case, 2007). In the group of Veterans wounded by fragments of DU in the First Gulf War, although the fragments continually solubilize over time releasing uranium, no adverse health effects have been documented for the 20 or more years these fragments have been in place (McDiarmid et al., 2009; McDiarmid et al., 2007; McDiarmid et al., 2006; McDiarmid et al., 2004; McDiarmid et al., 2000; McDiarmid, Squibb, Engelhart, Gucer, & Oliver, 2007; McDiarmid et al., 2001).

U.S. DEPARTMENT OF DEFENSE POLICY ON EMBEDDED FRAGMENTS

Depleted Uranium

Prior to 1990, there was no harmonized U.S. DOD policy on dealing with embedded fragment wounds. As noted earlier, standard surgical guidelines suggested leaving embedded metal fragments in place under the premise that they could be considered inert. However, the first extensive combat use of DU munitions in the First Persian Gulf War changed that thinking. Shortly after that conflict, the various services of the U.S. DOD established policies for assessing and treating DU fragment wounds. Because their personnel have the greatest risk of suffering embedded DU fragment wounds, the U.S. Army took the lead on developing procedures with which to identify and categorize DU exposure, assess the extent of exposure, and assure long-term patient follow-up care. Reevaluated every 2 years, this policy has developed a grading protocol to assess exposure to DU, as a result not only of embedded fragments but also of potential inhalation exposures (OTSG/MEDCOM, 2011). There are three categories of exposure (Levels I, II, and III). Personnel wounded by DU fragments or who were in or near a vehicle struck by DU munitions are assigned to Level I. In addition, first responders who enter a struck vehicle are also placed in this category. All individuals in Level I are required to have a 24-hr urine sample taken to measure their urinary uranium levels. Individuals who routinely enter vehicles that may contain DU residue are placed in Level II. These individuals also require a 24-hr urine bioassay to assess urine uranium levels. Level III includes potential incidental exposures that are infrequent and of short duration. Personnel categorized as Level III do not require a urine bioassay. However, if requested by the individual or their health care provider, a urine bioassay will be conducted.

The Army Policy memo (U.S. Army Public Health Command, 2012) on the management of personnel exposed to DU also describes the procedures to be followed for obtaining urinary uranium measurements from a 24-hr urine sample, how to properly report and record the results, the process for assuring that proper follow-up care is provided, and sources of additional information including fact sheets which can be used for risk communication efforts. Additional information on DU can be found on the DOD Deployment Health Clinical Center website (http://www.pdhealth.mil/du.asp).

Other Metals

The use of IEDs in the Iraq and Afghanistan conflicts, as well as the finding that a proposed alternative to DU induced rhabdomyosarcoma when implanted in a

TABLE 4.1
DOD Metals of Interest as per Health Affairs Policy Letter 07-029

Tungsten	Nickel	Cobalt
Lead	Copper	Uranium
Tin	Antimony	Iron

rodent model (Kalinich et al., 2005), increased the concern within the DOD as to the long-term health effects of embedded fragments. These concerns lead to the release of Health Affairs Policy Memo 07-029 (Policy on Analysis of Metal Fragments Removed from Department of Defense Personnel; 2007). The long-term risk from the expanded use of novel metal mixtures on the battlefield was addressed in the directive. The metals listed in Table 4.1 are designated to be of special concern if found in embedded fragments. Although the decision to surgically remove embedded fragments remains that of the medical personnel, once a fragment is excised, it becomes property of the U.S. Government. They are not to be disposed of or returned to the patient as a "souvenir." The policy memo further directs that the fragments are to be sent to a service-designated analytical laboratory for identification with the results of the analysis entered into the individual's medical record as well as in the newly established DOD Embedded Metal Fragment Registry. Occasionally, embedded fragments work their way out of the body over time. If this occurs, patients should retain and pass these fragments on to their primary care providers who should then submit them for analysis. Detailed packing and shipping information is available from the U.S. Army Public Health Command (2012) and the Joint Pathology Center (JPC; 2013).

LONG-TERM FOLLOW-UP OF INDIVIDUALS WITH EMBEDDED FRAGMENTS IN THE DEPARTMENT OF VETERANS AFFAIRS MEDICAL SYSTEM

Depleted Uranium Follow-Up Program

As a result of friendly-fire incidents involving DU during the First Gulf War, in 1993 the Depleted Uranium Follow-Up Program was established at the Veterans Affairs (VA) Medical Center in Baltimore, Maryland. Individuals with embedded DU fragments, as well as those who were in or around vehicles that had been struck with DU munitions, were asked to participate in the follow-up program. Every 2 years, this cohort is invited to Baltimore VA Medical Center where evaluations have included physical exams and complete histories covering medical, social, family, partner, and reproductive issues as well as occupational exposures. In addition, extensive laboratory assessments of hematological parameters, serum and urine chemistries, neuroendocrine status, semen analysis, and renal function have been conducted. Samples of blood and urine have been collected for uranium analysis. Mutations and chromosomal aberrations in peripheral blood lymphocytes have been assessed. Testing for neurocognitive function has been undertaken, and focus group/risk communication sessions have been conducted. To provide a high level of transparency, group data from these assessments are routinely published in the peer-reviewed medical literature (McDiarmid et al., 2009; McDiarmid, Engelhardt, et al., 2007; McDiarmid et al., 2006; McDiarmid et al., 2004; McDiarmid et al., 2000; McDiarmid, Squibb, et al., 2007; McDiarmid et al., 2001; Squibb et al., 2012). The effort of this program was later expanded to include Veterans from Operation Iraqi Freedom and Operation Enduring Freedom. In addition, the program offers urine uranium analysis for any Veteran who requests it and can provide assistance to primary care providers in interpreting results and answering questions related to DU exposure. The procedures pertaining to this service are found on the DVA website (DVA, n.d.).

Toxic Embedded Fragment Surveillance Center

The widespread insurgent use of IEDs in Iraq and Afghanistan has resulted in a large number of personnel suffering from blast effects. Traumatic brain injury (TBI) has been described as the "signature wound" of these conflicts (Hoge et al., 2008). Often overlooked is the fact that, in many of these cases, embedded fragment wounds will occur simultaneously, either from projectiles related to the IED itself, pieces of the destroyed vehicle, or other surrounding materials. IEDs often contain a heterogeneous assortment of material whose in vivo biokinetic and toxicologic properties are not known. This, along with the laboratory research results discussed previously, raises concern that these types of embedded fragments could lead to adverse health effects, both localized and systemic. In response, the DVA established the Toxic Embedded Fragment Surveillance Center in 2008 (http://www.publichealth.va.gov/exposures/toxic_fragments/surv_center.asp). Because of the success of the Depleted Uranium Follow-Up Program, the Toxic Embedded Fragment Surveillance Center was also established at the VA Medical Center in Baltimore, Maryland.

The mission of the center is to provide care and medical surveillance for Veterans with embedded fragments. Four major functions of the center help fulfill

TABLE 4.2
The Toxic Embedded Fragment Surveillance Center's Metal Toxicants of Interest

Aluminum	Arsenic	Cadmium	Chromium
Cobalt	Copper	Iron	Manganese
Nickel	Lead	Uranium	Tungsten
Zinc			

its mission: fragment identification and characterization, biomonitoring and medical surveillance, development of a registry to track Veterans with embedded fragments, consultations and assistance in interpreting results, and providing further information pertaining to risk communication. The basic framework of achieving these goals was developed from the experiences of the Depleted Uranium Follow-Up Program. However, the task is much more daunting because of the large number of U.S. personnel thought to have retained embedded fragments and the greatly increased list of metals of concern. As part of the center's program, this identification and characterization analysis is conducted on any excised fragments. In addition, urine samples are collected and analyzed for concentrations of 13 metal toxicants of interest listed in Table 4.2. These metals were chosen based on lists of metals frequently found in fragments and/or their potential toxicity (Gaitens, Dorsey, & McDiarmid, 2010). Along with these metals, analysis of urine samples for organic materials such as plastics and polymer components is also being considered. These urine results can provide information on the identity of the fragment and also the biokinetics of the fragments still remaining in the injured individual. Once the identity and biokinetic characteristics are obtained, surveillance for organ-specific toxicity can be initiated. Changes in the location or shape of the embedded fragments can be followed using standard medical imaging techniques. Taken together, this information can be used to determine if the embedded fragment is inducing effects which require a medical response. The data obtained through the surveillance program will also help in choosing which response would be most appropriate.

An important component of the center's mission is the establishment of an embedded fragment registry. The registry will allow VA health care professionals to identify Veterans who suffered embedded fragment wounds during their military service, to address health concerns associated with the embedded fragments, and, if necessary, to develop medical and surgical management guidelines for dealing with these types of injuries (Gaitens et al., 2010). The ability to easily track, monitor, and provide appropriate medical care and follow-up for Veterans with embedded fragment injuries is a major directive in the Presidential Task Force Report on the Returning Global War on Terror Heroes (DVA, 2010). A seamless link between DOD and DVA patient databases to allow transfer of embedded fragment information on wounded Veterans is critical to the ultimate success of this registry.

SAMPLE ANALYSIS

A key component of patient follow-up in both the DOD and DVA health care systems is the prompt and accurate analysis of urine samples for metal content and the identification and characterization of excised embedded fragments. For DOD personnel with potential exposure to DU, samples are to be forwarded to one of two analytical laboratories, depending on the branch of service of the wounded individual. The U.S. Army Public Health Command and the Biophysical Toxicology Laboratory of the JPC are the two DOD designated laboratories for analysis of DU in urine samples and excised fragments. Both labs used state-of-the-art inductively coupled plasma mass spectrometry methods to measure uranium content and differentiate natural uranium from DU. Briefly, in the inductively coupled plasma portion of the instrument, a metal-containing sample, usually in liquid form, is aerosolized and sent through a high-temperature plasma resulting in the generation of positively charged ions. The ionized sample then enters the mass spectrometer where the ions are separated based on their mass/charge ratio. Concentrations of the separated ions are then determined as a function of signal strength measured at a detector in the instrument. As a result of the ionization process, the sample is destroyed during analysis. Detailed instructions on collection and shipping of samples are available online from both laboratories (JPC, 2013; U.S. Army Public Health Command, 2012). These facilities are also the DOD-designated laboratories for fragment analysis in support of the Health Affairs Policy Letter 07-029 (Analysis of Metal Fragments Removed from DOD Personnel, 2007). Again, detailed instructions on collection and shipping are available online. Because sample preservation is important in these cases, the analytical method of choice for characterizing metal fragments is energy-dispersive x-ray fluorescence spectroscopy. In this technique, the sample is exposed to high-energy x-rays. This results in ionization of atoms in the sample and ejection of electrons producing an unstable atom. As the atom returns to a stable state, a photon is released. Measurement of the energy of the photon can be used to identify the excited atom and thus determine the elemental composition of the sample.

Identical techniques are used for fragment analysis in support of the DVA Depleted Uranium Follow-Up Program and the Toxic Embedded Fragment Surveillance Center because they rely on the Biophysical Toxicology Laboratory of the JPC for their analytical needs. In addition to the fragment analysis, the JPC-Biophysical Toxicology Laboratory offers unique analytical and molecular spectroscopy capabilities for the analysis of tissue-related specimens which may be obtained during fragment removal. A rough outline of how fragments are characterized when they are received in the analysis laboratory in shown in Figure 4.1. More detailed information on the fragment characterization process can be found elsewhere (Centeno et al., 2014).

CONCLUSIONS

Although advances in trauma care have greatly increased the survivability of battlefield injuries, the long-term health effects of the embedded metal fragments from these wounds have become a paramount concern. Although significant progress has been achieved assessing and managing embedded fragment injuries, many issues still remain unresolved. For example, metals and metal mixtures being developed for new munitions are not tested for potential adverse health effects if embedded as fragments. The inclusion of biokinetic and toxicity testing of these materials as embedded fragments could provide significant information on whether they have the potential to be a long-term health concern. The development of serum- or urine-based biomarker assessments of metal-induced adverse health effects would enhance the diagnostic ability of medical personnel such that prompt surgical or pharmacological interventions can be initiated.

Often, embedded fragment wounds are suffered in combination with another injury such as TBI or hemorrhage. Very little is known on whether the presence of embedded metals will adversely affect the recovery from these combined injuries. In addition, because the toxicological properties of many of the metals and metal mixtures found on the battlefield today have not been investigated, it is not known what, if any, effect they have on muscle repair and normal wound healing. Any negative effect would delay a return to duty or continuation of a normal active lifestyle. There is also scant information on potential interactions between metal released from embedded fragments and other metals in the body, either endogenous or from medical devices (e.g., surgical screws, artificial joints).

Although the policies describing the procedures required for tracking personnel with embedded fragment wounds have been in place for more than 5 years, better communication between the policy makers and those responsible for ensuring it is successful is needed. In particular, the requirement that all fragments removed from wounded personnel be sent for analysis needs to be strictly adhered to. Also, personnel tasked with this duty, as well as all those in the

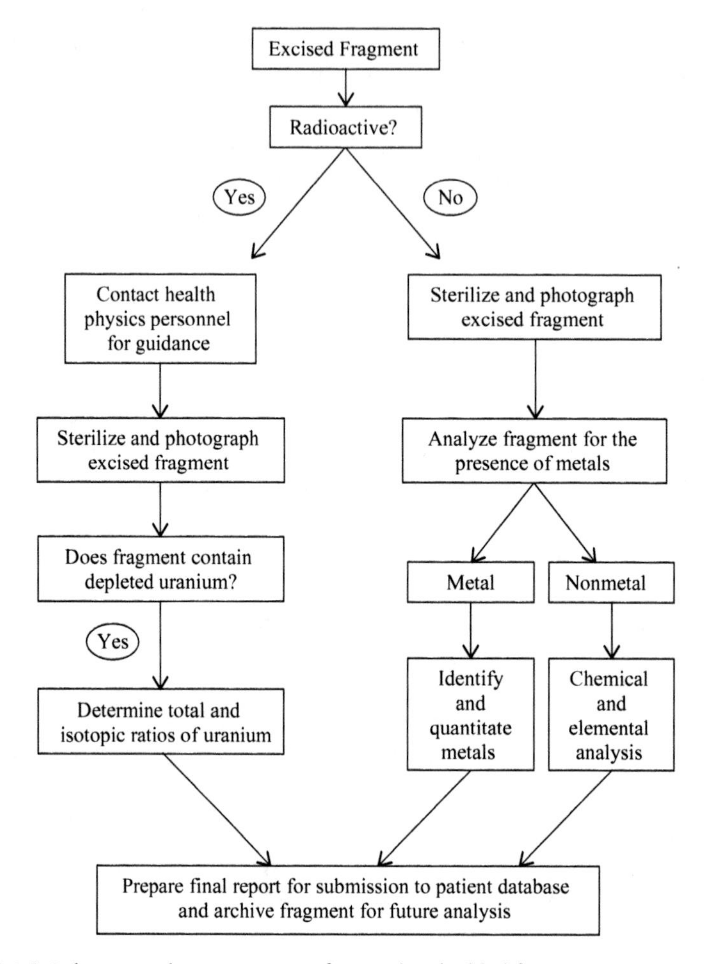

FIGURE 4.1 Laboratory characterization of excised embedded fragments.

transport chain, need to have a clear understanding of what analytical laboratory needs to receive the fragment and how to get it there.

Many embedded metal fragments may never be removed from the wounded individual. Because of the uncertainty regarding the long-term health effects of embedded metal fragments, it is imperative that all information be accurately recorded in the medical record. It is also critical that this information flows seamlessly and completely from the DOD patient databases to the DVA as the individual transitions from military to civilian life.

The long-term health effects of embedded metal fragments are not known. Although nursing professionals will be at the forefront in caring for these wounded individuals, both immediately after the trauma and during the healing and rehabilitation process, it is also critical that they ensure that the information concerning that injury be properly documented so that in the event of any fragment-related future health issue, that information is readily available.

DISCLAIMER

The views expressed do not necessarily represent the AFRRI, the Graduate School of Nursing, the Uniformed Services University of the Health Sciences, the JPC, or the U.S. Departments of Defense and Veterans Affairs.

REFERENCES

Akhtar, A. J., Funnye, A. S., & Akanno, J. (2003). Gunshot-induced plumbism in an adult male. *Journal of the National Medical Association*, *95*, 986–990.

Arfsten, D. P., Bekkedal, M., Wilfong, E. R., Rossi, J., III, Grasman, K. A., Healey, L. B., . . . Still, K. R. (2005). Study of the reproductive effects in rats surgically implanted with depleted uranium for up to 90 days. *Journal of Toxicology and Environmental Health. Part A*, *68*, 967–997.

Arfsten, D. P., Schaeffer, D. J., Johnson, E. W., Cunningham, J. R., Still, K. R., & Wilfong, E. R. (2006). Evaluation of the effect of implanted depleted uranium on male reproductive success, sperm concentration, and sperm velocity. *Environmental Research*, *100*, 205–215.

Arfsten, D. P., Still, K. R., Wilfong, E. R., Johnson, E. W., McInturf, S. M., Eggers, J. S., . . . Bekkedal, M. Y. V. (2009). Two-generation reproductive toxicity study of implanted depleted uranium (DU) in CD rats. *Journal of Toxicology and Environmental Health. Part A*, *72*, 410–427.

Arfsten, D. P., Wilfong, E. R., Bekkedal, M. Y. V., Johnson, E. W., McInturf, S. M., Eggers, J. S., . . . Still, K. R. (2007). Evaluation of the effect of implanted depleted uranium (DU) on adult rat behavior and toxicological endpoints. *Journal of Toxicology and Environmental Health. Part A*, *70*, 1995–2010.

Brewer, L., Fairbrother, A., Clark, J., & Amick, D. (2003). Acute toxicity of lead, steel, and an iron-tungsten-nickel shot to mallard ducks (Anas platyrhynchos). *Journal of Wildlife Diseases*, *39*, 638–648.

Castro, C. A., Benson, K. A., Bogo, V., Daxon, E. G., Hogan, J. B., Jacocks, H. M., . . . Shehata, C. W. (1996). *Establishment of an animal model to evaluate the biological effects of intramuscularly embedded depleted uranium fragments* (Tech. Rep. 96-3). Armed Forces Radiobiology Research Institute, Bethesda, MD.

Centeno, J. A., Rogers, D. A., van der Voet, G. B., Fornero, E., Zhang, L., Mullick, F. G., . . . Potter, B. K. (2014). Embedded fragments—A unique exposure situation and concerns of possible health effects. *International Journal of Environmental Research and Public Health*, *11*, 1261–1278.

Coon, T., Miller, M., Shirazi, F., & Sullivan, J. (2006). Lead toxicity in a 14-year-old female with retained bullet fragments. *Pediatrics*, *117*, 227–230.

Department of Defense. (2013). *Department of Defense casualty status report*. Retrieved from http://www.defense.gov/news/casualty.pdf

Dougherty, P. J., & Eidt, H. C. (2009). Wound ballistics: Minié ball vs. full metal jacketed bullets—A comparison of Civil War and Spanish-American War firearms. *Military Medicine*, *174*, 403–407.

Emond, C. A., & Kalinich, J. F. (2012). Biokinetics of embedded surrogate radiological dispersal device material. *Health Physics*, *102*, 124–136.

Eylon, S., Mosheiff, R., Liebergall, M., Wolf, E., Brocke, L., & Peyser, A. (2005). Delayed reaction to shrapnel retained in soft tissue. *Injury*, *36*, 275–281.

Farrell, S. E., Vandevander, P., Schoffstall, J. M., & Lee, D. C. (1999). Blood lead levels in emergency department patients with retained lead bullets and shrapnel. *Academic Emergency Medicine*, *6*, 208–212.

Fitsanakis, V. A., Erikson, K. M., Garcia, S. J., Evje, L., Syversen, T., & Aschner, M. (2006). Brain accumulation of depleted uranium in rats following 3- or 6-month treatment with implanted depleted uranium pellets. *Biological Trace Element Research*, *111*, 185–197.

Gaitens, J. M., Dorsey, C. D., & McDiarmid, M. A. (2010). Using a public health registry to conduct medical surveillance: The case of toxic embedded fragments in U.S. military Veterans. *European Journal of Oncology*, *15*, 77–89.

Hahn, F. F., Guilmette, R. A., & Hoover, M. D. (2002). Implanted depleted uranium fragments cause soft tissue sarcomas in the muscles of rats. *Environmental Health Perspectives*, *110*, 51–59.

Health Affairs. (2007). *Policy on analysis of metal fragments removed from Department of Defense personnel*. Retrieved from http://www.health.mil/libraries/HA_Policies_and_Guidelines/07-029.pdf

Hoge, C. W., McGurk, D., Thomas, J. L., Cox, A. L., Engel, C. C., & Castro, C. A. (2008). Mild traumatic brain injury in U.S. soldiers returning from Iraq. *New England Journal of Medicine*, *358*, 453–463.

International Agency for Research on Cancer. (1999). Monograph on the evaluation of carcinogenic risk to humans. *Surgical implants and other foreign bodies* (Vol. 74, pp. 113–229). Lyon, France: Author.

John, B. E., & Boatright, D. (1999). Lead toxicity from gunshot wound. *Southern Medical Journal*, *92*, 223–224.

Joint Pathology Center. (2013). *Operational instructions for the collection, handling and shipment of metal fragments removed from Department of Defense personnel*. Retrieved from http://www.jpc.capmed.mil/docs/metal_fragment_collection_instructions.pdf

Kalinich, J. F., Emond, C. A., Dalton, T. K., Mog, S. R., Colman, G. D., Kordell, J. E., . . . Clain, D. E. (2005). Embedded weapons-grade tungsten alloy shrapnel rapidly induces metastatic high-grade rhabdomyosarcomas in F344 rats. *Environmental Health Perspectives*, *113*, 729–734.

Kalinich, J. F., Vergara, V. B., & Emond, C. E. (2008). Urinary and serum metal levels as indicators of embedded tungsten alloy fragments. *Military Medicine*, *173*, 754–758.

Kane, M. A., Kasper, C. E., & Kalinich, J. F. (2009). Protocol for the assessment of potential health effects from embedded metal fragments. *Military Medicine*, *174*, 265–269.

Keegan, G. M., Learmonth, I. D., & Case, C. P. (2007). Orthopaedic metals and their potential toxicity in the arthroplasty patient: A review of current knowledge and future strategies. *Journal of Bone and Joint Surgery (British)*, *89*(5), 567–573.

Kelly, M. E., Fitzgerald, S. D., Aulerich, R. J., Balander, R. J., Powell, D. C., Stickle, R. L., . . . Bursian, S. J. (1998). Acute effects of lead, steel, tungsten-iron, and tungsten-polymer shot administered to game-farm mallards. *Journal of Wildlife Diseases*, *34*, 673–687.

Knox, J., & Wilkinson, A. (1981). Shrapnel presenting with symptoms 62 years after wounding. *British Medical Journal (Clinical Research Edition)*, *283*, 193.

Kraabel, B. J., Miller, M. W., Getzy, D. M., & Ringelman, J. K. (1996). Effects of embedded tungsten-bismuth-tin shot and steel shot on mallards (Anas platyrhynchos). *Journal of Wildlife Diseases*, *32*, 1–8.

Ligtenstein, D. A., Krijnen, J. L. M., Jansen, B. R. H., & Eulderink, F. (1994). Forgotten injury: A late benign complication of an unremoved shrapnel fragment—Case report. *Journal of Trauma, 36*, 580–582.

Lindeman, G., McKay, M. J., Taubman, K. L., & Bilous, A. M. (1990). Malignant fibrous histiocytoma developing in bone 44 years after shrapnel trauma. *Cancer, 66*, 2229–2232.

Manring, M. M., Hawk, A., Calhoun, J. H., & Andersen, R. C. (2009). Treatment of war wounds—A historical review. *Clinical and Orthopedic Related Research, 467*, 2168–2191.

McDiarmid, M. A., Engelhardt, S. M., Dorsey, C. D., Oliver, M., Gucer, P., Wilson, P. D., . . . Squibb, K. S. (2009). Surveillance results of depleted uranium-exposed Gulf War I Veterans: Sixteen years of follow-up. *Journal of Toxicology and Environmental Health, Part A: Current Issues, 72*, 14–29.

McDiarmid, M. A., Engelhardt, S. M., Oliver, M., Gucer, P., Wilson, P. D., Kane, R., . . . Squibb, K. S. (2007). Health surveillance of Gulf War I Veterans exposed to depleted uranium: Updating the cohort. *Health Physics, 93*, 60–73.

McDiarmid, M. A., Engelhardt, S. M., Oliver, M., Gucer, P., Wilson, P. D., Kane, R., . . . Squibb, K. S. (2006). Biological monitoring and surveillance results of Gulf War I Veterans exposed to depleted uranium. *International Archives of Occupational and Environmental Health, 79*, 11–21.

McDiarmid, M. A., Engelhardt, S., Oliver, M., Gucer, P., Wilson, P. D., Kane, R., . . . Squibb, K. S. (2004). Health effects of depleted uranium on exposed Gulf War Veterans: A ten-year follow-up. *Journal of Toxicology and Environmental Health, Part A: Current Issues*, 67, 277–296.

McDiarmid, M. A., Keogh, J. P., Hooper, F. J., McPhaul, K., Squibb, K., Kane, R., . . . Walsh, M. (2000). Health effects of depleted uranium on exposed Gulf War Veterans. *Environmental Research, 82*, 168–180.

McDiarmid, M. A., Squibb, K., Engelhardt, S., Gucer, P., & Oliver, M. (2007). Surveillance of Gulf War I Veterans exposed to depleted uranium: 15 years of follow-up. *European Journal of Oncology, 12*, 235–242.

McDiarmid, M. A., Squibb, K., Engelhardt, S., Oliver, M., Gucer, P., Wilson, P. D., . . . Jacobson-Kram, D. (2001). Surveillance of depleted uranium exposed Gulf War Veterans: Health effects observed in an enlarged "friendly fire" cohort. *Journal of Occupational and Environmental Medicine, 43*, 991–1000.

McQuirter, J. L., Rothenberg, S. J., Dinkins, G. A., Kondrashov, V., Manalo, M., & Todd, A. C. (2004). Change in blood lead concentration up to 1 year after a gunshot wound with a retained bullet. *American Journal of Epidemiology, 159*, 683–692.

McQuirter, J. L., Rothenberg, S. J., Dinkins, G. A., Manalo, M., Kondrashov, V., & Todd, A. C. (2001). The effects of retained lead bullets on body lead burden. *The Journal of Trauma, 50*, 892–899.

Miller, A. C., Stewart, M., & Rivas, R. (2010). Preconceptional paternal exposure to depleted uranium: Transmission of genetic damage to offspring. *Health Physics, 99*, 371–379.

Mitchell, R. R., Fitzgerald, S. D., Aulerich, R. J., Balander, R. J., Powell, D. C., Tempelman, R. J., . . . Bursian, S. J. (2001a). Hematological effects and metal residue concentrations following chronic dosing with tungsten-iron and tungsten-polymer shot in adult game-farm mallards. *Journal of Wildlife Diseases, 37*, 459–467.

Mitchell, R. R., Fitzgerald, S. D., Aulerich, R. J., Balander, R. J., Powell, D. C., Tempelman, R. J., . . . Bursian, S. J. (2001b). Reproductive effects and duckling survivability following chronic dosing with tungsten-iron and tungsten-polymer shot in adult game-farm mallards. *Journal of Wildlife Diseases, 37*, 468–474.

Mitchell, R. R., Fitzgerald, S. D., Aulerich, R. J., Balander, R. J., Powell, D. C., Tempelman, R. J., . . . Bursian, S.J. (2001c). Health effects following chronic dosing with tungsten-iron and tungsten-polymer shot in adult game-farm mallards. *Journal of Wildlife Diseases, 37*, 451–458.

Nguyen, A., Schaider, J. J., Manzanares, M., Hanaki, R., Rydman, R. J., & Bokhari, F. (2005). Elevation of blood lead levels in emergency department patients with extra-articular retained missiles. *Journal of Trauma*, *58*, 289–299.

Office of the Surgeon General/MEDCOM. (2011). Medical management of army personnel exposed to depleted uranium (DU). *OTSG/MEDCOM policy memo 11-047*. Retrieved from http://www.pdhealth.mil/downloads/OTSG_MEDCOM_Policy_11-047_Med_M.pdf

Osawa, R., Abe, R., Inokuma, D., Yokota, K., Ito, H., Nabeshima, M., & Shimizu, H. (2006). Chain saw blade granuloma: Reaction to a deeply embedded metal fragment. *Archives of Dermatology*, *142*, 1079–1080.

Parkhurst, M. A., Daxon, E. G., Lodde, G. M., Szrom, F., Guilmette, R. A., Roszell, L. E., . . . McKee, C. B. (2005). *Depleted uranium aerosol doses and risks*. Columbus, OH: Battelle Press.

Pellmar, T. C., Fuciarelli, A. F., Ejnik, J. W., Hamilton, M., Hogan, J., Strocko, S., . . . Landauer, M. R. (1999). Distribution of uranium in rats implanted with depleted uranium pellets. *Toxicological Sciences*, *49*, 29–39.

Rehani, B., & Wissman, R. (2011). Lead poisoning from a gunshot wound. *Southern Medical Journal*, *104*, 57–58.

Saruwatari, H., Kamiwada, R., Matsushita, S., Hashiguchi, T., Kawai, K., & Kanekura, T. (2009). Tungsten granuloma attributable to a piece of lawn-mower blade. *Clinical and Experimental Dermatology*, *34*, e268–e269.

Schenck, N. L., & Kronman, B. S. (1977). Hoarseness and mass in the neck 30 years after penetrating shrapnel injury. *Annals of Otology, Rhinology, and Laryngology*, *86*, 259.

Schuster, B. E., Roszell, L. E., Murr, L. E., Ramirez, D. A., Demaree, J. D., Klotz, B. R., . . . Bannon, D. I. (2012). In vivo corrosion, tumor outcome, and microarray gene expression for two types of muscle-implanted tungsten alloys. *Toxicology and Applied Pharmacology*, *265*, 128–138.

Squibb, K. S., Gaitens, J. M., Engelhardt, S., Centeno, J. A., Xu, H., Gray, P., & McDiarmid, M. A. (2012). Surveillance for long-term health effects associated with depleted uranium exposure and retained embedded fragments in US Veterans. *Journal of Occupational and Environmental Medicine*, *54*, 724–732.

Symonds, R. P., Mackay, C., & Morley, P. (1985). The late effect of grenade fragments. *Journal of the Royal Army Medical Corps*, *131*, 68–69.

Thomsen, P., & Gretzer, C. (2001). Macrophage interactions with modified material surfaces. *Current Opinion in Solid State Materials Sciences*, *5*, 163–176.

U.S. Army Public Health Command. (2012). *Radiobioassay collection labeling and shipping requirements. Technical guide 211*. Retrieved from http://phc.amedd.army.mil/PHC Resource Library/TG211_RadiobioassayCollectionLabelingandShippingRequirements.pdf

U.S. Department of Veterans Affairs. (n.d.) *Depleted uranium follow-up program*. Retrieved from http://www.publichealth.va.gov/exposures/depleted_uranium/followup_program.asp

U.S. Department of Veterans Affairs. (2010). *Screening and evaluation of Operation Enduring Freedom (OEF) and Operation Iraqi Freedom (OIF) veterans with embedded fragments*. Retrieved from http://www.va.gov/VHAPUBLICATIONS/ViewPublication.asp?pub_ID=2255

Yokel, R. A., Lasley, S. M., & Dorman, D. C. (2006). The speciation of metals in mammals influences their toxicokinetics and toxicodynamics and therefore human health risk assessment. *Journal of Toxicology and Environmental Health. Part B*, *9*, 63–85.

CHAPTER 5

Mantram Repetition

An Evidence-Based Complementary Practice for Military Personnel and Veterans in the 21st Century

Jill E. Bormann, Sally Weinrich, Carolyn B. Allard, Danielle Beck, Brian D. Johnson, and Lindsay Cosco Holt

ABSTRACT

Today in the digital age, with our advances in modern technology and communication, there are additional stressors for our military personnel and Veterans. Constant dangers exist both on and off the battlefield, unlike prior wars that had clearly-defined war zones. In addition, medical advances have assisted in saving the lives of many more gravely injured troops than ever previously possible. As the wars in Iraq and Afghanistan come to an end, large numbers of service men and women are returning home with multiple injuries. This group of Veterans has significantly higher rates of posttraumatic stress disorder (PTSD) and traumatic brain injury than ever before reported. Although existing PTSD therapies have been found to be highly effective for many Veterans, there is a substantial minority unsatisfactorily treated. Mantram repetition, an innovative, complementary, evidence-based treatment, is proving to be successful for these new Veterans. When used regularly it helps with "road rage, impatience, anger, frustration, and being out of control." A mantram is a brief, sacred word or phrase that embodies divine power or the greatest positive energy one can imagine (Easwaran, 2008a).

http://dx.doi.org/10.1891/0739-6686.32.79

Mantram repetition is a simple, quick, personal, portable, and private complementary practice that may be used as an adjunct to current treatments for PTSD. Growing research evidence supports mantram repetition's value for dissemination and adoption in the 21st century. This chapter summarizes Mantram Program research conducted from 2003 to 2014. It describes the health-related benefits of the Mantram Program in various populations. The current research focuses on benefits for managing psychological distress and promoting quality of life in Veterans. Future areas for research are suggested.

INTRODUCTION

The Mantram Program is an innovative approach to symptom and stress management for the 21st century. Never before in history have our technological breakthroughs in medicine been so rapidly applied to the battlefield, keeping more soldiers alive, and leaving them with greater physical, mental, and spiritual battle scars. For those who refuse or do not respond to medications or current evidence-based treatments for PTSD, complementary alternatives are being developed and tested to help manage the symptoms of trauma and injury. This chapter consists of five sections. In the first section, the practice of *mantram repetition* and the *Mantram Program* are described. In Section 2, Mantram Program delivery and dissemination strategies are presented. Section 3 briefly outlines the theoretical basis for mantram repetition efficacy. Section 4 describes Mantram Program research completed to date, including quantitative and qualitative studies as well as randomized clinical trials. Finally, possible directions for future research in military personnel and Veterans are outlined.

WHAT IS MANTRAM REPETITION?

Mantram repetition—a simple, quick, personal, portable, and private complementary practice—comes from the work of Sri Eknath Easwaran (1910–1999). He was a teacher of meditation who studied ancient wisdom traditions and translated them into practical practices for Westerners (Easwaran, 2008a, 2008b, 2005/2013). He defines a mantram as a "short, powerful, spiritual formula for the highest power we can conceive of" (Easwaran, 2008a, p. 12). There are similarities as well as differences between mantram (spelled with an *m*) and mantra (without an *m*). Both terms originate from Sanskrit and represent a word or phrase of power, strength, or comfort. They both represent a traditional holy name or characteristic that one aspires to. The differences come from how our modern society uses the word *mantra* to refer to *any* secular self-created sentence, affirmation, motto, or slogan that is repeated. In contrast, one's mantram (with an *m*) is a word or phrase defined as sacred or having divine power, originating from ancient wisdom traditions, and having a positive effect on the one who repeats it.

Mantram repetition alone can be taught in as little as 3–5 min. The first step is choosing a personalized mantram. A personalized mantram is more likely to be embraced, remembered, and practiced now and in the future. In our research and clinical courses, we provide a list of common mantrams.[1] After choosing a mantram, some people like to "test drive" one for a few weeks to experience it. This is permissible in the beginning, but once selected and established, a mantram is to be kept for the rest of one's life (Easwaran, 2008a). The goal is to make the practice of mantram repetition a habit that is easily brought into consciousness with little effort. Other programs may recommend multiple mantrams for different situations, but in this program, the recommendation is that "one mantram fits all (situations)." One mantram is used for everything, so it is important to choose one that is pleasant-sounding, compatible with one's personal beliefs, and easily remembered. Most people select a mantram based on its meaning, but it is actually more important to repeat the mantram with focused attention on the sounds of the word itself rather than think of its definition.

The second step is to memorize the mantram and repeat it silently, with *intention* and *commitment*. A mantram is to be repeated as often as possible and particularly at times of rest, relaxation, or when feeling neutral. Repeating it may seem artificial or mechanical at first, with little noticeable effect. Its therapeutic value comes with time.

The third step is practice. The practice of mantram repetition requires intentional, internal, focused attention. When the mind wanders, it is redirected to the mantram. In doing this, the speed and content of one's thinking can be interrupted. Over time and with consistent, committed effort, a mantram becomes a constant, invisible companion used to ward off unwanted thoughts, manage negative feelings, and interrupt inappropriate or unhelpful behaviors. In short, it is an effective tool for emotional and behavioral self-regulation.

To facilitate success in the early stages of practicing mantram repetition, it is recommended that it be done during quiet, nonbusy, and nonstressful times. Once a person can experience focused attention internally on his or her personal mantram in a quiet, nonbusy, nonstressful environment, that focus can later be practiced in a noisy, crazy, stressful environment. Other ways to further strengthen mantram practice can include writing the mantram over and over. This helps to increase focus and further instill one's mantram to memory. Some learners are also more kinesthetic and find that writing the mantram is especially useful when feeling scattered and unfocused. Purposely taking a "mantram walk" or a "mantram nap" are also times to intentionally and silently practice mantram repetition.

The goal of repeating a mantram is to develop a calm sense of concentration and focus. The time taken for this transition to occur varies with each individual. Multiple factors involved include a person's (a) current environment, (b) current mental state, and (c) depth of intention and commitment to a sustained daily practice. We all have experienced the obvious impact of the current environment. As already stated, one can focus much easier in a quiet, nonhurried, nonstressful environment compared to a noisy, busy, stressful environment. Similarly, we all have experienced the effect of varying mental states. A tired, stressed, and/or worried mental state of mind leads to increased difficulty in focusing in contrast to a rested, nonstressed, nonworried mental state of mind. Finally, a strong desire or intention to practice with dedicated commitment leads to a change in behavior much more quickly than weak desire or skepticism. Motivation is another way of describing intention. Our research documents that homeless persons are more motivated to practice mantram repetition than nonhomeless persons. We hypothesize that this increased use of mantram is directly related to the increased need or motivation in homeless persons to find help in contrast to nonhomeless persons.

Mantram repetition is portable and can be used in any situation that does not require special attention or concentration on the task at hand (i.e., solving problems, brainstorming, working on a difficult project that requires focus, or operating dangerous machinery). To make it readily available requires repeating it as often as possible during the day and before sleep at night. Fortunately, this is possible and practical because mantram repetition does not require a particular time or place, closed eyes, or any particular posture. Mantram repetition differs from sitting meditation because it is practiced as much as possible throughout the day without limits to location or time. Therefore, it has been described as an "in vivo mantra" (Wachholtz & Austin, 2013, p. 312).

THE MANTRAM PROGRAM

The exercise of mantram repetition and the Mantram Program are different. The "Mantram Program" teaches three specific practices—mantram repetition, slowing down, and one-pointed attention. These three practices work together synergistically. These three practices were taken from Easwaran's Eight Point Program (Easwaran, 2008b; for more information, see http://www.easwaran.org) and adapted into a health education course. All three practices are taught for calming the mind, relaxing the body, and connecting to one's inner spiritual resources (Easwaran, 2008a, 2005/2013).

The first practice now is mantram repetition as described in the section earlier. The second practice is slowing down—the opposite of "automatic pilot" on which many of us operate. We are bombarded with so much information that we do not have time to process it all, and we become overloaded. Slowing down sets a "pause time" or a break to reevaluate priorities, take a rest, or reflect on the present moment. Slowing down allows one to be in the present rather than worrying about the past or future. By being present-centered, one can intentionally attend to those things that are most important in the here and now (e.g., quality family time, relationships). It also allows time to more effectively evaluate stressors and choose a plan of action. Slowing down activities may also include making a list of priorities, evaluating how one's time is spent, and setting the highest priorities into motion based on one's values.

The third practice is one-pointed attention, the opposite of multitasking. The process of cultivating focused attention involves one's acceptance that it requires practice. This acceptance helps mitigate self-criticism. Focus is easier to obtain in quiet, nonbusy, nonstressful situations. Over time, however, with persistent practice and patience, one's ability to focus with one-pointed attention can be done in chaotic, stressful times. Furthermore, one-pointed attention is strengthened by repeating a mantram. This same one-pointed attention can then be transferred to doing new tasks, one at a time, such as listening to others without interrupting them, concentrating fully on studies or paperwork, or learning a new skill. One-pointed attention is like a form of mindfulness that, at first, is practiced by mentally repeating a mantram and, later, is applied to completing tasks or activities. Ultimately, all three practices of repeating a mantram, slowing down, and one-pointed attention reinforce each other. When taught in the Mantram Program, they are presented as three separate concepts, each with their own exercises for learning. When used, the three practices support and reinforce each other.

IMPLEMENTATION AND DISSEMINATION OF THE MANTRAM PROGRAM

We have designed the Mantram Program to include the following course materials: a manual, instructor guide, the book *Strength in the Storm* (Easwaran, 2013), a small blank journal for writing the mantram, and weekly exercises called "experiments." Participants are asked to conduct self-assessments each week related to personal awareness of their thoughts and thinking process, feelings of time pressure, and awareness of multitasking. Then, they are invited to share their experiences of obstacles and successes of program practices with their group or mantram facilitator each week.

The Mantram Program can be delivered in group or individual sessions, face-to-face, and via webinars or conference calls, depending on participants' needs and available resources. The face-to-face program was originally only 5 weeks long and included reading from *The Mantram Handbook* (Easwaran, 2008a) as described in some studies (Bormann, Becker, et al. 2006; Bormann et al., 2005; Yong, Kim, Park, Seo, & Swinton, 2011). Today, the face-to-face program consists of eight weekly sessions (90 min/week) with reading assignments from *Strength in the Storm* (Easwaran, 2005/2013). Bormann and colleagues developed a Veteran manual and instructor guide specifically addressing symptoms of PTSD, which has been used in research. A second more generic manual, the *All Purpose Mantram Manual*, and instructor guide have also been developed for wider use in populations without trauma.

The program can be delivered effectively in groups whereby participants share experiences and help each other. Our experience in delivering the program to Veterans who have suffered military sexual trauma (MST) or to those who refuse to attend *any* groups prompted us to provide individual sessions. This allows for greater privacy and sense of safety early in the process of recovery. Findings on the outcomes of individual program delivery are not yet available but are expected to be published in 2015. This study can be found on clinicaltrials.gov: http://clinicaltrials.gov/ct2/show/NCT01506323?term=Mantram+Repetition&rank=2

Another method of delivery has been via telephone conference calls. This was done successfully in groups of family caregivers of Veterans with dementia who found it difficult to leave their loved ones unsupervised (Bormann, Warren, et al., 2009). For this group, we delivered the Mantram Program with only two face-to-face meetings (Sessions 1 and 8), and the remaining sessions were conducted using conference calls. This method was so well received that monthly, supportive conference calls were continued.

Because repeating a word or phrase initially can seem "too simple" to be of any significance for many, all facilitators who teach mantram repetition are trained in and practice mantram repetition themselves. With practice, they can normalize potential skepticism in their participants and share personal experiences of the program's benefits. Sometimes, the term *mantram* itself is an obstacle for those who perceive it as belonging to a tradition or religion to which they do not subscribe, such as Buddhism or Hinduism. It has been referred to as *repetition of the Holy Name* by members of the Christian tradition (Oman & Driskill, 2003). All facilitators are encouraged to use *The Mantram Handbook* (Easwaran, 2008a) as a resource when teaching the program.

Because it is important to be culturally sensitive to spiritual differences, the Mantram Program includes mantrams from many different cultural and spiritual traditions. The word *mantram* can be replaced with other terms perceived as more acceptable, such as *rapid focusing tool* or *centering word*. To illustrate this, a small pilot study on the Mantram Program was conducted in a sample of predominantly African American women (81%) in North Carolina. To be sensitive to the participants' cultural and religious beliefs, the term *mantram* was replaced by *prayer word* in all course materials (Kemppainen, Bormann, & Bomar, 2012).

To make the Mantram Program more accessible to patients, it first must be available to and embraced by health care providers who want to teach it. To do this, the 8-week program has been condensed into six 1-hr live meetings delivered over the Internet. Sessions are presented every 2 weeks to allow for practice in between. Unpublished research on this program has demonstrated significant reductions in exhaustion, an aspect of burnout, from pre- to posttest that continued to decline when measured at 3-month follow-up (Leary, Bormann, Smith, Georges, & Andrews, 2013). Other improvements reported included higher levels of professional efficacy, another aspect of burnout; mindfulness attention awareness; and existential spiritual well-being. Lower levels of internal and external stress of conscience, a measure of the dissonance between one's ethical standards and actual standards of care, were also reported (Leary et al., 2013).

The VA San Diego Healthcare System is pilot testing the national dissemination of the Mantram Program within the Veterans Affairs (VA) health care system as "Portable Mindful Strategies for a Healthy Workforce." This is a new unsynchronized curriculum consisting of four self-learning modules and two live meetings that are designed to promote experiential learning and preserve content integrity. We also have developed a 2-day intensive Mantram Facilitator Training for those who are actively using the practices of the program and have the skills to lead groups or individual mantram sessions.

THEORETICAL LITERATURE

The Mantram Program has previously been described as a "portable, contemplative practice" to emphasize both its mobility and spiritual nature (Bormann, 2010). There are several hypothesized mechanisms that explain how the practice of mantram repetition works. In this section, we briefly review several theories that provide physiological, psychological, and spiritual explanations. We recognize that future growth in genomic and brain research will likely shed greater understanding on mechanisms of action.

Physiological Theories

On the surface, the practice of mantram repetition replicates the same two steps as Benson's relaxation response: (a) mentally repeating the word, sound, or phrase and (b) passively disregarding any other thoughts that intrude (Benson, 1993;

Benson, 1996). Relaxation is not generally experienced immediately because it requires practice for sustained periods during nonstressful moments, such as when waiting in line or before falling asleep. Over time and with daily practice, however, relaxation comes more quickly along with improved cardiovascular patterns (Bernardi et al., 2001) and heart rate dynamics (Peng et al., 2004).

Another proposed mechanism for the effect of mantram repetition is that it strengthens different neuropathways in the brain. One's ability to concentrate gets stronger with repetition. Using functional magnetic resonance imaging (fMRI), Lazar and colleagues (2005) demonstrated that meditation increased cortical thickness in the prefrontal cortex and right anterior insula. Subsequent research has confirmed this phenomenon of neuroplasticity whereby repeated meditative practices have improved the function and structure of the brain in areas that affect attention, fear, anger, and anxiety (Holzel et al., 2011; Lutz, Greischar, Rawlings, Ricard, & Davidson, 2004; Manna et al., 2010).

Thus, the practice of mantram repetition is that of redirecting attention away from intrusive thoughts or feelings and toward the mantram. By replacing disturbing memories and thoughts with the silent, frequent refocusing of attention on a spiritual word or phrase of comfort, an alternative reaction to the stress response can be generated. This requires some mental conditioning. Refocusing attention on a spiritual word/phrase is easier when feeling calm or less distressed, combined with the belief in a higher power or the spiritual element inherent in the word/phrase chosen.

Psychological Theories

Mantram repetition may also reduce PTSD symptoms by reconditioning. Repeating the mantram can become associated with pleasant or at least neutral emotional responses and initiate the relaxation response (Khusid, 2013). This is similar to how traumatic cues can elicit negative emotional responses and physiological arousal in PTSD. It is important to note that repetition of a mantram, as it is taught in the Mantram Program, is not a traditional "relaxation technique" per se, but rather, the sacred word becomes paired with sensations of calm and peace that comes from focusing the mind through practice. Over time, and with continued practice, the process becomes more automatic and the response can be elicited even in stressful situations, such as when exposed to traumatic triggers and intrusive thoughts. The intrusive memories and thoughts may, in turn, lose strength as individuals with PTSD learn that they can initiate a relaxation response even in situations of arousal. Mantram repetition may work then in two ways—by developing a conditioned response of relaxation to the mantram cue and potentially weakening the associations between traumatic triggers, negative emotional responses, and physiological arousal.

Theoretically, mantram repetition can affect PTSD symptomatology in several ways. To begin, the mantram itself can be used as a tool *during* the experience of traumatic reminders and intrusive thoughts. Mantram repetition provides a way to redirect individuals' attention away from these traumatic triggers, intrusive memories, and cognitive distortions (Vujanovic, Niles, Pietrefesa, Schmertz, & Potter, 2011). If individuals focus on the mantram, they are not reliving past circumstances, not worrying about future events, and not experiencing undue distress. The reprieve from these trauma-related triggers may not only encourage healthy coping through mantram use but may also slow down an individual's thought process to facilitate subsequent behaviors that are adaptive (Kemeny et al., 2012). Gaining confidence in one's ability to redirect attention at will and, therefore, modulate emotional reactivity suggests self-efficacy as another mechanism for managing PTSD symptoms (Oman & Bormann, 2013).

Mantram practice, like related forms of meditation, is believed to enhance mental clarity and decrease reactivity (Cahn, Delorme, & Polich, 2013; Cahn & Polich, 2006; Lutz et al., 2004). Mantram repetition is intended to heighten awareness of the thought process rather than transcend it. The goal of Transcendental Meditation, a popular meditation practice, is to transcend or rise above consciousness (Travis & Shear, 2010). In contrast, mantram repetition is intended to heighten awareness of one's consciousness and more specifically, one's thinking process. It allows for metacognition and furthers self-awareness.

Spiritual Theories

Another hypothesized mechanism of action is spiritual well-being. Spiritual well-being is an often neglected focus of inquiry in PTSD treatment. It is not unusual for those who have undergone traumatic events to forego any belief in divine power and gradually lose a sense of spiritual well-being (Fontana & Rosenheck, 2004). Two reviews have inspected more than 20 empirical studies examining religious and spiritual factors and relationships to trauma. They summarized that religious and spiritual factors are both correlated with positive recovery progression in persons who have undergone a traumatic event, but some results are mixed (Schaefer, Blazer, & Koenig, 2008; Shaw, Joseph, & Linley, 2005). We conducted research showing that spiritual well-being partially mediated PTSD symptom improvement. The Mantram Program was instrumental in increasing levels of existential spiritual well-being (Peterman, Fitchett, Brady, Hernandez, & Cella, 2002) in Veterans with PTSD. Spiritual well-being, in turn, partially mediated reductions in self-reported PTSD symptoms measured using the PTSD Checklist (PCL; Weathers, Litz, Herman, Huska, & Keane, 1993). With repeated practice, the silent refocusing of attention on a chosen spiritual phrase of comfort or inspiration may come to be an alternative reaction to the stress response

(Lang et al., 2012). Other researchers have found that dysphoria and immune functioning, as well as cardiovascular illness and life span, have each been related to religious and spiritual factors (Koenig, King, & Carson, 2012; Miller & Thoresen, 2003), including studies on Veterans (Koenig et al., 2012).

EVIDENCE-BASED MANTRAM RESEARCH

Dr. Bormann and other mantram research colleagues have conducted and published 17 Mantram Program or related studies since 2003 in both Veteran and nonveteran populations (see Table 5.1). For Veterans specifically, 10 different published or presented studies with more than 275 Veterans document the benefits of Mantram Program (Bormann, Hurst, & Kelly, 2013; Bormann, Liu, Thorp, & Lang, 2012; Bormann, Oman, et al., 2006; Bormann, Oman, Walter, & Johnson, (in press); Bormann et al., 2005; Bormann, Smith, Shively, Dellefield, & Gifford, 2007; Bormann, Thorp, Wetherell, & Golshan, 2008; Bormann, Thorp, Wetherell, Golshan, & Lang, 2013; Oman & Bormann, 2013; Plumb et al., 2014). The research trajectory of the Mantram Program serves as a model for development of future nursing interventions. This section presents published Mantram Program or similar research studies in the following order: (a) mixed methods with and without randomized designs, (b) randomized controlled trials (RCTs), (c) pretest–posttest research design studies, (d) qualitative-only designs, and (f) mediation studies.

Mixed-Methods Research

Mantram Program mixed-methods research (i.e., both quantitative and qualitative methods in one sample) has been conducted in four different studies. Three of these studies included RCTs and one used repeated measures design (see Table 5.1). In this section, we describe a completed RCT with Veterans diagnosed with PTSD (Bormann, Thorp, et al., 2013). Second, we explain a smaller RCT conducted in first-time military mothers and their spouses or partners (Hunter et al., 2011). Third, we present findings from an earlier RCT with adults living with human immunodeficiency virus (HIV) population (Bormann, Gifford, et al., 2006). Fourth, we highlight a mixed-methods study conducted with a repeated measures design in family caregivers of Veterans with dementia (Bormann, Warren, et al., 2009).

Mixed-Methods Randomized Controlled Trial in Veterans With PTSD

A mixed-methods RCT compared a treatment-as-usual (TAU) control to a 6-week (90 min/week) Mantram Program combined with TAU (Bormann, Thorp, et al., 2013; see Table 5.1). TAU included both medication and case management. Veterans with military-related PTSD were the targeted population. Results provide support for the reduction of PTSD symptom severity, both self-reported

TABLE 5.1

Findings Related to Mantram Program Research (2001–2013)

Author/Date	Sample	N	Design	Findings
Mixed methods with randomized controlled trials (RCTs)				
Bormann, Thorp, Wetherell, Golshan, & Lang, 2013	Veterans with PTSD	146	Randomized trial: experimental mantram group plus case management versus control case management–only group	↓ PTSD (self-report and clinician-assessed) ↓ Depression ↑ Mental health status ↑ Mindfulness ↑ Existential spiritual well-being No change: reexperiencing No change: avoidance No change: anxiety No change: somatization Satisfaction: moderate to high
Bormann, Hurst, et al., 2013	Veterans with PTSD	65	Qualitative interviews at 3 months follow-up in mantram group only	Themes included improving relationships, managing road rage, controlling symptoms of hyperarousal, relaxing/calming down, and dealing with insomnia, nightmares, and flashbacks.
Hunter et al., 2011	Military personnel (first-time mothers, spouses, or partners)	30	Randomized trial, experimental versus control pretest–posttest	Mantram used for pain management and feelings of "uncertainty" during labor
		9	Qualitative interviews with mantram and control mothers at 6 months follow-up	Mantram used for sleep Mantram practice sustainable at 6 months Satisfaction: moderate to high

(Continued)

TABLE 5.1
Findings Related to Mantram Program Research (2001–2013) (Continued)

Author/Date	Sample	N	Design	Findings
Bormann, Gifford, et al., 2006	Adults with HIV	93	Experimental mantram group versus active HIV educational control group	↓ Trait anger ↑ Faith/assurance ↑ Spiritual connectedness No change: stress No change: depression No change: trait anxiety Frequent mantram practice associated with ↓ Intrusive thoughts ↓ Depression ↑ Quality of life ↑ Total spiritual well-being Satisfaction: moderate to high
Kemppainen et al., 2012	Adults with HIV	32	Qualitative interviews in mantram group only	Major themes from using mantram Increasing calm and/or peace Mastering technique Changing viewpoint

TABLE 5.1
Findings Related to Mantram Program Research (2001–2013) (Continued)

Author/Date	Sample	*N*	Design	Findings
Mixed methods with one-group repeated measures				
Bormann, Warren, et al., 2009	Family caregivers of Veterans with dementia	16	Pretest, posttest, and 36 weeks follow-up	↓ Stress ↓ Depression ↓ Caregiver burden ↓ Rumination ↑ Quality of life
			Qualitative interviews at 36 weeks follow-up	Reported mantram repetition to manage Anger Anxiety Impatience Irritation Sadness/grief Insomnia Bored/tired Excited/overly happy
RCTs				
Bormann, Thorp, et al., 2008	Veterans with PTSD	29	Mantram group versus wait-list control group	↓ PTSD (self-report and clinician-assessed) ↓ Depression ↓ Mental health distress ↓ Anger expression ↑ Quality of life ↑ Mindfulness ↑ Spiritual well-being Satisfaction: moderate to high

(Continued)

TABLE 5.1

Findings Related to Mantram Program Research (2001–2013) (Continued)

Author/Date	Sample	*N*	Design	Findings
Plumb et al., 2014	Veterans with PTSD	45	Individual mantram versus individual present-centered therapy control	↓ Clinician-assessed PTSD ↓ Self-reported PTSD
Yong et al., 2011	Korean nurse managers	51	Mantram group versus educational control	↓ Burnout ↑ Spiritual well-being ↑ Spiritual integrity ↑ Leadership practice No change: job satisfaction
Wolf & Abell, 2003	Community-dwelling adults	61	Real-mantra group, placebo-mantra group, and no-treatment control × 3 time points	↓ Stress ↓ Depression
Pretest–posttest design studies				
Bormann et al., 2005	Veterans with chronic illness	62	Pretest–posttest	↓ Stress ↓ State-trait anxiety ↓ Trait anger ↑ Quality of life ↑ Total spiritual well-being ↑ Existential well-being No change: religious well-being No change: state anger

TABLE 5.1
Findings Related to Mantram Program Research (2001–2013) (Continued)

Author/Date	Sample	*N*	Design	Findings
Bormann, Becker, et al., 2006	Health care employees	42	Pretest–posttest	↓ Stress ↓ Trait anxiety ↓ Trait anger ↑ Quality of life ↑ Total spiritual well-being Mantram wrist counters associated with ↓ Trait anxiety ↑ Religious well-being ↑ Total spiritual well-being
Bormann et al., 2007	Veterans and health care employees	59	Mantram group only, pretest–posttest; mantram wrist counters as a covariate	↓ Stress ↓ Trait anger ↑ Quality of life ↑ Total spiritual well-being
Qualitative-only studies				
Bormann, Oman, et al., 2006	Veterans Health care employees	66	Qualitative	Decreasing stress in traffic and work Decreasing anxiety Decreasing feelings of out of control Decreasing interpersonal tension Decreasing insomnia Decreasing unwanted thoughts

(Continued)

TABLE 5.1
Findings Related to Mantram Program Research (2001–2013) (Continued)

Author/Date	Sample	*N*	Design	Findings
Richards, Oman, Hedberg, Thoresen, & Bowden, 2006	Nurses in workplace	12	Qualitative	Nurses reported using mantram, slowing down, and one-pointed attention to manage workplace stress.
Mediation studies				
Bormann et al., 2012	Veterans with PTSD	136	Mediation analysis	Mantram improves existential spiritual well-being; existential spiritual well-being partially mediates decreases in self-reported PTSD.
Bormann, Oman, Walter, & Johnson (in press)	Veterans with PTSD	66	Mediation analysis	Mantram program improves mindful attention; mindful attention mediates reductions in PTSD symptoms and improves psychological well-being; improvements in mindful attention were due to frequency of mantram repetition practice.
Oman & Bormann, 2013	Veterans with PTSD	132	Mediation analysis	Mantram improves self-efficacy for symptoms; increases in self-efficacy partially mediate decreases in PTSD.
Bormann & Carrico, 2009	Adults with HIV	93	Mediation of positive appraisal coping	Mantram improves positive appraisal coping; positive appraisal coping partially mediates decreases in trait anger long-term.

TABLE 5.1

Findings Related to Mantram Program Research (2001–2013) (Continued)

Author/Date	Sample	*N*	Design	Findings
Bormann, Aschbacher, Wetherell, Roesch, & Redwine, 2009	Adults with HIV	71	Path analysis	Mantram program increased faith/assurance, in which faith/assurance had delayed effect on decreasing salivary cortisol levels.

Note. PTSD = posttraumatic stress disorder; HIV = human immunodeficiency virus.

and clinician-assessed (Blake et al., 1990). There were reductions in depression symptoms after the Mantram Program with significance levels of $p < .05$ using the Brief Symptom Inventory-18 (Derogatis, 2000; Thorp et al., 2009). A post hoc analysis of the PTSD symptom clusters revealed significant reductions in hyperarousal ($p < .01$) and numbing ($p < .05$). There was little change in PTSD symptoms of reexperiencing and avoidance. Significant improvements were also found in mental health status ($p < .04$) but not physical health status (Ware, Kosinski, Turner-Bowker, & Gandek, 2002). There were significant improvements in existential spiritual well-being ($p < .001$). In contrast, results did not support the significance of Mantram Program for reduction of symptoms of somatization or anxiety. Two points of special importance from this study are (a) Veterans in the Mantram Program reported no adverse events and (b) they had a very low dropout rate of 6%. This is much lower than the 18%–21% dropout rate reported for other evidence-based PTSD treatments (Bradley, Greene, Russ, Dutra, & Westen, 2005; Imel, Laska, Jakupcak, & Simpson, 2013).

Details from the qualitative component of this RCT with 65 Veterans are highlighted here (Bormann, Hurst, et al., 2013). Findings provide strong evidence that the Mantram Program is an effective intervention for managing long-term, chronic PTSD symptoms. Almost all (97%) participants reported moderate to high satisfaction with the Mantram Program. Veterans diagnosed with PTSD report various uses for their mantram repetition. Sixty (92%) of the Veterans reported using mantram repetition effectively for (a) relaxing/calming down, (b) diverting attention away from the triggering incident, and (c) letting go of anger. Veterans reported various uses and situations whereby mantram repetition was a useful tool in managing symptoms. Some examples include managing road rage, controlling symptoms of hyperarousal, and dealing with insomnia and nightmares (Bormann, Hurst, et al., 2013). Other beneficial outcomes reported by the Veterans included "thinking clearly and rationally, focusing attention, refining mantram skills, slowing down, communicating thoughts and feelings more effectively, feeling in touch spiritually, and letting go of physical pain" (p. 769).

The following quote is one example of a Veteran's response:

> Well sometimes, when I have nightmares, I get really upset, frustrated, angry, and have a tendency to take it out on my wife. She's the closest one to me living in the house and the mantram helps me to, you know, calm myself down and apologize, and explain to her that it's me, not her. That really helps, because she's been really good at supporting me, putting up with my abuse.

Another way Veterans report using mantram repetition is prophylactically, that is, repeating it prior to stressful events. They use it in preparation of events where they anticipate having flashbacks or irritability. They use their mantram to mitigate these negative responses. In other words, mantram repetition buffers their emotional reaction to negative recalls (Bormann, Hurst, et al., 2013).

Mixed-Methods Randomized Controlled Trial in Childbearing

In a second RCT, first-time mothers and active duty military spouses and partners were seeking coping skills in preparation for childbirth (Hunter et al., 2011). The Mantram Program was delivered in three, 2-hr sessions over three weekends to accommodate participants. The control group was a standard community-based childbirth course. Satisfaction of the Mantram Program was moderate to high. Those who learned mantram repetition used it to manage feelings of uncertainty and pain during labor. Telephone interviews at 6 months postdelivery revealed that all mothers assigned to the Mantram Program were still practicing mantram repetition. They reported using mantram for managing insomnia and their emotions.

Mixed-Methods Randomized Controlled Trial in Adults With HIV

In another RCT in adults living with HIV, the Mantram Program showed significant reductions in trait anger ($p < .05$) and intrusive thoughts ($p < .04$) compared to an active HIV educational control group (Bormann, Gifford, et al., 2006). There was little change in depression, stress, and trait anxiety (see Table 5.1). In this study, the frequency of mantram practice was measured using wrist counters and daily logs (Bormann et al., 2007). Frequency of mantram practice was found positively associated with quality of life and existential spiritual well-being (meaning/peace and faith/assurance) and negatively associated with intrusive thoughts (Bormann, Gifford, et al., 2006). These findings provide empirical support for the hypothesized mechanism of redirecting attention away from negative, unwanted thoughts and toward the mantram to promote well-being (Vujanovic et al., 2011).

The qualitative component of this study contains specific quotes described by Kemppainen, Bormann, Shively, et al. (2012). Interviews conducted at 2 months follow-up demonstrated the sustainability of mantram repetition. Findings demonstrated that mantram repetition resulted in (a) feelings of calm and/or peace, (b) increasing personal awareness, and (c) managing physical symptoms, among others.

Mixed-Methods One-Group Repeated Measures in Family Caregivers

In another mixed-methods study, a group of 16 family caregivers of Veterans with dementia completed the Mantram Program (Bormann, Warren, et al., 2009). This program was delivered using telephone conference calls (see Table 5.1). Questionnaires were collected at preintervention, postintervention, and follow-up. Telephone interviews were conducted at week 36 postintervention to assess mantram use. Results demonstrated significant decreases in caregiver burden, stress, depression, and rumination (all $p < .04$) with increases in quality of life ($p < .04$). Results of the qualitative interviews are summarized in Table 5.1.

Randomized Controlled Trials

Four RCTs without qualitative interviews have been completed on the Mantram Program. Two were with Veterans with PTSD (Bormann et al., 2008; Plumb et al., 2014), one was with Korean nurse managers (Yong et al., 2011), and the fourth was with community-dwelling adults (Wolf & Abell, 2003). Three of the four studies had an active control group, and all demonstrated improvements in lowering psychological distress and improving well-being.

Veterans completing the group Mantram Program reported lower PTSD symptom severity and psychological distress while improving quality of life and spiritual well-being compared to a wait-list control group (Bormann et al., 2008; see Table 5.1). In another RCT, Veterans in the individually delivered Mantram Program reported significant reductions in PTSD symptom severity while controlling for spiritual well-being (Plumb et al., 2014). They were compared to a present-centered therapy control group (Frost, Laska, & Wampold, 2014). In the third study, Korean nurse managers in the Mantram Program reported heightened levels of spiritual integrity, spiritual well-being, and leadership practice while significantly decreasing burnout compared to an educational control group (Yong et al., 2011). Finally, a group of community-dwelling adults who recited a real mantra were compared to either a placebo-mantra or no-treatment control group. The placebo mantra was made up with nonsense Sanskrit syllables that resembled the rhythm and length of the real-mantra group. Depression and stress were decreased in both groups, but the lower depression levels were maintained at 4-week follow-up in the real-mantra group (Wolf & Abell, 2003).

Bormann's current research in Veterans with PTSD includes an RCT where the Mantram Program is delivered individually in eight, 1-hr weekly sessions compared to individual present-centered therapy (Frost et al., 2014). This study is located in two geographic areas: Bedford, Massachusetts and San Diego, California. Results will be available in 2015: http://clinicaltrials.gov/ct2/show/NCT01506323?term=Mantram+Repetition&rank=2

Pretest–Posttest Studies

Early research on the Mantram Program showed significant improvements in health outcomes using pretest–posttest, one-group research design studies (see Table 5.1). Two mantram pretest–posttest research studies document the effectiveness of the Mantram Program in chronically stressful situations. The populations were Veterans with chronic illnesses (Bormann et al., 2007) and health care providers in today's highly technical, stressful work environments (Bormann, Becker, et al., 2006). Both studies demonstrated improvements in lowering psychological distress and improving quality of life and spiritual well-being (see Table 5.1).

Qualitative Studies

Published qualitative research studies are a strength of the Mantram Program research. The three mixed-methods studies previously described included qualitative interviews conducted by telephone at 2 or 3 months posttreatment. In addition, two other published qualitative-*only* studies have been published on the Mantram Program. One was with a sample of both Veterans with chronic illness and health care providers (Bormann, Oman, et al., 2006). The other was in a sample of nurses (Richards et al., 2006; see Table 5.1). Veterans reported the effective use of the Mantram Program to manage symptoms of "impatience, anger, frustration, being upset, feeling disgruntled, and feeling out of control" (Bormann, Oman, et al., 2006, p. 507). They also cited mantram repetition as a help with insomnia and nightmares. Two other key points taught in the Mantram Program, one-pointed attention and slowing down, were identified by the health care employees and nurses who stated that they applied one-pointed attention to keep distractions at work from interfering with their concentration (Richards et al., 2006).

These qualitative-only studies were conducted in 36 health care employees, 30 Veterans with chronic illnesses (Bormann, Oman, et al., 2006), and 12 nurses (Richards et al., 2006). The telephone interviews, which ranged from 10 to 45 min, were conducted approximately 2 to 3 months postmantram intervention by trained research personnel (Flanagan, 1954). Another unpublished qualitative study in a small sample of mostly women African Americans (81%) was conducted in North Carolina. Mantram was replaced with *prayer word* and outcomes included hypertension and spiritual well-being (Kemppainen, Bormann, & Bomar, 2012). Findings demonstrated significant reductions in stress management. All these qualitative studies reveal specific and useful ways to use mantram repetition.

Mediation Studies

Five Mantram Program studies have been conducted to explore mechanisms of action using mediator or path analysis (Bormann, Aschbacher, et al., 2009; Bormann & Carrico, 2009; Bormann et al., 2012; (Bormann, Oman, Walter, & Johnson/in press) Oman & Bormann, 2013). This means that the Mantram Program mediated or changed a specific concept and, in turn, this changed concept positively influenced a second concept. An example is that an increase in spiritual well-being was found as a result of the Mantram Program in a sample of Veterans with PTSD (Bormann et al., 2012). Then, this increased spiritual well-being lowered self-reported PTSD symptom severity (see Table 5.1). Similarly, the Mantram Program increased levels of self-efficacy managing PTSD symptoms in Veterans with PTSD. Self-efficacy was found to mediate reductions in PTSD symptom severity. In the HIV study, increases in faith/assurance had a delayed effect of lowering salivary cortisol levels in those adults with HIV (Bormann, Aschbacher, et al., 2009), and positive reappraisal coping was found to mediate long-term reductions in trait anger (Bormann & Carrico, 2009).

In summary, all these Mantram Program studies have two important strengths: adequate sample sizes and various study designs. Adequate sample sizes prevent a Type II error, which commonly occurs in nursing research with small inadequate sample sizes (Polit & Beck, 2012). In addition, having numerous research designs to study the Mantram Program, specifically mixed methods and RCTs, provide greater confidence in the strength of evidence from study findings (see Table 5.1).

DIRECT NURSING CARE: USES FOR MANTRAM REPETITION

Differences in participants' reports highlight the wide variety of uses of mantram repetition in direct nursing care (Chan, 2014). When the participants answered a question about what was most useful from the Mantram Program, Veterans had different responses than health care workers. Veterans reported that they most often repeated their mantrams. In contrast, health care providers reported that they most often used one-pointed attention and slowing down from the Mantram Program. One-pointed attention taught them how to focus on the tasks at hand, and slowing down taught them how to be more present in their relationships with patients and families.

The versatility of the Mantram Program is demonstrated with these two differences. Mantram repetition can be used in many different situations for many different reasons. In the cited example, Veterans use mantram repetition to cope with events that trigger their PTSD symptoms from military trauma. In contrast, health care workers use one-pointed attention to concentrate and complete their work assignments with greater safety and efficiency. The health care workers' need for, and benefit from, one-pointed attention makes sense when one thinks of the highly interactive, demanding, constantly changing, and noisy work environment in today's health care system.

The authors believe that the Mantram Program could be useful in most areas of direct patient care for both providers and patients. Mantram repetition is also applicable for nurses with complex health care assignments that require focus and patience. Other uses are to help providers make transitions from one patient or procedure to another, allowing slight pause time to refocus. The Mantram Program has not been tested to date for its effect with physical symptoms which takes us to the next section, future research.

EVIDENCE-BASED RESEARCH NEEDED WITH MILITARY PERSONNEL AND VETERANS

Future areas for testing include military personnel and active duty. With the exception of one study in military childbearing couples (Hunter et al., 2011), the Mantram Program has not been tested with active duty military personnel. This is an important population for future testing. The types of stress and adrenaline experienced by today's military and combat Veterans are significantly different from previous wars. Today, they come home after multiple deployments; experience war conditions that are extremely unpredictable; and suffer from roadside bombs, civilian enemies, and suicide bombers. For military personnel and Veterans, there are five relevant characteristics of mantram repetition—simple, quick, personal, portable, and private—that describe the advantages of mantram repetition for today's soldier who is tomorrow's Veteran (Table 5.2).

Future military testing could include replication studies based on positive results reported from Veterans. Prior demonstrated effectiveness of Mantram Program with adults living with HIV (Bormann, Gifford, et al., 2006) may also be applicable. Both groups, current military personnel and adults living with HIV at the time the research was conducted, were in life-threatening situations. However, there are definite differences between the two groups. Hence, the need for future replication research with military personnel.

If the Mantram Program is found to be effective in military personnel, perhaps mantram repetition could serve to promote improved health outcomes

TABLE 5.2
Strengths of Mantram Repetition

Simple
Quick
Personal
Portable
Private

and wellness. Research needs to be conducted to determine if mantram repetition could prevent or decrease the intensity of both PTSD and depression in military personnel. The Mantram Program could also be tested as an intervention for suicide prevention and recovery from substance abuse.

For Veterans, the Mantram Program needs to be provided prior to or along with current recommended treatments for PTSD. These include prolonged exposure, cognitive processing therapy, cognitive behavioral therapy, eye movement and desensitization reprocessing, and psychopharmacology (Foa, Keane, & Friedman, 2010). Having a way to remain present while actively engaged in these evidence-based treatments may improve their effectiveness and reduce attrition. If the Mantram Program is proven as effective as other VA-recommended interventions, our Veterans would have another effective, simple, quick, and portable intervention they could use without the side effects that occur from medications.

Additional outcomes need to be tested with increased focus on physical symptoms. Suggested conditions for future testing include acute and chronic pain, tinnitus, spinal cord injury, and mild traumatic brain injury. The Mantram Program may provide additional coping practices for navigating the journey from severe physical injuries to rehabilitation. Examples include amputation of limbs, adjusting to new prosthesis, relearning activities of daily living in a wheel chair, or learning to adapt to a new way of life following injuries. Research on the Mantram Program needs to be tested in patients who deal with painful or difficult procedures such as wound care, burn dressing changes, and hyperbaric oxygen therapy, for example.

The Mantram Program itself has several areas to be tested, which include methods of delivery. The most frequently used method of delivery, a group, needs to be compared to other methods of delivery such as individually or by electronic means such as telephone conference calls or Internet delivery. The VA has recognized and currently provides peer support advocates. A peer educator and peer navigator have been documented to be effective in both colorectal and prostate cancer screening (Weinrich, Weinrich, Boyd, & Mettlin, 1998; Weinrich, Weinrich, Stromborg, Boyd, & Weiss, 1993). The use of peer advocates also needs to be tested with the Mantram Program.

Today, it is recognized that the needs of female Veterans differ from male Veterans. Females are a critical population for future Mantram Program research. Research is needed with both active duty as well as Veteran females. The need to conduct intervention research on females-only versus mixed-gender groups has been identified by the VA (Tsai, Mares, & Rosenheck, 2012; VA Office of Inspector General, 2012). Female-only Mantram Programs versus mixed-gender Mantram Programs need to be evaluated to determine the best outcomes. Could female-only groups provide better peer support and promote more access to care in contrast to mixed-gender groups? Both quantitative and qualitative studies are needed.

Unfortunately, many Veterans are dealing with the after effects of MST. To date, the Mantram Program has not been tested solely with MST survivors. This population is an important group to include in future research. MST is also a risk factor for homelessness (Balshem, Christensen, Tuepker, & Kansagara, 2011), another huge problem for returning Veterans. We do have preliminary data on homeless Veterans who have suffered MST. The Mantram Program was taught to 4 Veteran women who were part of a larger group of 29 homeless women who recently learned the Mantram Program. Positive results are pending. Larger studies with the Mantram Program delivered with the recommended 8-week format need to be conducted, both with MST survivors as well as homeless Veterans.

A greater focus on the recruitment of females into the Mantram Program needs to occur. Qualitative research needs to be conducted to determine what is important to females in order for them to enroll into the Mantram Program. Despite our efforts to recruit women, prior mantram studies have been composed of primarily male Veterans.

For this chapter, data on females who completed the Mantram Program is presented in the following text. The following unpublished results provide support for future Mantram Program research that targets females in both the active military and Veteran populations. Data were collected between 2001 and 2005. The sample sizes varied from 31 to 80 as new measures were added at different time periods. The findings contain both Veteran and nonveteran females (N = 106). All of the studies used a one-group, pretest–posttest design. Results using paired t tests show that there were significant decreases in perceived stress, trait anger, and state anxiety. There were significant increases in quality of life enjoyment and satisfaction and existential spiritual well-being. Results for these 106 females are shown in Table 5.3.

TABLE 5.3

Significant Improvements With Mantram Repetition in 109 Females

Concept	Sample Size (n)	Significance (p value)
Perceived stress	80	<.001***
State anger	50	*ns*
Trait anger	53	<.01**
State anxiety	31	<.02*
Trait anxiety	34	*ns*
Quality of life	73	*<.001****
Spiritual well-being	53	*ns*
Religious well-being	53	*ns*
Existential spiritual well-being	53	<.02*

Note. ns = not significant.
*$p < .05$. **$p < .01$. ***$p < .001$.

CONCLUSIONS

Despite our impressive technological advances that promote health and prevent disease, the wounds of war are an ever-evolving challenge. Each generation is tested with new weapons, strategies, and risks. The impending return of large numbers of Iraq and Afghanistan Veterans require diverse, more innovative, and low-cost therapies. Both male and female Veterans returning from these wars increasingly have complex, comorbid physical and psychological trauma; combat-related psychological trauma; and MST. Many return with unemployment, homelessness, and feelings of abandonment by the system designed to take care of them. Our health care system is not sufficiently prepared to care for these Veterans who often reject pharmacological interventions caused by side effects or trauma-focused therapies delivered in the traditional hospital or clinic setting. This generation is technologically advanced, and they deserve 21st-century health care from practitioners who understand what they have endured. The Mantram Program's Internet and individual delivery capabilities will likely attract many more of this generation's Veterans. The need for such interventions is great because it is estimated that by 2015, the total Veteran population in the United States will reach 21 million (U.S. Department of Veterans Affairs, Office of the Actuary, 2014).

The Mantram Program is a "one-size-fits-all" modality that is personal, portable, and private to each Veteran regardless of age, gender, race, spiritual belief, and education level. It is user-friendly and very adaptable. Larger RCTs are needed to target specific military and Veteran groups (e.g., active duty, younger, female, homeless, MST survivors) and provide sound evidence of treatment effectiveness. The future is promising for the Mantram Program providing concomitant and potentially stand-alone relief of many symptoms our military and Veterans are experiencing.

ACKNOWLEDGMENTS

Authors acknowledge all sources of funding that have contributed to the research studies described here. These include the Department of Veterans Affairs (VA), Veterans Health Administration, Office of Research and Development, Health Services Research and Development, Nursing Research Initiative (RI 04-041-1); VA San Diego Center of Excellence for Stress and Mental Health (CESAMH); National Institutes of Health/National Center of Complementary and Alternative Medicine (NIH/NCCAM), R21 AT01159; Sigma Theta Tau International Nursing Society, Gamma Gamma Chapter, San Diego State School of Nursing; Nurses of Veterans Affairs (NOVA) Foundation; and the San Diego State University School of Nursing's Institute of Nursing Research (#900521).

DISCLAIMER

The views expressed in this chapter are those of the authors and do not necessarily reflect the official policy or position of the Department of the Navy, Department of Defense, Department of Veterans Affairs, or the U.S. government.

NOTE

1. Some mantrams include "Om Shanti," which means peace; "Om Prema," which means love; "my God and my all," used by St. Francis of Assisi; "Rama," which invites eternal joy within and was used by Mahatma Gandhi; "Ave Maria" or "Jesus," from Christianity; and "O Wakan Tanka" or "Oh Great Spirit" from native American Indian tradition.

REFERENCES

Balshem, H., Christensen, V., Tuepker, A., & Kansagara, D. (2011). *A critical review of the literature regarding homelessness among Veterans* (Department of Veterans Affairs VA-ESP Project

#05-225). Washington, DC: Department of Veterans Affairs. Retrieved from http://www.hsrd.research.va.gov/publications/esp/homelessness.cfm

Benson, H. (1993). The relaxation response. In D. Goleman & J. Gurin (Eds.), *Mind/body medicine: How to use your mind for better health* (pp. 233–257). Yonkers, NY: Consumer Reports Books.

Benson, H. (1996). *Timeless healing*. New York, NY: Scribner.

Bernardi, L., Sleight, P., Bandinelli, G., Cencetti, S., Fattorini, L., Wdowczyc-Szulc, J., & Lagi, A. (2001). Effect of rosary prayer and yoga mantras on autonomic cardiovascular rhythms: Comparative study. *British Medical Journal*, *323*, 1446–1449. Retrieved from http://www.jstor.org/stable/25468612

Blake, D. D., Weathers, F. W., Nagy, L. M., Kaloupek, D. G., Charney, D. S., & Keane, T. M. (1990). *The Clinician-Administered PTSD Scale—IV*. Boston, MA: National Center for PTSD—Behavioral Science Division.

Bormann, J. E. (2010). Mantram repetition: A "portable contemplative practice" for modern times. In T. G. Plante (Ed.), *Contemplative practices in action: Spirituality, meditation, and health* (pp. 78–99). Santa Barbara, CA: ABC-CLIO.

Bormann, J. E., Aschbacher, K., Wetherell, J. L., Roesch, S., & Redwine, L. (2009). Effects of faith/assurance on cortisol levels are enhanced by a spiritual mantram intervention in adults with HIV: A randomized trial. *Journal of Psychosomatic Research*, *66*(2), 161–171. http://dx.doi.org/10.1016/j.jpsychores.2008.09.017

Bormann, J. E., Becker, S., Gershwin, M., Kelly, A., Pada, L., Smith, T. L., & Gifford, A. L. (2006). Relationship of frequent mantram repetition to emotional and spiritual well-being in healthcare workers. *Journal of Continuing Education in Nursing*, *37*(5), 218–224. Retrieved from http://www.jcenonline.com

Bormann, J. E., & Carrico, A. (2009). Increases in positive reappraisal coping during a group-based mantram intervention mediate sustained reductions in anger in HIV-positive persons. *International Journal of Behavioral Medicine*, *16*, 74–80. http://dx.doi.org/10.1007/s12529-008-9007-3

Bormann, J. E., Gifford, A. L., Shively, M., Smith, T. L., Redwine, L. Kelly, A., . . . Belding, W. (2006). Effects of spiritual mantram repetition on HIV outcomes: A randomized controlled trial. *Journal of Behavioral Medicine*, *29*(4), 359–376. http://dx.doi.org/10.1007/s10865-006-9063-6

Bormann, J. E., Hurst, S., & Kelly, A. (2013). Responses to mantram repetition program from Veterans with posttraumatic stress disorder: A qualitative analysis. *Journal of Rehabilitation Research and Development*, *50*(6), 769–784. http://dx.doi.org/10.1682/JRRD.2012.06.0118

Bormann, J. E., Liu, L., Thorp, S., & Lang, A. J. (2012). Spiritual wellbeing mediates PTSD change in Veterans with military-related PTSD. *International Journal of Behavioral Medicine*, *19*(4), 496–502. http://dx.doi.org/10.1007/s12529-011-9186-1

Bormann, J. E., Oman, D., Kemppainen, J. K., Becker, S., Gershwin, M., & Kelly, A. (2006). Mantram repetition for stress management in Veterans and employees: A critical incident study. *Journal of Advanced Nursing*, *53*(5), 502–512. http://dx.doi.org/10.1111/j.1365-2648.2006.03752.x

Bormann, J. E., Oman, D., Walter, K. H., & Johnson, B. D. (in press). Mindful attention increases and mediates psychological outcomes following mantram repetition practice in Veterans with posttraumatic stress disorder. *Medical Care: Special supplement on CAM use in Veterans and military personnel.*

Bormann, J. E., Smith, T. L., Becker, S., Gershwin, M., Pada, L., Grudzinski, A. H., & Nurmi, E. A. (2005). Efficacy of frequent, mantram repetition on stress, quality of life, and spiritual well-being in Veterans: A pilot study. *Journal of Holistic Nursing*, *23*(4), 395–414. http://dx.doi.org/10.1177/0898010105278929

Bormann, J. E., Smith, T. L., Shively, M., Dellefield, M. E., & Gifford, A. L. (2007). Self-monitoring of a stress reduction technique using wrist-worn counters. *Journal of Healthcare Quality*, *29*(1), 45–52. http://dx.doi.org/10.1111/j.1945-1474.2007.tb00175.x

Bormann, J. E., Thorp, S., Wetherell, J. L., & Golshan, S. (2008). A spiritually based group intervention for combat Veterans with PTSD: Feasibility study. *Journal of Holistic Nursing*, *26*(2), 109–116. http://dx.doi.org/10.1177/0898010107311276

Bormann, J. E., Thorp, S. R., Wetherell, J. L., Golshan, S., & Lang, A. J. (2013). Meditation-based mantram intervention for Veterans with posttraumatic stress disorder: A randomized trial. *Psychological Trauma: Theory, Research, Practice, and Policy*, *5*(3), 259–267. http://dx.doi.org/10.1037/a0027522

Bormann, J. E., Warren, K. A., Regalbuto, L., Glaser, D., Kelly, A., Schnack, J., & Hinton, L. (2009). A spiritually-based caregiver intervention with telephone delivery for family caregivers of Veterans with dementia. *Journal of Family and Community Health*, *32*(4), 345–353. http://dx.doi.org/10.1097/FCH.0b013e3181b91fd6

Bradley, R., Greene, J., Russ, E., Dutra, L., & Westen, D. (2005). A multidimensional meta-analysis of psychotherapy for PTSD. *American Journal of Psychiatry*, *162*, 214–227.

Cahn, B. R., Delorme, A., & Polich, J. (2013). Event-related delta, theta, alpha and gamma correlates to auditory oddball processing during Vipassana meditation. *Social Cognitive and Affective Neuroscience*, *8*(1), 100–111. http://dx.doi.org/10.1093/scan/nss060

Cahn, B. R., & Polich, J. (2006). Meditation states and traits: EEG, ERP, and neuroimaging studies. *Psychological Bulletin*, *132*, 180–211. http://dx.doi.org/10.1037/0033-2909.132.2.180

Chan, R. R. (2014). Mantra meditation as a bedside spiritual intervention. *Medsurg Nursing*, *23*(2), 84–88.

Derogatis, L. R. (2000). *Brief Symptom Inventory (BSI) 18: Administration, scoring, and procedures manual*. Minneapolis, MN: NCS Pearson.

Easwaran, E. (2008a). *The mantram handbook: A practical guide to choosing your mantram and calming your mind*. Tomales, CA: Nilgiri Press.

Easwaran, E. (2008b). *Passage meditation: Bringing the deep wisdom of the heart into daily life* (3rd ed.). Tomales, CA: Nilgiri Press.

Easwaran, E. (2005/2013). *Strength in the storm: Transform stress, live in balance & find peace of mind*. Tomales, CA: Nilgiri Press.

Flanagan, J. C. (1954). The critical incident technique. *Psychological Bulletin*, *51*(4), 327–358. http://dx.doi.org/10.1037/h0061470 28

Foa, E. B., Keane, T. M., & Friedman, M. J. (2010). *Effective treatments for posttraumatic stress disorder: Practice guidelines from the International Society for Traumatic Stress Studies*. New York, NY: Guilford Press.

Fontana, A., & Rosenheck, R. (2004). Trauma, change in strength of religious faith, and mental health service use among Veterans treated for PTSD. *Journal of Neurological and Mental Disorders*, *192*(9), 579–584. http://dx.doi.org/10.1097/01.nmd.0000138224.17375.55

Frost, N. D., Laska, K. M., & Wampold, B. E. (2014). The evidence for present-centered therapy as a treatment for posttraumatic stress disorder. *Journal of Traumatic Stress*, *27*, 1–8.

Holzel, B. K., Carmody, J., Vangel, M., Congleton, C., Yerramsetti, S. M., Gard, T., & Lazar, S. W. (2011). Mindfulness practice leads to increases in regional brain gray matter density. *Psychiatry Research*, *191*(1), 36–43. http://dx.doi.org/10.1016/j.pscychresns.2010.08.006

Hunter, L., Bormann, J., Belding, W., Sobo, E. J., Axman, L., Reseter, B. K., . . . Miranda, V. (2011). Satisfaction with the use of a spiritually based mantram intervention for childbirth-related fears in couples. *Journal of Applied Nursing Research*, *24*, 138–146. http://dx.doi.org/10.1016/j.apnr.2009.06.002

Imel, Z. E., Laska, K., Jakupcak, M., & Simpson, T. L. (2013). Meta-analysis of dropout in treatments for PTSD. *Journal of Clinical and Consulting Psychology*, *81*(3), 394–404.

Kemeny, M. E., Foltz, C., Cavanagh, J. F., Cullen, M., Giese-Davis, J., Jennings, P., . . . Ekman, P. (2012). Contemplative/emotion training reduces negative emotional behavior and promotes prosocial responses. *Emotion*, *12*(2), 338–350. http://dx.doi.org/10.1037/a0026118

Kemppainen, J., Bormann, J., & Bomar, P. (2012, April). *The efficacy of a spiritually based mantram repetition program on hypertension in African Americans living in rural Southeastern North Carolina*. Paper presented at the Sigma Theta Tau International Nursing Society, Nu Omega Research Day, University of North Carolina Wilmington, Wilmington, NC.

Kemppainen, J., Bormann, J. E., Shively, M., Kelly, A., Becker, S., Bone, P., . . . Gifford, A. L. (2012). Living with HIV: Responses to a mantram intervention using the critical incident research method. *Journal of Alternative and Complementary Medicine*, *18*(1), 76–82. http://dx.doi.org/10.1089/acm.2009.0489

Khusid, M. (2013). Self-care mindfulness approaches for refractory posttraumatic stress disorder. *Psychiatric Annals*, *43*(7), 340–344. http://dx.doi.org/10.3928/00485713-20130703-11

Koenig, H., King, D., & Carson, V. B. (2012). Handbook of religion and health (2nd ed.); Oxford University Press, New York, NY.

Lang, A. J., Strauss, J. L., Bomyea, J., Bormann, J. E., Hickman, S. D., Good, R. C., & Essex, M. (2012). The theoretical and empirical basis for meditation as an intervention for PTSD. *Behavior Modification*, *36*(6), 757–784. http://dx.doi.org/10.1177/0145445512441200

Lazar, S. W., Kerr, C. E., Wasserman, R. H., Gray, J. R., Greve, D. N., Treadway, M. T., . . . Fischl, B. (2005). Meditation experience is associated with increased cortical thickness. *Neurological Report*, *16*(17), 1893–1897. Retrieved from http://www.ncbi.nlm.nih.gov/pmc/articles/PMC1361002/

Leary, S., Bormann, J. E., Smith, T. L., Georges, J., & Andrews, T. (2013, April). *Internet-delivered mantram repetition program for burnout in healthcare workers*. Paper presented at the Western Institute of Nursing 46th Annual Communicating Nursing Research Conference, Anaheim, CA.

Lutz, A., Greischar, L., Rawlings, N. B., Ricard, M., & Davidson R. J. (2004). Long-term meditators self-induce high-amplitude synchrony during mental practice. *Proceedings of the National Academy of Science*, *101*(46), 16360–16373. Retrieved from http://www.pnas.org_cgi_doi_10.1073_pnas.0407401101

Manna, A., Raffone, A., Perrucci, M. G., Nardo, D., Ferretti, A., Tartaro, A., ...Romani, G. L. (2010). Neural correlates of focused attention and cognitive monitoring in meditation. *Brain Research Bulletin*, *82*(1–2), 45–56. http://dx.doi.org/10.1016/j.brainresbull.2010.03.001

Miller, W. R., & Thoresen, C. E. (2003). Spirituality, religion, and health: An emerging research field. *American Psychologist, 58*(1), 24–35. http://dx.doi.org/10.1037/0003-066X.58.1.24

Oman, D., & Bormann, J. (2013, March). *Mantram repetition fosters self-efficacy in Veterans for managing PTSD: A randomized trial*. Paper presented at the 34th Annual Meeting of the Society of Behavioral Medicine, San Francisco, CA.

Oman, D., & Driskill, J. D. (2003). Holy name repetition as a spiritual exercise and therapeutic technique. *Journal of Psychology and Christianity*, *22*(1), 5–19. Retrieved from http://www.caps.net

Peng, C. K., Henry, I. C., Mietus, J. E., Hausdorff, J. M., Khalsa, G., Benson, H., . . . Goldberger, A. L. (2004). Heart rate dynamics during three forms of meditation. *International Journal of Cardiology*, *95*, 19–27. http://dx.doi.org/10.1016/j.ijcard.2003.02.006

Peterman, A. H., Fitchett, G., Brady, M. J., Hernandez, L., & Cella, D. (2002). Measuring spiritual wellbeing in people with cancer: The Functional Assessment of Chronic Illness Therapy—Spiritual Well-Being Scale (FACIT-Sp). *Annals of Behavior Medicine*, *24*(1), 49–58.

Plumb, D. N., Bormann, J. E., Beck, D. J., Glickman, M. E., Zhao, S., Osei-Bonsu, P. E., . . . Elwy, A. R. (2014, May). *Meditation-based mantram repetition program for Veterans with PTSD:*

A randomized controlled trial in the VA Healthcare System. Paper presented at the International Research Congress on Integrative Medicine and Health, Miami, FL.

Polit, D. F., & Beck, C. T. (2012). *Nursing research: Generating and assessing evidence for nursing practice* (9th ed.). Philadelphia, PA: Wolters Kluwer/Lippincott Williams & Wilkins.

Richards T. A., Oman, D., Hedberg, J., Thoresen, C. E., & Bowden, J. (2006). A qualitative examination of a spiritually-based intervention and self-management in the workplace. *Nursing Science Quarterly, 19*(3), 231–239. http://dx.doi.org/10.1177/0894318406289490

Schaefer, F. C., Blazer, D. G., & Koenig, H. G. (2008). Religious and spiritual factors and the consequences of trauma: A review and model of the interrelationship. *International Journal of Psychiatry Medicine, 38*(4), 507–524.

Shaw, A., Joseph, S., & Linley, P. A. (2005). Religion, spirituality, and posttraumatic growth: A systematic review. *Journal of Mental Health and Religious Culture, 8*(1), 1–11. http://dx.doi.org/10.1080/1367467032000157981

Thorp, S., Bormann, J. E., Wetherell, J. L., Golshan, S., Gershwin, M., & Kelly, A. (2009). *Effects of a spiritually-based mantram intervention on psychological distress in Veterans with PTSD.* Paper presented at the 2009 Anxiety Disorders Association of America Annual Conference, Santa Ana Pueblo, NM.

Travis, F., & Shear, J. (2010). Focused attention, open monitoring and automatic self-transcending: Categories to organize meditations from Vedic, Buddhist and Chinese traditions. *Conscious Cognition, 19*(4), 1110–1118. http://dx.doi.org/10.1016/j.concog.2010.01.1007

Tsai, J., Mares, A. S., & Rosenheck, R. A. (2012). Do homeless Veterans have same needs and outcomes as non-veterans? *Military Medicine, 177*(1), 27–31.

VA Office of Inspector General. (2012). Audit of VHA's homeless providers grant and per diem program 11-00334-115; 1–39.

Vujanovic, A. A., Niles, B., Pietrefesa, A., Schmertz, S. K., & Potter, C. M. (2011). Mindfulness in the treatment of posttraumatic stress disorder among military Veterans. *Professional Psychological Research and Practice, 42*(1), 24–31. http://dx.doi.org/10.1037/a0022272

Wachholtz, A. B., & Austin, E. T. (2013). Contemporary spiritual meditation: Practices and outcomes. In K. I. Pargament (Ed.), *American Psychological Association handbook of psychology, religion, and spirituality* (Vol. 1, pp. 311–327). http://dx.doi.org/10.1037/14045-017

Ware, J. E., Kosinski, M., Turner-Bowker, D. M., & Gandek, B. (2002). *User's manual for the SF-12v2 Health Survey with a supplement documenting SF-12 Health Survey*. Lincoln, RI: QualityMetric.

Weathers, F. W., Litz, B. T., Herman, J. A., Huska, J. A., & Keane, T. M. (1993). *PTSD Checklist (PCL): Reliability, validity and diagnostic utility*. Paper presented at the Proceedings of the 9th Annual Conference of International Society for Traumatic Stress Studies, Chicago, IL.

Weinrich, S. P., Weinrich, M. C., Boyd, M. D., & Mettlin, C. (1998). Increasing prostate cancer screening in African American men with peer educator and Client Navigator Educational Interventions. *Journal of Cancer Education, 13*, 213–219.

Weinrich, S. P., Weinrich, M. C., Stromborg, M., Boyd, M. D., & Weiss, H. (1993). Using elderly educators to increase colorectal cancer screening. *The Gerontologist, 33*(4), 401–406.

Wolf, D. B., & Abell, N. (2003). Examining the effects of meditation techniques on psychosocial functioning. *Research on Social Work Practice, 13*(1), 27–42. http://dx.doi.org/10.1177/104973102237471

Yong, J., Kim, J., Park, J., Seo, I., & Swinton, J. (2011). Effects of a spirituality training program on the spiritual and psychosocial well-being of hospital middle manager nurses in Korea. *Journal of Continuing Education in Nursing, 42*(6), 280–288. http://dx.doi.org/10.3928/00220124-20101201-04

CHAPTER 6

Impact of Deployment on Military Families

Janice Agazio, Petra Goodman, and Diane L. Padden

ABSTRACT

To date, approximately 300,000 families including 700,000 children have been affected by the increased and repeated number of deployments in support of the Global War on Terror in Iraq and Afghanistan since 2001. The purpose of this review is to discuss the impact of these deployments on family members of active duty and reserve/guard personnel. A search of literature across the years of military conflicts reveals waves of studies emerging after World War II, the Vietnam conflict, Desert Storm/Shield, and now the most recent wars. Study designs most frequently include qualitative exploratory, survey methods, and program evaluations. The field is limited by small scale projects, service- and facility-specific samples, and knowledge extracted from related topics. More research is needed to achieve a more comprehensive understanding across the trajectory of the deployment experience for both service personnel and family members as well as long-term outcomes.

More than 2 million service members (SMs) have been deployed in support of Operation Iraqi Freedom (OIF), Operation Enduring Freedom (OEF), and Operation New Dawn (OND) since the Global War on Terror (GWOT) began well over a decade ago (White House, 2011). There are more than 3.6 million

http://dx.doi.org/10.1891/0739-6686.32.109

SMs within the total force of the Armed Services. Total force SMs include all those currently serving on active duty as well as the Reserve components which consist of SMs in the National Guard and Reserves. According to best estimates available on the Internet, since 2001, 2,333,972 American military servicemen and women have been deployed in support of OEF, OIF, or both. Furthermore, "according to the Defense Manpower Data Center, nearly half, or 977,542, of those who have served in Iraq or Afghanistan have been deployed more than once" (Department of Defense [DOD], 2012). Approximately 44% of the total force is married with children; thus, the total military force personnel and their families encompass greater than 5.3 million individuals within the U.S. population. Although the number and length of deployments have been steadily declining, the number of individuals affected since the GWOT began is substantial. Although active duty troops are usually stationed at or near military bases or posts, Reserve Component personnel of the Armed Services are "local citizens" dispersed across the United States and may not reside near military facilities. It has long been acknowledged that SM performance is affected by the stability and support from their families (Clever & Segal, 2013). With this in mind, understanding the impact of deployment on the family is paramount in how best to provide effective support and services. During the past 13 years, the knowledge regarding the effects of deployment on military families has increased because of multiple studies by nurses and from other disciplines in understanding how military families are impacted by, and cope with, deployment separations.

LITERATURE METHODOLOGY

An extensive literature review was conducted using a combination of research databases and lay literature to include PubMed, CINAHL, Academic Premier, Dissertation Abstracts, and Google Scholar. The key terms used to search for the research literature included military family, military spouse, military child, nursing research, deployment, and war. The search resulted in a combination of research, theoretical, programmatic, and government documents. The search included publications from 1990 to 2013 to capture early studies following Operation Desert Storm/Desert Shield (ODS/DS).

MILITARY CULTURE AND CHALLENGES

When considering the impact of deployment on families, it is necessary to first review and understand some of the challenges within the military culture. The unique characteristics of military life are well documented and include geographic mobility, periodic family separations, risk of injury of death or the service members (SMs), and adaption to the military culture (Rosen, Durand, & Martin, 2000). These cultural characteristics lead to four major stressors for military families which include frequent relocation, family separation, the possibility of danger and/or death, and adaptation to the military as an institution. The extent to which military family members can successfully adapt to the conditions of military life is related to SM retention, morale, and job performance. Since the GWOT began more than a decade ago, there has been an increased operational tempo, or pace, leading to more frequent deployment separations in the active duty component and an increase in the mobilization and deployments of the reserve component. Although deployment results in family separation, not all deployments are equal. Deployments may differ in nature and dangerousness of the mission, location, length of time, planned or unplanned, amount of information available to families, and amount of public attention and/or support. Wartime deployment is particularly stressful for military families. The state of war in and of itself brings family stressors unique to the war both during the actual time deployed and upon return throughout the reintegration process. During the deployment, family members may have limited knowledge of SM's current location/situation and limited communication with the SM. The prolonged anticipation of potential trauma and/or death to the SM brings additional stress and emotional sequelae for family members (Padden & Agazio, 2013).

Stages of Family Deployment

All families preparing for a deployment separation go through a process defined by the stages of preparation, survival, and reunion. Each stage represents different stressors and adjustments for the military member and family members left behind. First described by Logan (1987), and refined by Peebles-Kleiger and Kleiger (1994), and more recently by Pincus, House, Christenson, and Adler (2001), the cycle of deployment incorporates stages modeled on those of Kübler-Ross of the emotional cycle for families and the military member experiencing deployment. As the family learns of an impending deployment, the first stage, *predeployment*, occurs over a 1- to 2-week period marked by tension, protest, and anger. During this stage, preparations are made for deployment; family members feel "on edge" and may exhibit some emotional and physical withdrawal in anticipation of the separation while the SM experiences prolonged absences during the preparation. As departure becomes imminent, the family may experience more detachment and withdrawal because family members feel increasingly frightened by the impending loss of the military member and use increased emotional detachment as a protective mechanism. The second stage, *deployment*, is marked by emotional disorganization occurring during the first 6 weeks following departure. The family experiences symptoms of sadness, despair, tension, depression, and sometimes even relief that the deployment has finally occurred after such a busy time of preparation. Wives, or remaining spouses usually feel overwhelmed by having all the responsibility of parenting and household management during this initial adjustment period. As the remaining spouse learns to cope, the third stage, referred to as *sustainment*, begins around the first month of the deployment until about a month before redeployment. During the actual deployment, families learn how to adjust to the separation and communication lines are established. As the deployment nears an end, the SM and family again experience turmoil in the *redeployment* stages marked by the anticipation of homecoming because activity becomes focused on reuniting the military member with the family and preparations are focused on preparing themselves and the home.

The stage of *reunion/postdeployment* begins upon arrival of the military member home and lasts for up to 6 weeks following as the family becomes reacquainted with each other, negotiates changes in roles, reestablishes intimacy, and responds to perceived changes in each other that occurred during the deployment. Most families, according to Peebles-Kleiger and Kleiger (1994), have stabilized again about 12 weeks out from the deployment. They note that separations under wartime deployments represent more of a stressor and conflict for the families than the more routine separations which occur throughout a military career. Therefore, stages may take much longer to move through. Families subjected to wartime deployments may experience more difficult adjustments because danger is more imminent for the military member, less may be known about the environment or circumstances of the deployment, and information about or communication with the military member may be more difficult. Most of the research on which the stages are based have been elicited from the heretofore more common deployment of male military members away from their nonmilitary wives and children. The stages span the trajectory of the experience from notification of impending deployment through return to their family for all SMs, men and women.

MILITARY FAMILY RESEARCH

Research has shown that "a soldier's family problems can affect his duty or combat performance, increase his absence without leave (AWOL) risk, and lead to retention difficulties. The well-being of the family unit "directly impacts upon the soldiers' readiness, retention, and overall effectiveness" (Amen, Jellen, Meryes, & Lee, 1988, p. 441). In general, most research on military family separations/deployment has focused on normal rotations incurring separations for overseas assignments, peacekeeping operations, and more recently during wartime.

The first studies of the effect of war separation on families were conducted during World War II (Boulding, 1950; Hill, 1949; Rosenbaum, 1944). The purpose at that time was to determine the effects of the absence of the husband-father on families.

They determined that the event in itself did produce a crisis; however, the hardship of the event, the resources of the family to cope with the event, and the family's definition of the event all contributed to the family's ability to adjust to the separation. Findings from this preliminary work on war-induced separation was further developed and empirically tested (McCubbin, Dahl, Lester, Benson, & Robertson, 1976; McCubbin, Hunter, & Dahl, 1975) and subsequently used in application to assist military families during deployment separation (McCubbin, 1979; McCubbin & McCubbin, 1987; McCubbin, McCubbin, Thompson, Han, & Allen, 1997). The Gulf War, also known as Operation Desert Storm/Desert Shield, during the 1990s also spawned research exploring the effects of deployment on families, in particular on the military spouse and children left behind. The current conflicts have been ongoing since 2001. Multiple studies are currently emerging in the dissertation and extant literature addressing recurrent and new issues identified as related to deployments in Iraq and Afghanistan. Protective factors, such as resilience, and risk factors, such as deployment characteristics, are frequent variables included in the most recent studies as programs and intervention outcomes are evaluated for the family, child, and spouse (Palmer, 2008).

Research on Military Spouse

Knowledge of the effects of deployments on spouses has also recently increased because of the large numbers of married SMs who have deployed in support of OIF and OEF. Although military spouses have also voiced positive aspects of deployment, a substantial number of spouses experience challenges not only during deployment but also pre- and postdeployment (American Psychological Association, 2007). Spouses cite experiencing increased distress, anxiety, depression, posttraumatic distress, and adjustment difficulties (Booth, Wechsler, & Bell, 2007; Gewirtz, Polusny, DeGarmo, Khaylis, & Erbes, 2010; Hoge, Auchertonie, & Milliken, 2006; Lapp et al., 2010; Lester et al., 2010; Mansfield et al., 2010; Nelson-Goff, Crow, Reisbig, & Hamilton, 2007, 2009; Padden, Connors, & Agazio, 2011a, 2011b; Patzel, McBride, Bunting, & Anno, 2013; Renshaw, Rodrigues, & Jones, 2008; Sayers, Farrow, Ross, & Oslin, 2009; SteelFisher, Zaslavsky, & Blendon, 2008; Tollefson, 2008). Furthermore, in a study of military spouses with a deployed SM, Padden and colleagues (2011b) reported that perceived stress secondary to deployment accounted for 52% of the variance in mental well-being. These findings indicate that changes in psychological health secondary to stressors of deployment are prominent issues. Moreover, Burton, Farley, and Rhea (2009) found that increased levels of depression, anxiety, and stress are frequently associated with somatization for spouses. The top five somatic complaints were feeling tired or having little energy, trouble sleeping, menstrual cramps and problems with the menstrual cycle, back pain, and heart palpitations. The degree of impairment is also remarkable. In studies surveying the level of distress, 20%–46% of spouses met the screening criteria for moderate to severe depression and generalized anxiety disorders, as per the *Diagnostic and Statistical Manual of Mental Disorders* (4th ed., text rev.; *DSM-IV-TR*) criteria (Eaton et al., 2008; Warner, Appenzeller, Warner, & Grieger, 2009).

Studies report that spouses of deployed SMs experience secondary traumatic stress (STS; Nelson-Goff et al., 2007, 2009). STS is defined as clinically significant levels of posttraumatic stress symptoms (PTSS) without a history of direct trauma (Ting, Jacobson, Sanders, Bride, & Harrington, 2005). Rates of STS range from 2% to 61% (Melvin, Gross, Hayat, Jennings, & Campbell, 2012; Nelson-Goff et al., 2007, 2009; Renshaw et al., 2008). Melvin and colleagues (2012) reported a rate of 34% of STS in female spouses with deployed SMs. However, the rate decreased to 2% when controlled for the presence of previous trauma history. Therefore, previous traumas could have accounted for the higher rate of STS in the female spouses of deployed SMs.

Demographic variables, specific to the deployment, have been implicated as influencing psychological well-being. Lara-Cinisomo and colleagues (2012) reported that the emotional well-being of the spouses is dependent on the military service, whether on active duty or in the reserve component, rank, and length of deployment. Navy spouses experienced lower well-being than Army spouses, and National Guard spouses experienced lower well-being than Active Duty spouses. In terms of rank, junior enlisted spouses reported more problems than higher rank enlisted and officers. Finally, longer deployments have been reported as related to lower well-being. In a study of Army spouses, Mansfield and colleagues (2010) reported that lengthy deployments were associated with increased mental health diagnoses such as anxiety disorders, depressive disorders, sleep disorders, acute stress disorders, and adjustment disorders. Moreover, SteelFisher and colleagues (2008) found that deployment extensions adversely affected spouses' psychological well-being.

Parenting stress has been reported to be related to deployments, particularly length of deployments (Everson, Darling, & Herzog, 2013). When an SM deploys, the remaining spouse must function as a single parent for the duration of the deployment. The added responsibilities to encompass the role and tasks of the deployed parent may result in parenting strain, which, in turn, may negatively affect parental coping (Everson et al., 2013). Parental stress may be further heightened if the added responsibilities impact not only the parenting role but also other roles and responsibilities. In a qualitative study of military spouses, some reported that the parenting impacted their professional careers for they had to either give up work because of parental obligations or change work schedules to accommodate parenting responsibilities (Lara-Cinisomo et al., 2012). Moreover, parenting stress has been linked to child abuse cases reported among military spouses during deployment (Gibbs, Martin, Kupper, & Johnson, 2007). In a descriptive case series of substantiated incidents of parental child maltreatment in 1,771 families of enlisted Army soldiers who experienced at least one deployment between September 2001 and December 2004, the overall rate of child maltreatment was 42% higher during deployment. The rates of child neglect were almost twice as high. Among female civilian spouses, the rate of maltreatment during deployment was more than three times greater, the rate of child neglect was almost four times greater, and the rate of physical abuse was nearly twice as great (Gibbs et al., 2007).

Deployments have also been reported as straining marital relationships. Factors such as length and frequency of deployments and SMs' psychological conditions such as PTSS, posttraumatic stress disorder (PTSD), depression, anxiety, and dissociation have strained military relationships resulting in lower rates of marital satisfaction and intimacy (Allen, Rhoades, Stanley, & Markman, 2010; deBurgh, White, Fear, & Iversen, 2011; Knobloch & Theiss, 2012; Lara-Cinisomo et al., 2012; Mansfield et al., 2010; McLeland, Sutton, & Schumm, 2008; Melvin et al., 2012; Nelson-Goff et al., 2007; Sayers et al., 2009). Lara-Cinisomo and colleagues (2012) also found that the psychological health of the spouse was related to marital relationships in that spouses with poorer mental health experienced more relationship hassles. In addition, Melvin and colleagues (2012) reported that coercion or violence between the spouses further compromised the relationship between PTSS and marital relationships. Individuals with higher levels of violence and coercions reported lower couple functioning.

In an exploratory qualitative study, Knobloch and Theiss (2012) identified issues experienced by military couples particularly during the post-deployment transition. The questions focused on diverse changes to their relationship, issues of relational uncertainty, and interference in their daily routines. In terms of changes to their relationships, some participants reported no changes, whereas others indicated that their relationship grew closer or that they valued their relationship more. However, some participants cited negative issues. Participants reported problems reconnecting, difficulty communicating, increased independence and burden of decision making, changes in finances and employment, changes in sexual behavior, problems reintegrating the SM into daily life, heightened conflict, and separation or divorce. In terms of relational uncertainty, participants voiced concerns about commitment, reintegration, household stressors, personality changes, sexual behavior and infidelity, the health of the SM, and communication. Finally, individuals indicated that partner interference was related to everyday routines, household chores, control issues, feeling smothered, parenting, partner differences, social networks and social activities, and not having enough time to spend together.

To manage the stress generated by deployment challenges, the spouses relied on their resiliency and coping mechanisms. Resilience is a dynamic interaction between the characteristics and abilities of an individual which facilitate effective coping, recovery, and normal functioning during times of significant stress (Rutter, 1993). Resilience has been posited as a protective factor. Melvin and colleagues (2012) found that resilience was a positive predictor of couple functioning even when individual posttraumatic stress levels were high. Coping strategies primarily related to self-reliance and social supports (Lara-Cinisomo et al., 2012; Patzel et al., 2013). Self-reliance in the form of trying to control their own environment and establishing priorities to determine what needs to get done and what could be let go was one method for coping with overwhelming responsibilities. Acceptance, positive reframing, avoidance, distraction by staying busy, and focusing on work or other interests were other notated coping methods (Dimiceli, Steinhardt, & Smith, 2010; Lara-Cinisomo et al., 2012; Patzel et al., 2013; Wheeler & Torres-Stone, 2009). Finally, self-care such as exercising was implemented by some of the spouses to cope with the stressors of deployment. However, support was also described as helping the spouses to cope. Spouses sought social support from family and friends; spoke about the importance of religion, prayer, and the church family; and maintained contact with the deployed SM. Examining the use of problem- and emotion-focused coping, Padden and colleagues (2011a, 2011b) reported that coping styles were also related to various demographic variables such as the spouses and SMs' ages and the number of years on active duty. In general, younger spouses and SMs with less time on active duty used more evasive and emotional coping than confrontive coping methods (Blank, Adams, Kittelson, Connors, & Padden, 2012; Padden, 2011a, 2011b). One could stipulate that this is related to the lack of knowledge and experience with military resources and other resources.

Research on Military Children

Children's reactions to military separation/deployment have been studied for several years. Most of the early studies occurred after the Vietnam War and during the decades following with a focus on normative separations such as shipboard duty or extended unaccompanied overseas assignments such as humanitarian missions. Early research focused primarily on paternal separation because fathers were more likely to be the deployed parent, but since ODS/DS in the 1980s, mothers are just as likely to be deployed as fathers for military duties (Birgenheier, 1993). Since the GWOT began in 2001, approximately 1.2 million American children and youth younger than the age of 18 years have a parent on active duty and an additional 739,916 whose parents are in the reserve component (Department of Defense [DOD], 2010). Best estimates available on the Internet indicate that at least 700,000 children had one or both parents deployed during the recent conflicts (ABC News, 2011). Of these children, it is estimated that children younger than 5 years of age represent at least 40% of those with parents who have deployed (Flake, Davis, Johnson, & Middleton, 2009). These authors note that parental deployments have included 95,187 dual military families, 74,086 single parents, and 102,053 families with special health care needs. Coupled with normative separations expected for training, ship duty, and overseas rotations, military children often experience multiple separations over the course of their childhood.

Developmental Theory Application

For the most part, more attention has been directed toward the effects on school-aged children and teens, and only recently to the effects on younger children. Most studies that consider younger children's reactions are assessed from the parent's viewpoint, with less known regarding the child's thoughts and feelings regarding the parental separation.

Children's reactions to separations from their parents are influenced by many factors and shaped by their ability to cognitively understand why a parent may be absent in his or her life at different periods. As infants, children are forming attachments with both parents through consistent provision of nourishment, affection, and meeting of physical needs. Erikson (1963) sees infancy as a time when infants are egocentric, focused on having their needs met, and establishing trust in the caregivers. Piaget (Ball, Bindler, & Cowan, 2010) posits that learning in this period is primarily through the senses as the brain and nervous system mature for more complex learning. Through trial and error, children develop a sense of permanence in objects and persons external to themselves. In the toddler years, children begin to exert a sense of self-achievement and autonomy in exerting their will on their surroundings. Learning continues to be primarily sensorimotor and rudimentary language skills are present, such as 1–2 word responses or demands, that is, "me want" (Erikson, 1963). Young children "do not yet have the language, emotional regulatory capacity, or coping skills to effectively express and moderate strong emotions" (Mulrooney & Williams, 2011, p. 2) so that it is unclear what and how they experience separation from a parent at this early age. Preschoolers have more understandable and advanced language development, but their thinking is, according to Piaget (Ball et al., 2010), pre-operational, characterized by magical thinking and fantasy driven. Military children may feel something they said or did caused the parent to leave or imagine circumstances much more horrific than the actual threat. Preschoolers may be more aware of danger in a wartime environment, for example, but less able to "accurately assess or understand the specifics of the threat" (Paris, DeVoe, Ross, & Acker, 2010, p. 613). The transition from preschool to school-aged children reach what Piaget (Ball et al., 2010) describes as operational thought and brings a concrete ability to understand sequencing of events, such as, "Daddy is soldier, daddy has to go away to fight for his country." School-aged children and adolescents have a more realistic understanding of the consequences which may result from a deployment. Jensen, Martin, and Watanabe (1996) documented some increase in psychological symptoms for school-aged children during deployments but not significantly as compared to other children without deployed parents. On the other hand, adolescents may demonstrate acting-out and risk-taking behaviors related to the vulnerability of moving between childhood and adulthood. According to the DOD report from 2010, adolescents have demonstrated "more depressive symptoms, . . . decreased academic performance, . . . and peer relationship problems . . ." (p. 21) related to parental deployment. Because of their increased maturity, adolescents are often asked to shoulder more household responsibilities resulting in more disruption to their normal routines. Their routines are once again disrupted on return of the SM as responsibilities may shift back to the returning parent. Despite the stress of military life and deployment separations, military children, in particular school-aged children and adolescents, demonstrate resiliency which serves as a protective factor.

Research Regarding Effects of Deployment on Military Children

Research regarding the effects of deployment on military children has primarily focused on both qualitative and/or quantitative studies of school-aged and adolescent children (Paris et al., 2010) or parental perceptions of the effects for most developmental levels. Developmental level as well as type of deployment can influence the experience of separation. In addition, as noted by Chartrand and Siegel (2007) and Chartrand, Frank, White, and Shope (2008), children may have different experiences depending on whether the parent is active duty or reserve component. Reserve troops are often located in communities outside and away from military bases. Their children would remain in a familiar community perhaps closer to extended family and friends but may lack support provided on military posts such as family support networks, and families may face "pay cuts, job loss, and changes in medical insurance" (Chartrand & Siegel, 2007, p. 2) not experienced by active duty families. Active duty families on the other hand may be stationed far away from family support systems, leaving wives (or husbands) feeling isolated and alone during separations. Flake and colleagues (2009) noted that 30%–50% of families may relocate back to hometowns to be close to other family members during an extended deployment. With the lengthy involvement in Iraq and Afghanistan recently, many publications have appeared in the literature describing the effects of wartime deployments on children (Andres & Moelker, 2010; Applewhite & Mays, 1996; Aranda, Middleton, Flake, & Davis, 2011; Barker & Berry, 2009; Chandra et al., 2009; Cozza, 2011; Cozza, Chun, & Polo, 2005; Cozza et al., 2010; Levin & van Hoorn, 2009; Lincoln & Sweeten, 2011). Interestingly, few are research-based and those that are either continue to sample the older child or adolescent or seek parental impressions of the effects on the child. Clinically based theoretical articles abound addressing the effect on the younger-aged child; however, it is unclear if a research base undergirds these discussions.

Lincoln, Swift, and Shorteno-Fraser (2008) described the reactions and response to separation based on age and developmental level. They noted that infant response is related to the stress and anxiety displayed by the remaining caregivers. The infant may react "by becoming more irritable and unresponsive, vulnerable to sleep disruption, eating problems, and increased periods of crying" (p. 987). Toddlers may display more resistive behaviors and perhaps become clingier. Preschoolers may regress "to behaviors that they have previously outgrown" (p. 987). School-aged children have more awareness of what is happening and the potential danger faced by the deploying parent. For this reason, perhaps, most studies of military children's reaction to deployment have focused on school-aged children or adolescents (Huebner, Mancini, Wilcox, Grass, & Grass, 2007; Lincoln & Sweeten, 2011).

In their review article, DeVoe and Ross (2012) note that, in young children, deployments may interrupt normal development and maintenance of relationships with the absent parent. The young child may miss the opportunity to bond with the deployed parent or experience interruption of that bond during the separation. Children in the preschool years, because of the magical thinking common in this age group, may feel responsibility for the deployment separation related to perhaps some misbehavior on their part or negative thoughts about the deployed parent (Lester & Bursch, 2011; Lester et al., 2010; Maholmes, 2012). Stress and guilt may lead to somatic symptoms such as stomachaches or behavior problems. School-aged children may also exhibit behavioral or academic problems in response to the deployment. In their systematic review of nine studies of military children, White, de Burgh, Fear, and Iversen (2011) confirmed that "children of deployed parents are at higher risk than their civilian counterparts, which may reflect the multiple stressors that military children face" (p. 211).

Some limitations they noted in the research to date included the retrospective point of view of most studies, garnering only maternal perceptions, and usually focused on a limited number of variables without considering confounding variables; primary use of cross-sectional designs; and use of small convenience samples.

There are some earlier studies of separation related to deployments in support of ODS completed during the 1990s demonstrating unique stressors for children and for their families (Amen et al., 1988; Black, 1993; Blount, Curry, & Lubin, 1992; Jensen et al., 1996; Lester & Bursch, 2011; Lester et al., 2010; Maholmes, 2012; Pierce & Buck, 1998; Pierce, Vinokur, & Buck, 1998; White et al., 2011; Zeff, Lewis, & Hirsch, 1997). According to Kelley and colleagues (2001), the degree to which the children experience stress depends on several factors including previous experience with separations, the nature of the deployment, the parent's emotional development, satisfaction with the military, stability of the marriage, and most importantly, the developmental level of the child. Interestingly, Jensen and colleagues (1996) found not only younger children experiencing higher depression but also a marked increase for boys making them especially vulnerable to deployment effects. This study was particularly valuable because the researchers had collected data on the children prior to the war's beginning, allowing them to "prospectively evaluate the impact of wartime deployment by comparing follow up ratings" (Cozza et al., 2005, p. 373).

More recently, in one of the few studies including younger aged children, Flake and colleagues (2009) noted that children 5–12 years of age experiencing a separation reacted using more internalizing behaviors such as whining, being anxious, and more frequent crying rather than externalizing behaviors such as acting out or school difficulties. "Children of younger-aged parents, short duration of marriage, and lower SES were at higher risk for having psychosocial symptoms" (p. 276). With 42% of the parents reporting significant parenting stress, a major finding from this study was that children appeared to pick up on parenting stress such that "the most significant predictor of child psychosocial functioning during wartime deployment was parenting stress" (p. 271). In contrast, Chartrand and colleagues (2008) reported children aged 3 years and older demonstrated higher externalizing behaviors for those whose parent was deployed in comparison to children whose parent was not currently deployed. The authors claimed this was the first study to demonstrate "that children aged 3 years or older with a deployed parent exhibit increased behavioral symptoms compared with peers without a deployed parent after controlling for caregiver stress and depressive symptoms" (p. 1009). The inclusion of the effect on younger children and a comparison group for children who did not have a deployed parent was a unique aspect of this study. However, like many studies of military children, data were only collected from parents regarding their perceptions of child behavior as a marker of the effects of the deployment.

On a more positive note, Ryan-Wenger (2002) demonstrated the resilience of military children in comparison with a group of civilian children. She found no difference in levels of anxiety or psychopathology when considering the threat of war. Comparably, Applewhite and Mays (1996) demonstrated that psychosocial functioning in military children did not differ based on maternal or paternal separations. Although the authors noted the contradictory nature of their findings regarding maternal versus paternal separation, this study was limited by a convenience sample dependent on recall of the child's first extended separation. Despite the work of these researchers, understanding how younger children experience deployment has been limited by the focus on older children, primarily collected from the maternal (or stay-at-home parent's) perception of the child's reaction, collected during normative separations or for the limited Gulf War separations, and primarily focused on paternal deployments.

State of Science for Nursing Research

The research to date on military families has primarily been conducted by psychologists, social workers, physicians, chaplains and to a lesser degree, nurses. Many advances in nursing science regarding military family deployment impacts can be attributed to the funding the Tri-Service Nursing Research Program (TSNRP) has provided for multiple studies following ODS/DS and during the current conflicts. One of the earliest studies was conducted by Birgenheier (1993) who explored the behavioral difficulties of military children during a separation, and in particular, differences between mother and father separations.

Also following ODS/DS, one of the most prolific nurse scientists, Pierce conducted a series of studies on military women that included family effects and was also one of the first to include maternal deployments rather than just father separations. Pierce and colleagues (1998) conducted a comprehensive study considering the effects of deployment on mothers and children. They used a quantitative survey design measuring strains in major life domains to include job strain, financial strain, parenting strain, depression, ability to provide for children during deployment, anxiety symptoms, children's adjustment problems, and life changes as major variables in the study. The sample included active duty Air Force mothers participating in the study approximately 2 years after the Gulf War. Mothers reported difficulty providing comprehensive care for their children. Of the children with married mothers, 77% stayed with fathers or stepfathers, 21% stayed with mother's parents or siblings, and 2% stayed with paternal grandparents. For children who stayed with extended family, 67% changed residence at the time of the separation, 73% changed schools, and 7% were separated from one or more siblings. Mothers in the reserves or guard forces and officers reported greater difficulties in finding care for their children during the deployment. Interestingly, the mothers "who had experienced more difficulty in finding care, scored lower in their role and emotional functioning and reported more symptoms of depression and anxiety" 2 years following the deployment (Pierce & Buck, 1998, p. 3).

Messecar (1998) conducted a qualitative study to describe family stress associated with wartime separation. She identified three patterns of the separation experience organized around the core variable of uncertainty. Her pattern typography illuminated different strategies by which families manage the uncertainty during deployment and provided suggested clinical interventions and policy implications to support family coping. In 2005, Messecar extended her research to consider the experiences of National Guard family reintegration following deployment in the GWOT. Again, using qualitative methods, she included 45 guard and family member participants. Her findings led to recommendations for structuring reintegration activities supportive of family time and needs. Opportunities such as "couples retreat" types of activities can be beneficial but could also be more stressful if perceived to be burdensome related to time impacts and child care issues.

McNulty (2003) explored the health care needs of deployed family members stationed in Okinawa while they were separated from their spouses. With 299 wives and 89 children participating, this study revealed decline in family functioning for deployed families over the course of the separation as compared to family members who were not experiencing deployment separation. Although there were some limits to generalization because of an 80% Marine sample of only female spouses, her study was unique in exploring the deployment experience for those whose stress was compounded by being stationed outside the United States in an isolated area. McNulty (2006) continued to use a sample stationed outside of the continental United States in a follow-up study comparing families in Hawaii experiencing reintegration as they returned from Iraq and Afghanistan. This study compared National Guard and Reserve families to those who were active duty Army family members. Unfortunately, at this time, the results from this study were not available.

Resiliency in families and in military children has been reported frequently in the literature, and nurse researchers have also used that as a focus. Russek (2003) conducted a cross-sectional mixed methods study with U.S. Army Reserve family members and friends who provided dependent child care during deployment. Also focusing on children, White (2004) was funded by TSNRP to test the effectiveness of a coping skills intervention for children whose parents had been deployed on a shipboard assignment for at least 6 months. This project explored whether the "My Deployment Activity Book" coupled with weekly stress and coping activities would affect coping, stress symptoms, and behavior by comparing pre- and postdeployment scores.

Most recently, Melvin and colleagues (2012) focused on couples after reintegration to describe the relationship between PTSS and couple functioning with further exploration to differentiate between single SM couples as compared to dual military members. Baumann and Smith (2012) also focused on coming home using a case study approach to interpret the experience of one military family using Parse's human becoming family model. This project illustrated not only the challenges faced during the reintegration period but also highlighted some needs for support, health care services, and resource needs for military families.

Moving to a consideration of the effects on military children, Marter (2013) received a TSNRP predoctoral award to explore the link between deployment factors and parenting stress. Her correlational design will employ dyad comparisons (Navy couples with a male military member and female civilian spouse) to test the effects of deployment characteristics, social support, and spirituality in determining direct or mediating effects on parenting stress.

Also, concerned about the impact of deployment on families, Agazio and colleagues (2013) using grounded theory explored parenting and relationship effects in her research of deployment of military mothers and how they maintained their relationship with their children over the deployment trajectory. Her team identified useful strategies mothers used to support the process of "preserving the sacred maternal bond" that emerged as the core concept. She was funded in 2013 to extend this work into family research with a mixed methods study of the effects of deployment on young children. This project will include interviews with the deployed and stay-at-home parent or caregiver and an art-based interview with the younger aged child. In addition, measures of parenting stress and family functioning will be used to potentially create a typology of child impact based on these descriptive measures.

Ternus (2010) has focused her research on the adolescent and their experiences during parental deployments. She found that longer deployments were associated with greater risk for adolescents to engage in increased risk behaviors.

Outside of TSNRP-funded studies, the literature also contains publications from other nurses within academia and from those with prior military experience and/or interested in family-related military issues. In recent years, multiple dissertations have appeared in *Dissertation Abstracts International*. For example, Suarez (2011) explored healthy lifestyle behaviors, deployment factors, and adjustment within military spouses. Within her sample of 158 female military spouses, she identified a small percentage who were engaged in healthy behaviors and did not identify any significant predictors of adjustment. Similarly, Padden and colleagues (2011a, 2011b) have developed a program of research considering the health promotion of military female spouses especially in terms of coping with deployment. In this same area, Miramontes (2008) used unstructured interviews to explore the experiences of nine military wives and identified four major themes: anticipating disconnecting, preparing for disconnecting, being disconnected, and reconnecting that appear to mirror the states of deployment previously reported in the literature. Kotlowski (2009) used quantitative methods to identify relationships between psychological stressors and selected demographic and deployment characteristics. Looper (2012) considered a reservist population in her dissertation research especially focused on the reintegration period. In contrast to Miramontes (2008), Looper (2012), using Roy's adaptation model as her theoretical basis, discerned different deployment stages as coping methods were modified as demands increased and changed. In general, the area of exploring the effects of deployment on the marital relationship has been actively researched by nurses.

IMPLICATIONS FOR NURSING

As previously indicated, deployments are stressful for military families. Although there are positive aspects related to deployment, deployments also pose many challenges for families compromising their overall well-being. The literature documents numerous negative health outcomes of family members such as anxiety, depression, marital conflicts, parental stress, postviolence, somatization, behavioral and academic problems, and others. Therefore, families with deployed SMs should be identified as being at risk and provided targeted support.

Support should also be considered in view of the stage of deployment. Challenges posed by deployment surface prior to the actual deployment beginning during the predeployment process and extending through postdeployment, 3–6 months after the actual deployment. Each stage is characterized by specific tasks and challenges that the family is experiencing. Knowledge of the specific stage of deployment will provide guidance to nurses on specific areas for assessment, implementation of appropriate care, and potential referral for services.

Given that research has shown that family members are at high risk for developing psychological disorders, it is essential for nurses to be adept at assessing for symptoms related to psychological distress. Nurses should screen for psychological and behavioral problems prior to deployments and routinely throughout and following deployments so that problems can be detected as early as possible. Once identified, care should be provided to help the family member and protect the other family members from any adverse outcomes related to the family member experiencing the behavioral health problems. In addition, family members should be assessed for high-risk and maladaptive behaviors such as the increased use of alcohol, tobacco, and/or illicit substances and potential suicide ideation. Moreover, because of the increase in child abuse and domestic violence in deployed families, members need to be assessed for evidence of these potential issues within the family.

Once a family member has screened positive for risk of violence, nurses need to ensure that the family member and, if necessary, the family receive adequate and appropriate treatment and referrals. This highlights the importance of communication between nurses and primary care providers and mental health professionals. Based on the location of the family whether near a military installation or not, nurses need to ensure that family members have access to behavioral health care services. Additional information regarding the locations and contact numbers for local Veterans Administration facilities and other resources should also be provided to the family.

To mitigate adverse outcomes, nurses should identify and bolster positive resources such as resiliency and effective coping strategies that families may have cultivated perhaps throughout exposure to multiple deployments to promote successful adaptation. To supplement their positive strategies, families should be informed of additional support in the form of stress management and other programs to facilitate management of deployment challenges. Educating family members on how to identify and increase families' personal resources through self-care, social supports, and access to services will further facilitate adjustment and overall family well-being during deployment.

Spouses experiencing parental stress should be provided parental support through existing services. Additional child care services may be needed to provide the parent with respite time. Service-specific resources such as Family Readiness Groups in the Army, Fleet and Family in the Navy, and Family Support Centers in the Air Force, developed specifically to support families of deployed SMs, may need to be contacted to provide support to the parent. If such resources are not available locally, collaboration with units may highlight local child care resources. Finally, nurses need to assess if parental stress places the spouses at risk for child abuse or neglect.

The findings related to marital strains underscore the need for nurses to address marital relationships as well. During assessments, nurses need to inquire about marital relationships, particularly when evidence of psychological distress is present in one or both of the partners. Postdeployment, the SM should also be present so that perspectives of both individuals can be assessed. In addition, communication between the SM and the spouse or partner should also be evaluated to allow assessment of interactions between them. Couples should be informed that because of the disruption and challenges posed by deployment, time should be allotted for readjustment. Couples should be informed of the kinds of issues they may encounter so that they are better equipped to deal with them if and when they arise. In time of conflict, couples should be encouraged to seek counseling through chaplain services or other local counseling services. Finally, couples experiencing interpersonal conflict and behavioral health issues should be assessed for intimate partner violence to identify those at risk and to link them to services.

Similar to the parents, research reports that children experience psychological distress and behavioral problems. Nurses need to be able to establish trusting relationships with children so that they feel safe in discussion of their feelings. Nurses need to encourage children to express their thoughts and feelings regarding the deployment and its impact on the family. Children need to be reassured that their feelings are normal. If children express guilt for the deployment, they need to be reassured that they were not the reason for the departure of the deployed parent. Interventions for children need to be developmentally appropriate. For young children, visual aids such as pictures may be needed to help the child understand. By understanding the challenges posed by deployments and the potential consequential issues, nurses can intervene to maximize the care and support for military families with deployed SMs.

RECOMMENDATIONS FOR FUTURE RESEARCH

Despite the growing body of literature focused on the experience of the military family and individual family members during deployment, in particular, spouses and children, gaps and questions remain regarding the most effective programs, services, and resources. Most of the studies reviewed were cross-sectional, examining single points in time. Longitudinal studies are needed to evaluate family adjustment across the stages of deployment and to develop and test interventions to maximize family adjustment. In addition, longitudinal studies to assess the long-term effects and the impact of reported influential variables such as age, gender, military component, and others on family outcomes are needed. Particularly in reference to children, additional studies investigating the specific impact based on the age and gender of the child are warranted to develop appropriate interventions.

The literature has documented that families experience multiple challenges. Further research related to specific challenges and how those challenges are impacted by other factors, and, in turn, influence family well-being need to be conducted. Based on findings, interventions to maximize positive aspects and eliminate or minimize negative aspects need to be developed and tested.

In addition, although it is important to identify factors impacting families, it is also important to explore how families can overcome any adverse effects and how providers can help them to avoid long-term negative outcomes.

Because of reports of increased partner violence in families with a deployed SM, future research exploring the relationship between marital relationships and SM and spousal behavioral health issues and subsequent intimate partner violence is needed. The results could inform strategies to identify those at risk and link them to services.

Furthermore, there is a need for greater understanding of how factors such as resilience and coping function as protective variables. Interventions designed to increase resilience and adaptive coping need to be tested. In addition, predeployment interventions training family members to establish or expand on existing protective factors need to be developed and tested. Palmer (2008) suggests that marital status, routine relocations and assignments outside of the United States, and differences based on rank and military status are understudied variables in how they may modify or affect resilience and/or act as a risk factor.

Multiple programs have been developed and are being tested as interventions for pre-, during, and post-deployment participation. The literature appears to be mixed in assessing the outcomes. Some articles used findings from related research to judge potential effectiveness with military families, whereas others are just beginning to report research findings and outcomes. More research needs to be conducted to determine which programs are most effective and consistent in achieving and protecting family cohesion and functioning.

More research is needed in considering the deployment experience for single parents, dual military, blended families, maternal deployments, families with special needs children or infants, and reserve/guard families (DOD, 2010). In addition, with the number of wounded warriors returning from the recent conflicts, more research is needed to explore the effects of PTSD, amputations, traumatic head injury, and other injuries and/or rehabilitative processes on the family and family members (Chandra & London, 2013; Herzog, Everson, & Whitworth, 2011).

And finally, some metasynthesis and meta-analytic studies are needed to synthesize and assess findings from the smaller and site-specific studies which are predominant in the current scientific literature. Coordination needs to occur between services not only to avoid duplication of studies but also to ensure representation across the different services and more generalizability of findings. Veteran family research needs to be better integrated with that conducted with active duty and reserve forces to better articulate the trajectory of the complete military family experience (Clever & Segal, 2013).

CONCLUSION

Millions of military families have been affected by GWOT. We need to understand the effect of these lengthy and multiple deployments on these families, particularly as they continue to struggle with the challenges long after the deployments and wars have ceased. As the literature indicates, research to understand the effects of these challenges, how they function, and what factors moderate the effects have been conducted. However, we need to expand on these findings through continued research to develop knowledge to develop research-based guidelines for best practices, which facilitates successful resolution of the challenges and promotes the well-being of these families. Continued research will acknowledge the military service and sacrifice of these families. As health care providers, nurses play not only a key role in the provision and facilitation of appropriate care and support for the families, but also a role in the continued completion of such research.

REFERENCES

ABC News. (2011). *U.S. Veterans by the numbers*. Retrieved from http://abcnews.go.com/Politics/us-veterans-numbers/story?id=14928136#1

Agazio, J., Hillier, S., Throop, M., Goodman, P., Padden, D., Greiner, S., & Turner, A. (2013). Mothers going to war: The role of nurse practitioners in the care of military mothers and families during deployment. *Journal of the American Association of Nurse Practitioners*, *25*, 253–262.

Allen, E. S., Rhoades, G. K., Stanley, S. M., & Markman, H. J. (2010). Hitting home: Relationships between recent deployment, post-traumatic stress symptoms, and marital functioning for Army couples. *Journal of Family Psychology*, *24*, 280–288. http://dx.doi.org/10.1037/a0019405

Amen, D. G., Jellen, L., Meryes, E., & Lee, R. E. (1988). Minimizing the impact of deployment separation on military children: Stages, current preventive efforts, and system recommendations. *Military Medicine*, *153*(9), 441–446.

American Psychological Association. (2007). *The psychological needs of U.S. military service members and their families: A preliminary report*. Washington, DC: Author.

Andres, M. D., & Moelker, R. (2010). There and back again: How parental expectations affect children's adjustments in the course of military deployments. *Armed Forces and Society*, *37*(3), 418–447. http://dx.doi.org/10.1177/0095327X10390461

Applewhite, L. W., & Mays, R. A. (1996). Parent-child separation: A comparison of maternally and paternally separated children in military families. *Child and Adolescent Social Work Journal*, *13*(1), 23–39.

Aranda, M. C., Middleton, L. S., Flake, E., & Davis, B. E. (2011). Psychosocial screening in children with wartime-deployed parents. *Military Medicine*, *176*(4), 402–407.

Ball, J. W., Bindler, R. C., & Cowan, K. J. (2010). *Child health nursing* (2nd ed.). New York, NY: Pearson Education.

Barker, L. H., & Berry, K. D. (2009). Developmental issues impacting military families with young children during single and multiple deployments. *Military Medicine*, *174*(10), 1033–1040.

Baumann, S. L., & Smith, D. G. (2012). Coming home revisited: Family life and military deployment. *Nursing Science Quarterly*, *25*(3), 267–271.

Birgenheier, P. S. (1993). Parents and children: War and separation. *Pediatric Nursing, 19*(5), 471–476.

Black, W. G. (1993). Military-induced family separation: A stress reduction intervention. *Social Work, 38*(3), 273–280.

Blank, C., Adams, L., Kittelson, B., Connors, R., & Padden, D. (2012). Coping behaviors used by Army wives during deployment separation and their perceived effectiveness. *Journal of the American Academy of Nurse Practitioners, 24*(11), 660–668. http://dx.doi.org/10.1111/j.1745-7599.2012.00766.x

Blount, B. W., Curry, A., Jr., & Lubin, G. I. (1992). Family separations in the military. *Military Medicine, 157*(2), 76–80.

Booth, B., Wechsler, S. M., & Bell, D. B. (2007). *What do we know about Army families?* Retrieved from http://www.army.mil/fmwrc/documents/research/WhatWeKnow2007.pdf

Boulding, E. (1950). Family adjustments to war separation and reunion. *The Annals of the American Academy of Political and Social Science, 272*, 59–68.

Burton, T., Farley, D., & Rhea, A. (2009). Stress-induced somatization in spouses of deployed and non-deployed service men. *Academy of Nurse Practitioners, 21*, 332–339.

Chandra, A., Lara-Cinisomo, S., Jaycox, L. H., Tanielian, T., Burns, R. M., Ruder, T., & Han, B. (2009). Children on the homefront: The experience of children from military families. *Pediatrics, 125*, 16–25.

Chandra, A., & London, A. S. (2013). Unlocking insights about military children and families. *Future of Children, 23*(2), 187–198. http://www.futureofchildren.org

Chartrand, M. M., Frank, D. A., White, L. F., & Shope, T. R. (2008). Effect of parents' wartime deployment on the behavior of young children in military families. *Archives of Pediatrics and Adolescent Medicine, 162*(11), 1009–1014.

Chartrand, M. M., & Siegel, B. (2007). At war in Iraq and Afghanistan: Children in U.S. military families. *Ambulatory Pediatrics, 7*(1), 1–2.

Clever, M., & Segal, D. R. (2013). The demographics of military children and families. *Future of Children, 23*(2), 13–39. http://www.futureofchildren.org

Cozza, S. J. (2011). Children of military service members: Raising national awareness of the family health consequences of combat deployment. *Archives of Pediatric and Adolescent Medicine, 165*(11), 1044–1046.

Cozza, S. J., Chun, R. S., & Polo, J. A. (2005). Military families and children during Operation Iraqi Freedom. *Psychiatric Quarterly, 76*(4), 371–378.

Cozza, S. J., Guimond, J. M., McKibben, J. B., Chun, R. S., Arata-Maiers, T. L., Schneider, B., . . . Ursano, R. J. (2010). Combat-injured service members and their families: The relationship of child distress and spouse-perceived family distress and disruption. *Journal of Trauma Stress, 23*(1), 112–115.

deBurgh H. T., White, C. J., Fear, N. T., & Iversen, A. C. (2011). The impact of deployments to Iraq and Afghanistan on partners and wives of military personnel. *International Review of Psychiatry, 23*(2), 192–200.

Department of Defense. (2010). *Demographics 2010: Profile of the military community.* Retrieved from http://www.militaryhomefront.dod.mil/12038/Project%20Documents/MilitaryHOMEFRONT/Reports/2010_Demographics_Report.pdf

Department of Defense. (2012). *2011 demographic report*. Washington, DC: Office of the Deputy Under Secretary of Defense.

DeVoe, E. R., & Ross, A. (2012). The parenting cycle of deployment. *Military Medicine, 177*(2), 184–190.

Dimiceli, E. E., Steinhardt, M. A., & Smith, S. E. (2010). Stressful experiences, coping strategies, and predictors of health-related outcomes among wives of deployed military service men. *Armed Forces and Society, 36*, 351–373.

Eaton, K. M., Hoge, C. W., Messer, S. C., Whitt, A. A., Cabrera, O. A., McGurk, D., . . . Castro, C. A. (2008). Prevalence of mental health problems, treatment need, and barriers to care among primary care-seeking spouses of military service members involved in Iraq and Afghanistan deployments. *Military Medicine, 173*, 1051–1056.

Erikson, E. H. (1963). *Childhood and society* (2nd ed.). New York, NY: Norton.

Everson, R. B., Darling, C. A., & Herzog, J. R. (2013). Parenting stress among U.S. Army spouses during combat-related deployments: The role of sense of coherence. *Child and Family Social Work, 18*, 168–178. http://dx.doi.org/10.1111/j.1365-2206.2011.00818.x

Flake, E. M., Davis, B. E., Johnson, P. L., & Middleton, L. S. (2009). The psychosocial effects of deployment on military children. *Journal of Developmental and Behavioral Pediatrics, 30*(4), 271–278.

Gewirtz, A. H., Polusny, M. A., DeGarmo, D. S., Khaylis, A., & Erbes, C. R. (2010). Posttraumatic stress symptoms among National Guard soldiers deployed to Iraq: Associations with parenting behaviors and couple adjustment. *Journal of Consulting and Clinical Psychology, 78*(5), 599–610.

Gibbs, D. A., Martin, S. L., Kupper, L. L., & Johnson, R. E. (2007). Child maltreatment in enlisted soldiers' families during combat-related deployments. *Journal of the American Medical Association, 298*(5), 528–535.

Herzog, J. R., Everson, R. B., & Whitworth, J. D. (2011). Do secondary trauma symptoms in spouses of combat-exposed National Guard soldiers mediate impacts of soldiers' trauma exposure on their children? *Child and Adolescent Social Work, 28*, 459–473.

Hill, R. (1949). *Families under stress: Adjustment to the crisis of war separation and reunion*. New York, NY: Harper & Brothers.

Hoge, C. W., Auchertonie, J. L., & Milliken, C. S. (2006). Mental health problems, use of mental health services, and attrition from military service after returning from deployment to Iraq or Afghanistan. *Journal of the American Medical Association, 295*, 1023–1032. http://dx.doi.org/10.1001/jama.295.9.1023

Huebner, A. J., Mancini, J. A., Wilcox, R. M., Grass, S. R., & Grass, G. A. (2007). Parental deployment and youth in military families: Exploring uncertainty and ambiguous loss. *Family Relations, 56*, 112–122.

Jensen, P. S., Martin, D., & Watanabe, H. (1996). Children's response to parental separation during Operation Desert Storm. *Journal of the American Academy of Child and Adolescent Psychiatry, 35*(4), 433–441.

Kelley, M. L., Hock, E., Smith, K. M., Jarvis, M. S., Bonney, J. F., & Gaffney, M. A. (2001). Internalizing and externalizing behavior of children with enlisted Navy mothers experiencing military-induced separation. *Journal of the American Academy of Child and Adolescent Psychiatry, 40*(4), 464–471.

Knobloch, L. K., & Theiss, J. A. (2012). Experiences of U.S. military couples during the post-deployment transition: Applying the relational turbulence model. *Journal of Social and Personal Relationships, 29*(4), 423–450.

Kotlowski, C. (2009). An exploratory study of military deployment and its impact on marriage and family of soldiers. *Dissertation Abstracts International*. (UMI No. 3375978)

Lapp, C. A., Taft, L. B., Tollefson, T., Hoepner, A., Moore, K., & Divyak, K. (2010). Stress and coping on the home front: Guard and reserve spouses searching for a new normal. *Journal of Family Nursing, 16*(1), 1–23.

Lara-Cinisomo, S., Chandra, A., Burns, R. M., Jaycox, L. H., Tanielian, T., Ruder, T., & Han, B. (2012). A mixed-method approach to understanding the experiences of non-deployed military caregivers. *Maternal Child Health Journal, 16*, 374–384. http://dx.doi.org/10.1007/s10995-011-0772-2

Lester, P., & Bursch, B. (2011). The long war comes home. *Psychiatric Times*, *28*(7), 26–29.

Lester, P., Peterson, K., Reeves, J., Knauss, L., Glover, D., Mogil, C., . . . Beardslee, W. (2010). The long war and parental combat deployment: Effects on military children and at-home spouses. *Journal of the American Academy of Child and Adolescent Psychiatry*, *49*(4), 310–320.

Levin, D. E., & van Hoorn, J. (2009). Out of sight, out of mind, or is it? The impact of the war on children in the United States. *Childhood Education*, *85*(6), 342–346.

Lincoln, A. J., & Sweeten, K. (2011). Considerations for the effects of military deployment on children and families. *Social Work in Health Care*, *50*(1), 73–84.

Lincoln, A., Swift, E., & Shorteno-Fraser, M. (2008). Psychological adjustment and treatment of children and families with parents deployed in military combat. *Journal of Clinical Psychology*, *64*(8), 984–992. http://dx.doi.org/10.1002/jclp.20520.

Logan, K. V. (1987). The emotional cycle of deployment. *U.S. Navy Proceedings*, *113*, 43–47.

Looper, R. R. (2012). Adaptation and coping processes as reported by Army reservists and their families throughout one year following the soldier's deployment to combat locations. *Dissertation Abstracts International*. (UMI No. 3547248)

Maholmes, V. (2012). Adjustment of children and youth in military families: Toward developmental understandings. *Child Development Perspectives*, *6*(4), 430–435. http://dx.doi.org/10.1111/j.1750-8606.2012.00256.x

Mansfield, A. J., Kaufman, J. S., Marshall, S. W., Gaynes, B. N., Morrissey, J. P., & Engel, C. C. (2010). Deployment and the use of mental health services among U.S. Army wives. *The New England Journal of Medicine*, *362*, 101–109.

Marter, A. (2013). Link between deployment factors and parenting stress in military families. Retrieved from http://interimwebserver.usuhs.edu/cgi-bin/tsnrp/search_studies.cgi?id=384

McCubbin, H. (1979). Integrating coping behavior in family stress theory. *Journal of Marriage and the Family*, *41*, 237–244.

McCubbin, H., Dahl, B., Lester, G., Benson, D., & Robertson, M. (1976). Coping repertories of families adapting to prolonged war-induced separations. *Journal of Marriage and the Family*, *38*, 461–471.

McCubbin, H., Hunter, E., & Dahl, B. (1975). Residuals of war: Families of prisoners of war and servicemen missing in action. *Journal of Social Issues*, *31*, 161–182.

McCubbin, M., & McCubbin, H. (1987). Family stress theory and assessment. In H. I. McCubbin & A. I. Thompson (Eds.), *Family assessment inventories for research and practice* (pp. 3–25). Madison, WI: University of Wisconsin.

McCubbin, H., McCubbin, M., Thompson, A., Han, S., & Allen, C. (1997). Families under stress: What makes them resilient. *Journal of Family and Consumer Sciences*, *89*(3), 2–11.

McLeland, K. C., Sutton, G. W., & Schumm, W. R. (2008). Marital satisfaction before and after deployments associated with the global war on terror. *Psychological Reports*, *103*, 836–844.

McNulty, P. A. (2003). Does deployment impact the health care use of military families stationed in Okinawa, Japan? *Military Medicine*, *168*(6), 465–470.

McNulty, P. A. (2006). Impact of soldier reunification on families—A longitudinal study. Retrieved from http://interimwebserver.usuhs.edu/cgi-bin/tsnrp/search_studies.cgi?id=287

Melvin, K. C., Gross, D., Hayat, M. J., Jennings, B. M., & Campbell, J. C. (2012). Couple functioning and post-traumatic stress symptoms in U. S. Army couples: The role of resilience. *Research in Nursing and Health*, *35*, 164–177. http://dx.doi.org/10.1002/nur.21459

Messecar, D. (1998). Guard and reserve spouse separation during the Persian Gulf War: Coming to terms with uncertainty. *Journal of Family Nursing*, *4*, 309–333.

Messecar, D. (2005). Family reintegration following Guard deployment. Retrieved from http://interimwebserver.usuhs.edu/cgi-bin/tsnrp/search_studies.cgi?id=280

Miramontes, J. (2008). The experience of military wives whose spouses have been deployed to a combat zone. *Dissertation Abstracts International*. (UMI No. 1462939)

Mulrooney, K., & Williams, D. S. (2011). *Increasing understanding of infants and young children in military families through focused research*. Los Angeles, CA: USC Center for Innovation and Research on Veterans and Military Families. Retrieved from http://cir.usc.edu

Nelson-Goff, B. S., Crow, J. R., Reisbig, A. M. J., & Hamilton, S. (2007). The impact of individual trauma symptoms of deployed soldiers on relationship satisfaction. *Journal of Family Psychology*, *21*, 344–353.

Nelson-Goff, B. S., Crow, J. R., Reisbig, A. M. J., & Hamilton, S. (2009). The impact of soldiers' deployments to Iraq and Afghanistan: Secondary traumatic stress in female partners. *Journal of Couple and Relationship Therapy*, *8*, 291–305.

Padden, D., & Agazio, J. (2013). Caring for military families across the deployment cycle. *Journal of Emergency Nursing*, *39*(6), 562–569.

Padden, D., Connors, R. A., & Agazio, J. (2011a). Determinants of health promoting behaviors in military spouses during deployment separation. *Military Medicine*, *176*(1), 26–34.

Padden, D., Connors, R. A., & Agazio, J. (2011b). Stress, coping, and well-being in military spouses during deployment separation. *Western Journal of Nursing Research*, *33*(2), 247–267.

Palmer, C. (2008). A theory of risk and resilience factors in military families. *Military Psychology*, *20*, 205–217.

Paris, R., DeVoe, E. R., Ross, A. M., & Acker, M. L. (2010). When a parent goes to war: Effects of parental deployment on very young children and implications for intervention. *American Journal of Orthopsychiatry*, *80*(4), 610–618.

Patzel, B., McBride, M., Bunting, J., & Anno, T. (2013). Life goes on: The experiences of wives of multiply-deployed National Guard soldiers. *Issues in Mental Health Nursing*, *34*, 368–374.

Peebles-Kleiger, M. J., & Kleiger, J. H. (1994). Re-integration stress for Desert Storm families: Wartime deployments and family trauma. *Journal of Traumatic Stress*, *7*(2), 173–193.

Pierce, P. F., & Buck, C. L. (1998). Wartime separation of mothers and children: Lessons from Operations Desert Shield and Desert Storm. *Military Family Issues: The Research Digest*, *2*(2), 1–4.

Pierce, P. R., Vinokur, A. D., & Buck, C. L. (1998). Effects of war-induced maternal separation on children's adjustment during the Gulf War and two years later. *Journal of Applied Social Psychology*, *28*(14), 1286–1311. http://dx.doi.org/10.1111/j.1559-1816.1998.tb01677.x

Pincus, S., House, R., Christenson, J., & Adler, L. (2001). The emotional cycle of deployment: A military family perspective. *U. S. Army Medical Department Journal*, 139–145.

Renshaw, K. D., Rodrigues, C. S., & Jones, D. H. (2008). Psychological symptoms and marital satisfaction in spouses of Operation Iraqi Freedom Veterans: Relationships with spouses' perceptions of Veterans' experiences and symptoms. *Journal of Family Psychology*, *22*, 586–594.

Rosen, L. N., Durand, D. B., & Martin, J. A. (2000). Coping with the unique demands of military family life. In J. Martin, L. N. Rosen, & L. R. Sparacino (Eds.), *The military family: A practical guide for human service providers* (pp. 55–72). Westport, CT: Praeger.

Rosenbaum, M. (1944). Emotional aspects of wartime separations. *The Family*, *24*, 337–341.

Russek, J. (2003). *Resiliency in Army Reserve families before deployment*. Retrieved from http://interim-webserver.usuhs.edu/cgi-bin/tsnrp/search_studies.cgi?id=233

Rutter, M. (1993). Resilience: Some conceptual considerations. *Journal of Adolescent Health*, *14*, 598–611.

Ryan-Wenger, N. A. (2002). Impact of the threat of war on children in military families. *Journal of Pediatric Health Care*, *16*(5), 245–252.

Sayers, S. L., Farrow, V. A., Ross, J., & Oslin, D. W. (2009). Family problems among recently returned military Veterans referred for a mental health evaluation. *Journal of Clinical Psychiatry*, *70*, 163–170.

SteelFisher, G. K., Zaslavsky, A. M., & Blendon, R. J. (2008). Health-related impact of deployment extensions on spouses of active duty Army personnel. *Military Medicine, 173*, 221–229.

Suarez, N. J. (2011). Exploring healthy lifestyle behaviors, deployment factors, and adjustment among military spouses. *Dissertation Abstracts International*. (UMI No. 3485490)

Ternus, M. P. (2010). Support for adolescents who experience parental military deployment. *Journal of Adolescent Health, 46*, 203–206.

Ting, L., Jacobson, J. M., Sanders, S., Bride, B. E., & Harrington, D. (2005). The Secondary Traumatic Stress Scale (STSS): Confirmatory factor analysis with a national sample of mental health social workers. *Journal of Human Behavior in the Social Environment, 11*, 177–194. http://dx.doi.org/10.1300/J137v11n03_09

Tollefson, T. T. (2008). Supporting spouses during a military deployment. *Family and Community Health, 31*(4), 281–286.

Warner, C. H., Appenzeller, G. N., Warner, C. M., & Grieger, T. (2009). Psychological effects of deployments on military families. *Psychiatric Annals, 39*(2), 56–63.

Wheeler, A., & Torres-Stone, R. (2009). Exploring stress and coping strategies among National Guard spouses during times of deployment: A research note. *Armed Forces and Society, 36*, 545–557.

White, M. (2004). *Coping intervention for children of deployed parents*. Retrieved from http://interim-webserver.usuhs.edu/cgi-bin/tsnrp/search_studies.cgi?id=261

White, C. J., de Burgh, H. T., Fear, N. T., & Iversen, A. C. (2011). The impact of deployment to Iraq or Afghanistan on military children: A review of the literature. *International Review of Psychiatry, 23*, 210–217. http://dx.doi.org/10.3109/09540261.2011.560143

White House. (2011). Strengthening our military families—Meeting America's commitment. *White House Report*. http://www.whitehouse.gov/ondcp/military-veterans

Zeff, K. N., Lewis, S. J., & Hirsch, K. A. (1997). Military family adaptation to United Nations operations in Somalia. *Military Medicine, 162*, 384–387.

CHAPTER 7

Investigations on the Relationship Between the Autonomic Nervous System and the Triggering of Malignant Hyperthermia

A State-of-the-Science Review

Susan M. Perry

ABSTRACT

Early research in malignant hyperthermia (MH) focused on the autonomic nervous system (ANS) as a primary trigger of the syndrome. This hypothesis was based on the initial signs and symptoms of MH such as tachycardia, cardiac arrhythmias, hypertension, and signs of increased metabolism in patients who developed MH. Supporting these early links between MH and the ANS were case reports from anesthesia providers who reported that patients who subsequently developed MH after a nontriggering previous anesthetic had appeared unusually stressed prior to the surgical procedure in which they triggered. There is no disagreement in the scientific community that a primary disorder in MH lies in the inability to control myoplasmic calcium levels in skeletal muscles. However, considering the variability in genetic and clinical presentation, the timing of intraoperative triggering, and the unexplained phenomenon of nonanesthetic triggering, the identification of cofactors in MH triggering remains paramount. A careful review of existing research supports the hypothesis that the autonomic nervous

http://dx.doi.org/10.1891/0739-6686.32.135

system plays a significant role as a cofactor in the triggering and progression of an MH episode. If a differentiation can be made and a link can be demonstrated between abnormalities in receptor sensitivity for or release, reuptake, or metabolism of catecholamines in malignant hyperthermia susceptible individuals, we may be able to use these as additional markers/predictors of disease.

INTRODUCTION

Although first described more than 50 years ago, malignant hyperthermia (MH) continues to present to the anesthesia and medical research communities as a complicated and multifaceted spectrum disorder. In humans, MH is an autosomal inherited disorder that predisposes to a life-threatening hypermetabolic syndrome. In susceptible individuals, the commonly used inhalational anesthetics and the depolarizing muscle relaxant succinylcholine may induce an accelerated metabolism which leads to a potentially fatal syndrome (Nelson & Flewellen, 1983). The incidence of intraoperative triggering varies between 1:15,000 in the pediatric population and 1:50,000 for adults undergoing general anesthesia (Nelson & Flewellen, 1983). However, this estimate is possibly understated because it only reflects reported cases of MH and only those displayed in a more fulminate manner.

A fulminate episode is characterized by tachypnea, hypercarbia, tachycardia, muscle rigidity, rhabdomyolysis, metabolic acidosis, hyperkalemia, and hyperthermia. However, these are nonspecific signs with no single sign being specifically diagnostic for MH (Muldoon, Deuster, Brandom, & Bunger, 2004). Further complicating the diagnosis is that pharmacogenetic triggers may be administered to the susceptible individuals without causing an MH episode. Without the definitive treatment of dantrolene sodium and discontinuation of all triggering agents, mortality is in excess of 70% (Muldoon et al., 2004).

Although most malignant hyperthermia susceptible (MHS) individuals are asymptomatic prior to triggering, others have a history of variable skeletal muscle abnormalities with documented basal increases in creatine kinase (Sambuughin et al., 2001). This variation in clinical phenotype is hypothesized to be the consequence of unresolved genetic- and environmental-related factors (Muldoon et al., 2004). Identification prior to surgery is difficult and usually only possible if a family history of the disease is known or if the patient reports a prior suspicious metabolic response to general anesthetics. Currently, the only definitive diagnosis of malignant hyperthermia susceptible (MHS) requires a surgical biopsy of the vastus lateralis to measure the muscles' response to halothane and caffeine via the caffeine halothane contracture test (CHCT; Larach, 1989). The CHCT has a diagnostic sensitivity of 97% and a specificity of 78% (Allen, Larach, & Kunselman, 1998). Genetic studies have demonstrated that the RyR1 gene, located on chromosome

19q13.1, is the primary locus responsible for MH susceptibility (McCarthy et al., 1990; MacLennan et al., 1990). In a skeletal muscle, the RyR1 receptors function in the sarcoplasmic reticulum to trigger myofibril contraction by elevating the myoplasmic Ca^{2+} levels (Mackrill, 1998). Mutations in the RyR1 linked to MH cause the channel to respond with increased sensitivity to activators such as 4-chloro-m-cresol (4-CmC), caffeine, and inhalational anesthetics (Hamilton & Serysheva, 2009). In response to these activators, the RyR1 channel is unable to control intracellular levels of Ca^{2+}. More than 50% of MHS genetic linkages are estimated to be associated with the RyR1 gene. However, with more than 300 different mis-sense RyR1 mutations found in patients with positive CHCT, or presumptive clinical diagnoses for MH, genetic testing lacks the sensitivity and specificity to be used as a screening tool for this disease (Vukcevic et al., 2010).

MALIGNANT HYPERTHERMIA AND THE AUTONOMIC NERVOUS SYSTEM

Early research in MH focused on the autonomic nervous system (ANS) as a primary trigger of the syndrome. This hypothesis was based on the initial signs and symptoms of MH such as tachycardia, cardiac arrhythmias, hypertension, and signs of increased metabolism in patients who developed MH. These signs are not specifically related to the RyR1 receptor and the excessive Ca^{2+} release in skeletal muscles but could be associated with the adrenergic receptor response. Supporting these early links between MH and the ANS were case reports from anesthesia providers, who reported that patients who subsequently developed MH after a nontriggering previous anesthetic, had appeared unusually stressed prior to the surgical procedure in which they triggered. These finding suggested that emotional or physiological stress and the related ANS response to stress may provide an explanation for the variability in MH triggering in the surgical population.

There is no disagreement in the scientific community that a primary disorder in MH lies in the inability to control myoplasmic calcium levels in skeletal muscles (Nelson, 2003). However, considering the variability in genetic and clinical presentation, the timing of intraoperative triggering and the unexplained phenomenon of nonanesthetic triggering, the identification of cofactors in MH triggering remains paramount.

After a review of the existing literature, it is the hypothesis of the author that the ANS plays a significant role as a cofactor in the triggering and progression of an MH episode. The author also finds evidence in the literature to support the hypothesis that the primary physiological triggering mechanism for inhalational agents may vary substantially from that of the depolarizing muscle relaxant succinylcholine. If a differentiation can be made and a link can be demonstrated between abnormalities in receptor sensitivity for or release, reuptake, or metabolism of catecholamines in MHS individuals, we may be able to use these as additional markers/predictors of disease.

The first step in this process is to review the state of the science linking abnormal adrenergic responses to and increased intracellular Ca^{2+} release, which is the known alteration in MH triggering (Perry, Muldoon, Bunger, & Kasper, 2012). In this review involving the relationship between the ANS, an MH will include clinical case study reports and experimental studies using both animal and human models. In the following presentation of literature, we will investigate the possible link between the ANS and MH in the presence of various known triggers and hormonal substrates.

THE PORCINE MODEL

Much of the early research involving the role of stress and the involvement of the ANS in triggering of MH was done using the porcine model. MHS swine are homozygous for the genetic mutation in the RyR1 gene and can develop fulminate MH not only in response to the known triggers of general anesthetics and succinylcholine but also to environmental heat and stress (porcine stress syndrome).

In investigating MH in the porcine model, Williams, Snyderman, and Lefkowitz (1976) developed a hypothesis implicating norepinephrine (NE) as a major factor in MH, both as an existing physiological abnormality in the swine and as a trigger. They postulated that the MHS swine has a continually increased metabolism as a result of excessive NE release on its abnormally affected MHS muscle. According to this hypothesis, the MHS pig has a continually increased heat production and metabolic activity that it controls by its own homeostatic mechanisms. However, when some additional factors such as general anesthetics, a hot environment, fighting, coitus, or stresses occur, the animal cannot control the additional heat production and acute fulminate MH occurs (Williams, 1988).

In the 1970s and 1980s, researchers used the swine model to investigate the role of the ANS by measuring differences in catecholamine levels, testing the ability to trigger the pig to MH using adrenergic agonist, as well as attempting to prevent MH using adrenergic receptor blockers and drugs which depleted stores of catecholamines in the peripheral and central nervous systems. These different research approaches are presented in the sections that follow.

MHS Swine Have Increased Plasma Catecholamine Levels

In the mid-1970s, the British research group of Lucke, Hall, and Lister (1976) performed several studies designed to investigate the effect of the ANS on porcine MH.

In their first study, they examined the metabolic and physiological changes in MHS pigs. Using the same anesthetizing method for all of their studies, seven pigs were maintained under thiopental anesthesia and mechanically ventilated with oxygen. Five of the pigs were triggered to MH using two doses of succinylcholine, followed by halothane, whereas two swine received two doses of succinylcholine alone. The authors reported a significant increase in plasma catecholamines in the MHS pigs after triggering ($p < .001$). Mean control levels of catecholamines at baseline were 1.6 μg/L and increased to 7.4 μg/L after the first dose of succinylcholine. Catecholamines continued to increase to 44.6 μg/L before death. The authors also reported a highly significant correlation ($r = .846$, $p < .001$) between the log of the total plasma catecholamine and lactate levels in the MHS pigs (Lucke et al., 1976). They summarized as follows: "The log-linear nature of this relationship provides supporting evidence for our contention that the catecholamine increase is associated with, if not directly attributable to, a product of metabolism" (p. 303).

During the same period, another research group, Gronert, Milde, and Theye (1976), also examined the effect of the ANS on MHS swine. In a study published in 1976, these researchers examined the effect of halothane and succinylcholine on MHS pigs (normal controls were used for comparison). This study, which did not specify how catecholamines were measured, showed an increase in catecholamine levels in the MHS swine, compared with MH-normal (MHN) controls, when triggering agents were administered.

In 1982, Davis, Gehrke, Williams, Gehrke, and Gerhardt performed an experiment in MHS and non-MHS pigs exposed to halothane. Using precolumn derivatization and high-performance liquid chromatography, they measured differences in plasma levels of NE, dopamine, and serotonin. All of the MHS swine were found to have significantly higher levels of NE, with the largest increase "eightfold during times of intense peripheral vasoconstriction and body temperature rise." The authors suggest that other researchers who failed to find a definite role for NE in the development of MH had used less sensitive measurement methods (Davis et al., 1982).

These three investigations demonstrate that in MHS swine, there is an increase in plasma catecholamines during an episode of MH. This supports the hypothesis stated earlier that the ANS is involved in the hypermetabolic pathology of MH. The subsequent review of the literature will help to elucidate the specific involvement of the somatic nervous system (SNS) and suggest some possible methods used to mitigate these effects.

Adrenergic Receptor Agonist and Blockade

The research group of Lister, Hall, and Lucke (1976), having demonstrated the presence of increased catecholamines in the MHS swine, performed their next study to examine the effect of adrenergic blockade on MH triggering and outcome. For this study, six Pietrain MHS swine were fed reserpine and then exposed to a "two-dose succinylcholine challenge" (two doses of succinylcholine given 15 min apart). Three of the 6 swine were effectively depleted of catecholamines and did not trigger to MH when given succinylcholine. The three that were not effectively depleted did not survive the challenge and died. In addition, survivors had significantly lower levels of plasma catecholamines than the group that did not survive (0.14 μg/L vs. 1.23 μg/L; Lister et al., 1976).

Subsequently, researchers used 10 Pietrain pigs and infused either the α-adrenergic blocker phentolamine or the β-adrenergic blocker propranolol prior to the succinylcholine challenge. The authors titrated various doses of each blocking drug to determine the effective dose. Swine given an infusion of 50 μg/kg/min of phentolamine initially responded to succinylcholine with muscle fasciculation but did not develop fatal MH. In addition, the researchers found that although the α-adrenergic blocked pigs had an initial increase in plasma catecholamines, their levels subsequently decreased. In addition, infusions of concentrations of phentolamine lower than 50 μg/kg/min were not successful in preventing the MH episode, suggesting that the α-adrenergic receptors must be completely blocked to prevent MH (Lister et al., 1976).

MHS swine randomized to the β-adrenergic blocking propranolol (40 μg/kg/min) did not survive the succinylcholine challenge. Researchers summarized as follows: "The important finding of this experiment was that although neither reserpine nor phentolamine altered the initial muscle response to suxamethonium, they prevented the further stimulation of muscle metabolism found in fatal MH" (Lister et al., 1976). Investigators postulated that the α-adrenergic receptor might increase the release of acetylcholine at the presynaptic motor nerve terminal and play a large part in the extreme reaction in skeletal muscles of MHS individuals. The ability of phentolamine to block the MH episode supports this theory. The authors also suggested the possibility that the motor endplate in MHS swine may contain a larger preponderance of receptors (Lister et al., 1976).

Continuing with their exploration of the ANS and MH in 1977, Hall, Lucke, and Lister successfully demonstrated the ability of adrenergic agonists to induce fulminate MH in the absence of any other known triggering agent. Comparing the MHS Pietrain pigs to a control group of large, white pigs, they administered infusions of noradrenaline, noradrenaline with phentolamine, or noradrenaline with propranolol. MHS pigs receiving noradrenaline alone developed a small increase in body temperature but did not trigger MH. However, with no other triggering agent administered, MHS pigs developed a fatal hyperthermia when phenylephrine or noradrenaline were given to pigs pretreated with propranolol. This sensitivity to α-adrenergic stimulation was not evidenced in the control group and was supported by Dyer who found the affinity of the α-adrenergic receptor in an isolated aortic vascular rings preparation from MHS swine was 2.6 times more sensitive than in controls (Dyer, 1982; Hall et al., 1977).

These studies support the hypothesis that hormonal influences from the central nervous system may play a significant role in the triggering of MH and that the α-adrenergic agonists may be a significant cofactor in the triggering of MH. In addition, it is suggested that the β-adrenergic agonism may offer some essential component to recovery in the face of a fulminate episode. This is also supported by unpublished findings from the author who found increased sensitivity in the α response to NE in human B cells (Perry et al., 2012). To examine this more closely, we will look at studies that demonstrate the effects of a central blockade.

Neuromuscular Blockade: MH and the Neuromuscular Junction

In 1976, the British research group, this time led by Hall, examined the effect of neuromuscular blockade on the triggering of MHS swine. Investigators demonstrated that when the nondepolarizing muscle relaxant tubocurarine was given to the pigs prior to the succinylcholine challenge, they exhibited no muscle fasciculation or hypermetabolic response to succinylcholine (Hall, Lucke, & Lister, 1976).

However, when pigs were given tubocurarine prior to halothane, they suffered a fatal episode of MH. This is a significant finding and supports the possibility that "the depolarization of the motor end-plate is necessary for the triggering action of succinylcholine" (Hall et al., 1976, p. 1137). Investigators also reported that MHS swine not treated with the nondepolarizer showed extremely strong and prolonged fasciculation when given succinylcholine. They suggest that this may be the effect of increased number of receptors, or other functional abnormalities, at the motor endplate in MHS swine. In discussing a possible link between elevated catecholamines in those that triggered, the authors wrote, "We have postulated that one effect of the large increase in plasma catecholamine concentration in MH may be to induce an increase in acetylcholine release at the neuromuscular junction and stimulate muscle metabolism even further" (Lister et al., 1976).

In this same year, Short, Paddleford, McGrath, and Williams conducted an extensive study to examine the effects of various anesthetic combinations on MHS swine. The researchers used 53 swine which were first screened by a short halothane challenge and found to be MHS. The MHS swine were separated into four groups. The MHS swine in the first group did not trigger to MH until halothane was introduced. A second group of swine received pancuronium, prior to the administration of succinylcholine. These MHS swine had no increase in heart rate or temperature and did not develop MH following the administration of succinylcholine. The authors suggested that succinylcholine alone was not a trigger; however, the interaction of succinylcholine on an unidentified cofactor results in triggering MH.

A third group of MHS swine received reserpine, and the fourth group received methyldopa prior to being administered halothane. The use of methyldopa, as well as reserpine, provided protection against development of MH (Short et al., 1976). Methyldopa prevents the release of NE from presynaptic terminal, and reserpine blocks the release of NE from central and peripheral sites, including the adrenals. These finding again provides strong evidence of an interaction between the ANS and MH. The next section investigates the ability to use a central blockade of the ANS to prevent triggering of MH.

Central Nervous System Blockade

In 1978, the team led by Lucke investigated the effects of bilateral adrenalectomy and bretylium on MHS swine given halothane anesthesia. The drug bretylium prevents the release of NE from the peripheral nervous system and when combined with bilateral adrenalectomy, results in a complete adrenergic blockade. None of the swine treated with both an adrenalectomy and bretylium triggered to MH. The authors noted that the adrenalectomy alone was "nearly as effective as the adrenalectomy with bretylium, indicating a primary role of the adrenal medulla over that of the peripheral SNS" (Lucke, Denny, Hall, Lovell, & Lister, 1978). The authors surmised that the ability of the total sympathetic blockade to prevent halothane-induced MH implicates the ANS as a cofactor in the reaction of skeletal muscles to MH-triggering agents. They also suggest that, in the face of an adrenergic blockade, the MHS skeletal muscles may be unable respond to a known trigger with a metabolic response sufficient to trigger MH (Lucke et al., 1978).

The research team of Kerr, Wingard, and Gatz (1975) examined the possibility that a central blockade of the central nervous system (CNS) could prevent MH. In their experiment, halothane was administered to a group of MHS swine. All swine triggered to MH and were rescued before development of a fatal episode. With swine acting as their own controls, the team administered a continuous epidural block to the MHS pigs and reexposed them to halothane.

The purpose of the epidural was to prevent an autonomic response to any stimuli via central blockade of the CNS. Pigs that received the epidural blockade did not trigger to MH when the halothane was administered. In addition, the researchers noted that even MHS pigs with only a partial block triggered more slowly than they did in the control phase of the experiment. The authors stated, "Malignant hyperthermia in susceptible swine was completely blocked by epidural anesthesia with lidocaine. These studies indicate the importance of the nervous system in the triggering of malignant hyperthermia" (Kerr et al., 1975).

In these two studies, we see a clear demonstration that the ANS plays a key role in the initiation of MH and that a complete sympathectomy may be used to prevent halothane MH in the porcine model.

Primary Versus Secondary Role/Halothane Versus Succinylcholine Triggering

Although many researchers believe that the ANS plays a primary role in MH, others define the role of the ANS as secondary. Gronert and Theye in 1976 published a study entitled, "Halothane Induced Porcine Malignant Hyperthermia." The purpose of the study was to identify which physiological changes occurred first in MHS swine triggered with halothane. Their results indicated that an increase in lactate levels was the first significant difference found in the MHS pigs and that although catecholamine levels did increase, there was not a significant increase until 30 min after triggering. This is in stark difference to previous studies, including two by Gronert listed in the previous section, which showed immediate increases in levels of plasma catecholamines. However, in this study, the researchers did not use succinylcholine. This may reflect the reason for different findings and supports previous suggestions which perhaps the varied involvement in the ANS depends on the triggering agent presented to the MHS swine.

This same research group conducted other studies on the issue of MH and the SNS; however, the methods that were used for anesthetizing the swine and maintaining them during their studies do not allow for comparison with other researchers conducting similar studies at the same time. For example, this group used nitrous oxide and phenobarbital for anesthesia (Gronert, Milde, & Theye, 1977). In addition, at times, they added the cholinergic drug, atropine on induction, and transfused the swine with blood or supported their hemodynamics during the studies. The other researchers on this subject did not use nitrous and gave no adjunct therapy to swine during their studies. The use of these adjuncts, in the opinion of the author, makes any comparison with the work of other researchers in this article very difficult.

HUMAN STUDIES/CASE REPORTS

In 1975, R. F. W. Moulds in a letter published in the *Lancet* outlined a case for MH being a "manifestation of a generalized stress syndrome" in both humans and pigs. His underlying theory was that "abnormalities in the calcium storing muscle cells could also be present in the catecholamine secretory cells." He further wrote, "All the features necessary for the perpetuation of this cycle during malignant hyperpyrexia are probably exaggerations of normal responses rather than completely atypical responses."

Katz and Krich published a case report in 1976 of a patient who experienced MH 7 hr after initial induction of general anesthesia. For the patient's next surgery, a spinal anesthetic was chosen. They described the preanesthetic anxiety of the patient as "very stressed." They also describe the spinal as "spotty" with only an initial L2 level. The patient did not trigger during the anesthetic but did suffer a "hyperthermic" event 5 hr after the completion of the surgery. The authors suggested it was the stress that led to trigger in the second instance.

A case report by Gronert, Thompson, and Onofrio (1980) presented a 42-year-old male who reported stress-induced episodes of "fever, aching joints and sweats that lasted for several days." According to the authors, the symptoms were relieved with dantrolene. They suggested that the patient was experiencing a hypermetabolic response to stress and that perhaps even the patient's diabetic pattern was "secondary to increased circulating levels of catecholamines or adreno-cortical stimulation." Of interest also was their suggestion that perhaps humans did actually experience more episodes of MH than were reported because we have the ability to recognize early symptoms and more easily control the episodes of awake MH (Gronert et al., 1980).

In 1981, Wingard published a series of case studies on six patients who had experienced possible MH episodes as a response to stress alone. Wingard suggested that frequently, patients who are MHS do not trigger to anesthetics, although they can demonstrate a hyperpyretic response and signs of MH without triggers. However, these reports remain anecdotal because the patients had not been positively identified as MHS by CHCT, and genetic profiling was not yet available (Wingard, 1981).

A 1983 case report by Grinberg, Edelist, and Gordon described three patients that had nontriggering anesthetics to avoid MH and yet developed MH after surgery and "well into the postoperative period." The authors stated their belief that postoperative pain and hypothermia contributed to the trigger of the episodes.

In a 1988 case report, Britt described several family members in an MHS family. She outlined a history of several anesthetic-related and nonanesthetic-related incidences. She stated her theory that stress was a triggering factor for several of the reactions, one of which was fatal (Britt, 1988).

As previously discussed, humans are capable of experiencing MH-like episodes of MH which are unrelated to the intraoperative anesthetic triggers usually associated with an episode. In a recent commentary by Gronert, Tobin, and Muldoon (2011), the group outlined several authenticated cases of MHS individuals who experienced awake episodes of MH, subsequently found to be positive for MH via either genetic or CHCT testing. The authors' state, "There is indisputable evidence that humans susceptible to MH have stress related abnormal responses in the absence of exposure to triggering agents."

Recently, there have been multiple published reports of children triggering to MH as a result of exercise, environmental stress, or concomitant with viral illness (Tobin, Challa, Nelson, & Sambuughin, 2001). These include a 12-year-old boy who survived an anesthesia-related MH episode and later experienced a fatal hyperthermic event while playing football several months after the initial episode (Tobin et al., 2001). Groom et al. (2011) presented two case studies of ultimately fatal outcomes from MH. The first case described a male who had survived an inoperative MH episode at age of 7 months. Between 7 months and 9 years of age, he continued to exhibit numerous awake episodes of MH. At times, the child triggered to obvious environmental or viral factors; however, at other times there was no obvious causative factor identified. Ultimately, at age 9 years, he died on the way to the emergency department. The second child was a female who had exhibited two episodes of muscle rigidity and high temperatures once in response to exercise and the other in response to mild viral infections. The last episode resulted in cardiac arrest. In both children, genetic sequencing of the RyR1 revealed identical de novo mutations on the RyR1 receptor gene (Groom et al., 2011).

The advent of molecular genetics and the successful linking of mutations in the RyR1 and dihydropyridine receptors to MH susceptibility in humans have provided an avenue for improved identification of those MHS individuals who experience an MH episode in the absence of known anesthetic triggers. The genetic approach promises to lead to a better understanding of the potential role of stress in triggering MH in humans.

Human Experimental Studies

In 1981, Campbell, Ellis, Evans, and Chem compared the thermoregulatory, hormonal, and metabolic responses to stress in patients diagnosed as MHS compared to normal/control subjects; the stress test involved physical exercise and cooling. No consistent differences were found between MHS and control subjects. In particular, there was no clear evidence of an enhanced sympathetic adrenal response in MHS patients.

In contrast, Willner, Cerri, and Wood (1981) explored the role of the adrenergic signaling system in muscle from MHS individuals and their relatives. Cyclic AMP (cAMP), adenylate cyclase (AC), and phosphodiesterase (PDE) were measured. Their sample consisted of 18 survivors of MHS episodes and 15 relatives of MH survivors. These researchers found that "basal AC activity was abnormally increased in muscle of MH 'reactors' (meaning susceptible) and those relative with abnormal single-fiber responses to caffeine compared to control muscle."

They also found that increased AC activity occurred in the muscles of MHS subjects when they were asymptomatic. The authors stated, "The normal function of AC provides an explanation for this paradox . . . although activity of AC can be readily measure in vitro, cAMP is synthesized at a relatively low rate in vivo and in the absence of physiological stimulants it is rapidly degraded by PDE. The usually asymptomatic myopathy associated with MH is therefore associated with abnormality of an enzyme that normally requires stimulation to be catalytically active. Catecholamine secretion and anesthetics could provide that stimulation" (Willner et al., 1981, p. 1122).

This same research group had performed a previous study in 1979 entitled, "Malignant Hyperthermia: Abnormal Cyclic AMP Metabolism." In this study, the researchers examined skeletal muscles biopsies of children who had exercise-provoked hyperthermia or anesthesia-provoked MH and found increased cAMP content in their muscle samples. The authors suggested that these findings were supportive of the possibility that circulating catecholamines, as well as halothane, could act in MHS humans to trigger "a genetic defect expressed in the plasmalemma" and that "abnormal SR calcium transport could be a consequence of this defect" (Willner et al., 1979).

Stanec and Stefano (1984) performed an experimental study of 10 MHS and 10 non-MHS subjects given a Bruce protocol treadmill test. Each individual was exercised to his or her maximum exertion level and then tested for levels of cAMP. Statistically, significant results included the findings that MHS individuals reached their maximum predicted increase in heart rate and systolic blood pressure earlier than normal subjects and reported feeling "exhausted" earlier than non-MHS controls. When levels of cAMP were measured at baseline before exercise, the MHS sample had higher levels of cAMP but not to a statistically significant degree. However, cAMP increased to statistically significant higher levels in the MHS group during the exercise tests, and the duration of the increased in the cAMP levels in the MHS group, up to 2 hr after the test was completed, did reach statistically significant levels (Stanec & Stefano, 1984).

Human B Lymphocytes and Malignant Hyperthermia

In 1999, a new acceptable model was found for study of MH in humans when it was demonstrated that human B cells, from two cell lines, DAKIKI and human primary CD19 (+), expressed RyR1, RyR2, and RyR3 in 56%, 22%, and 0%, respectively, whereas T cells from the same samples ($N = 9$), expressed RyR1, RyR2, or RyR3 in significantly lower levels. The RyR1 receptors present in these cell lines were identical with that found in skeletal muscles (Hosoi et al.,

2001). This was the first research finding that established the possibility that human B lymphocytes could be used as a model to examine RyR1 function in immune cells.

In 2002, Sei et al. demonstrated that B lymphocytes from MHS individuals exhibited significantly increased Ca^{2+} emissions in response to the RyR1 agonists 4-CmC and caffeine when compared to MHN controls. This supported the idea that there was dysregulation in Ca^{2+} homeostasis in MHS individuals and that this was related to the RyR1. Using 50 mM caffeine or 400 μM 4-CmC in fluo-3 prepared B cells, the researchers reported a significantly increased fluorescence in B cells from MHS patients when compared to controls with a correlation between response to agonists and Ca^{2+} release (Sei, Gallagher, & Daly, 2001). Girard et al. (2001) demonstrated that immortalized Epstein-Barr virus (EBV) B cells from an MHS patient with a defined mutation exhibited a slightly larger fraction of total releasable intracellular Ca^{2+} pool when exposed to 400 or 600 μM of 4-CmC as compared to controls.

McKinney, Butler, Mullen, and Klein (2006) used DAKIKI and normal human B cell lines, as well as mixed population of lymphocytes obtained from MHS and normal pigs to compare the effects of 4-CmC on RyR1-mediated Ca^{2+} release. Ca^{2+} was measured fluorometrically with fura-2 AM for cells in suspension and with fluo-4 in single cells using confocal microscopy. They reported that B lymphocytes from MHS swine were more sensitive to the RyR1 agonist 4-CmC than normal swine, and this was demonstrated by using fura-2 AM dye to measure calcium (McKinney et al., 2006).

These investigations demonstrated that human B lymphocytes provide a valid and acceptable scientific model, which can be used to delineate differences between MHS and MHN individuals in the sensitivity of RyR1 agonist–induced Ca^{2+} release. The identification of this model opens the door to the further exploration of role which the ANS may play in the triggering of MH in the human model.

B Lymphocytes and the Adrenergic Nervous System

To investigate the effects of ANS catecholamine release on human B cells, it is necessary that the B cells express adrenergic receptors. The presence of adrenergic receptors on human B lymphocytes has been established by Aarons, Nies, Gal, Hegstrand, and Molinoff (1980); Ricci and colleagues (1999); Maisel, Harris, Rearden, and Michel (1990); and Williams, Snyderman, and Lefkowitz (1976).

Examining of the effect of isoproterenol, epinephrine, and NE on human B lymphocytes, researchers found that the β-adrenergic agonist isoproterenol was the most effective in stimulating the AC production in these immune cells. The authors stated that their results "provided an experimental approach to the study of states of altered sensitivity to catecholamines at the receptor level in man" (Williams et al., 1976). In addition, Redwine, Jenkins, and Baum (1996) demonstrated that increased stress in individuals resulted in a change in the activity of, and density in, β_2-adrenergic receptors on human B lymphocytes.

Ricci et al. demonstrated the expression of α_1 receptors on human lymphocytes in 1999. This group used reverse transcription–polymerase chain reaction (RT-PCR), radio-ligand binding assay techniques, as well as the use of specific α_1 antibody to prevent the binding of the pharmacological α-specific agonist prazosin. They found the expression of three α_1-receptor subtypes on human peripheral lymphocytes.

Taken together, these studies support the concept that human B lymphocytes provide an effective model from which to study RyR1-mediated Ca^{2+} release in response to pharmacological reagents and catecholamines in MHS and MHN B cells.

NEW INITIATIVES: BRING THE SCIENCE FORWARD

In 2012, a research grant was received by the author from the American Association of Nurse Anesthetist Foundation to reestablish research into the question of a link between the triggering of MH and the adrenergic stress response in humans. A research team from the Uniformed Services Graduate School of Nursing and Medical School collaborated to measure fura-2 calcium emissions in response to the RyR1 agonist 4-CmC in human B lymphocytes from MHS and non-MHS subjects. This study was the first experiment of its kind to explore the relationship between the catecholamine responses on intracellular calcium response in the MHS population. Results from this study are complete and are awaiting publication. It is our belief that this research will support the previous findings of earlier researchers on the role of the adrenergic response in MH triggering and reopens the door to the exploration of this phenomenon.

SUMMARY

As shown in the studies mentioned earlier, known MH triggers such as inhalational anesthetics and succinylcholine do not always trigger humans to MH. Furthermore, the literature reflects that humans can trigger to MH and MH-like episodes without these agents. Multiple studies point to a possible link between the ANS stress response and the triggering of MH in MHS patients.

Most literature reviews limit themselves to studies conducted within the last 10 years. However, after an extensive literature search on "SNS and MH" and "catecholamines and MH," I was struck by the paucity of research in this area after the mid-1980s. Although there was a flow of research in this area in the late 1970s and 1980s, most research after 1980s exploring the issue was done primarily in the veterinary community on MHS swine. The connection between the RyR1 receptor and MH occurred in the late 1980s. It is possible that the identification of the RyR1 gene resulted in redirection away from the role of the ANS.

After careful review of the literature, the definitive answer as to what is the common pathway involved in the triggering of an MH event remains undefined. In their article entitled "Is There a Link Between Malignant Hyperthermia and Exertional Heat Illness" (EHI), Muldoon and colleagues (2004) examined the relationship between the two syndromes. In their overview, they discuss variability as a "striking characteristic" of the disease MH. In addition, the cases they outline in their study clearly outline instances of MHS patients developing exercise-induced MH episodes in the absence of triggering pharmacological agents. These researchers suggest that MH "stems from an interaction between genes and environmental factors" and that "5%–8% develop symptoms with exercise emotional stress and/or environmental heat exposure" (Capacchione & Muldoon, 2009; Muldoon et al., 2004). This link between EHI and MH is currently being examined more carefully with the preponderance of evidence leading closer to a definitive link (Groom et al., 2011; Nishio et al., 2009; Ryan & Tedeschi, 1997; Tobin et al., 2001; Wappler et al., 2001).

The studies on cAMP, although done more than 20 years ago, are interesting in suggesting a possibility that the relationship between MH and EHI is one of a continuum, which may involve many levels of increasing hyperthermic syndromes. If this is the case, the early researchers such as Gronert were correct in suggesting that in humans, the awareness of symptoms may work to control the onset of the hyperthermic events.

Understanding of the SNS and what the literature suggests as to possible abnormalities in production of, receptor affinity for, and metabolism of catecholamines presents several possibilities for the influence of the ANS as a cofactor in the triggering of MH. Any trigger, pharmacological or environmental, which leads to a stress reaction in the MHS individuals, would trigger a release of NE. Although the RyR1 receptor is the primary calcium channel in skeletal muscles, the RyR2 isoform of the channel is primarily found in cardiac muscle. Discussing the mutations in the RyR2 receptor and its role in sudden cardiac death noted that the genetic mutations coding for catecholaminergic polymorphic ventricular tachycardia (CPVT), familial polymorphic ventricular tachycardia, and arrhythmogenic right ventricular dysplasia type 2 are found to cluster in the same three receptor channel regions found in the RyR1 receptor in individuals with MHS. He further explains that this is related to a hypersensitivity to adrenergic signaling (Marks, 2002).

In a recent review article, MacLennan and Zvaritch (2011) discussed the possibility of common triggering mechanisms for both CPVT and MH propose there is evidence that among other triggering mechanisms there is a link in the "adrenergic stimulation resulting from emotional or physical stress." Taken with the findings of this study, further research is required to examine the exact mechanism for this shared hypersensitivity in ryanodine receptors in both cardiac myocytes and B lymphocytes and how this translates to a possible hypersensitivity in skeletal muscles from MHS samples.

A new model for examining the relationship between stress and the triggering of MH in humans may now exist in the murine model. Several research groups are experimenting with knock-in mice models. The R163C RyR1 knock-in mouse has been validated for study of MH in humans (Yang et al., 2006). The T4826I RyR1 knock-in mouse exhibits triggering to MH in response to inhalational agents and environmental heat stress which appears to be gender-dependent (Yuen et al., 2012), and the Baylor University group headed by Dr. Susan Hamilton is currently working with the Y522S knock-in mouse which exhibits an MH response to elevated environmental temperatures, caffeine, and anesthetic agents (Chelu et al., 2006). These murine models present exciting opportunities for expanded research into the triggering and treatment, diagnosis, and possible prevention of EHI and MH.

The availability of new models in which to explore the role of the ANS in the spectrum disorders of EHI and MH is exciting. It is possible that future research into the role of the ANS in MH lies in the exploration of the relationship between the autonomic and nicotinic receptors and their sensitivity to catecholamines and acetylcholine to validate the early research done on the porcine and human models of the previous decades.

Many questions remain to be explored. Is there a demonstrated primary role for the ANS in the triggering, presentation, and/or control of MH? As suggested in the swine model of MH and in human case reports, what specific roles do the α- and/or β-adrenergic receptors play in triggering or control of MH? Is there a difference in the role of the ANS in the triggering mechanism when patients are exposed to inhalational agents, depolarizer, EHI, or other stressors? In addition, there were many metabolic variations in both the swine and human studies, well described by researchers investigating the relationship between the ANS and MH (Gronert & Theye, 1976; Gronert, Theye, Milde, & Tinker, 1978; Hall et al., 1977; Lister et al., 1976; Lucke et al., 1976; Lucke et al., 1978). Although equally important in a comprehensive review of MH, they are beyond the scope of this chapter. We believe the answers to all of these remaining questions may be found in future research using the lymphocyte and murine models.

ACKNOWLEDGMENTS

The author would like to acknowledge Dr. Sheila Muldoon, Dr. Christine Kasper, and Dr. Rolf Bunger for their significant collaboration in the preparation of this review and analysis.

DISCLAIMER

The views expressed in this chapter are those of the author and do not reflect the official policy or position of the Department of the Air Force, the Department of Defense, the Uniformed Services University, or the U.S. government.

REFERENCES

Aarons, R. D., Nies, A. S., Gal, J., Hegstrand, L. R., & Molinoff, P. B. (1980). Elevation of β-adrenergic receptor density in human lymphocytes after propranolol administration. *Journal of Clinical Investigations*, *65*, 949–957.

Allen, G. C., Larach, M. G., & Kunselman, A. R. (1998). The sensitivity and specificity of the caffeine-halothane muscle contracture test. North American Malignant Hyperthermia Group. *Anesthesia & Analgesia, 69,* 579–588.

Britt, B. A. (1988). Combined anesthetic and stress-induced malignant hyperthermia in two offspring of malignant hyperthermic-susceptible parents. *Anesthesia & analgesia*, *67*, 393–396.

Campbell, I. T., Ellis, F. R., Evans, R. T., & Chem, C. (1981). Metabolic rate and blood hormone and metabolite levels of individuals susceptible to malignant hyperpyrexia at rest and in response to food and mild exercise. *Anesthesiology*, *55*, 46–52.

Capacchione, J. F., & Muldoon, S. M. (2009). The relationship between exertional heat illness, exertional rhabdomyolysis, and malignant hyperthermia. *Anesthesia and Analgesia*, *109*(4), 1065–1069. http://dx.doi.org/101213/ane.Ob013e3181a9d8d9

Chelu, M. G., Goonasekera, S. A., Durham, W. J., Tang, W., Lueck, J. D., Riehl, J., . . . Hamilton, S. L. (2006). Heat and anesthesia induced malignant hyperthermia in a RyR1 Knock-in mouse. *Federation of American Societies for Experimental Biology*, *20*(2), 329–330.

Davis, T. P., Gehrke, C. W., Jr., Williams, C. H., Gehrke, C. W., & Gerhardt, K. O. (1982). Precolumn derivatization and high-performance liquid chromatography of biogenic amines in blood of normal and malignant hyperthermic pigs. *Journal of Chromatography*, *228*, 113–122.

Dyer, D. C. (1982). Evidence for differences in α-adrenergic receptor affinity in stress susceptible swine. *Experientia*, *38*, 1343–1344.

Girard, T., Cavagna, D., Padovan, E., Spagnoli, G., Urwyler, A., Zorzato, F., & Treves, S. (2001). B-lymphocytes from malignant hyperthermia-susceptible patients have an increased sensitivity to skeletal muscle ryanodine receptor activators. *The Journal of Biological Chemistry*, *276*(51), 48077–48082.

Grinberg, R., Edelist, G., & Gordon, A. (1983). Postoperative malignant hyperthermia episodes in patient who received "safe" anaesthetics. *Canadian Anaesthesiology Society Journal*, *30*(3, Pt. 1), 273–276.

Gronert, G. A., Milde, J. H., & Theye, R. A. (1976). Porcine malignant hyperthermia induced by halothane and succinylcholine: Failure of treatment with procaine or procainamide. *Anesthesiology*, *44*(2), 124–132.

Gronert, G. A., Milde, J. H., & Theye, R. A. (1977). Role of sympathetic activity in porcine malignant hyperthermia. *Anesthesiology*, *47*(5), 411–415.

Gronert, G. A., & Theye, R. A. (1976). Halothane-induced porcine malignant hyperthermia: Metabolic and hemodynamic changes. *Anesthesiology, 44*(1), 36–43.

Gronert, G. A., Theye, R. A., Milde, J. H., & Tinker, J. H. (1978). Catecholamine stimulation of myocardial oxygen consumption in porcine malignant hyperthermia. *Anesthesiology, 49,* 330–337.

Gronert, G. A., Thompson, R. L., & Onofrio, B. M. (1980). Human malignant hyperthermia: Awake episodes and correction by dantrolene. *Anesthesia and Analgesia, 59*(5), 377–378.

Gronert, G. A., Tobin, J. R., & Muldoon, S. M. (2011). Malignant hyperthermia: Human stress triggering. *Biochimica et Biophysica Acta, 1813*(12), 1–2. http://dx.doi.org/10.1016/j.bbamcr.2011.08.001

Groom, L., Muldoon, S. M., Brandom, B. W., Bayarsaikhan, M., Bina, S., Lee, H. S., . . . Dirksen, R. T. (2011). Identical de novo mutation in the type 1 ryanodine receptor gene associate with fata, ress induced malignant hyperthermia in two unrelated families. *Anesthesiology, 115*(5), 938–944.

Hall, G. M., Lucke, J. N., & Lister, D. (1976). Porcine malignant hyperthermia IV: Neuromuscular blockade. *British Journal of Anaesthesia, 48,* 1135–1141.

Hall, G. M., Lucke, J. N., & Lister, D. (1977). Porcine malignant hyperthermia V: Fatal hyperthermia in the Pietrain pig, associated with the infusion of alpha-adrenergic agonists. *British Journal of Anaesthesia, 49,* 855–863.

Hamilton, S. L., & Serysheva, I. I. (2009). Ryanodine receptor structure: Progress and challenges. *The Journal of Biological Chemistry, 284,* 4047–4051.

Hosoi, E., Nishizaki, C., Gallagher, K. L., Wyre, H. W., Matsuo, Y., & Sei, Y. (2001). Expression of the ryanodine receptor isoforms in immune cells. *The Journal of Immunology, 167,* 4887–4894.

Katz, J. D., & Krich, L. B. (1976). Acute febrile reaction complicating spinal anaesthesia in a survivor of malignant hyperthermia. *Canadian Anaesthesia Society Journal, 23*(3), 285–289.

Kerr, D. D., Wingard, D. W., & Gatz, E. E. (1975). Prevention of porcine malignant hyperthermia by epidural block. *Anesthesiology,* 42(3), 307–331.

Larach, M. G. (1989). Standardization of the caffeine halothane muscle contracture test. North American Malignant Hyperthermia Group. *Anesthesia and Analgesia, 69,* 511–515.

Lister, D., Hall, G. M., & Lucke, J. N. (1976). Porcine malignant hyperthermia. III: Adrenergic blockade. *British Journal of Anaesthesia, 48,* 831–838.

Lucke, J. N., Denny, H., Hall, G. M., Lovell, R., & Lister, D. (1978). Porcine malignant hyperthermia VI: The effects of bilateral adrenalectomy and pretreatment with bretylium on the halothane-induced response. *British Journal of Anaesthesia, 50,* 241–246.

Lucke, J. N., Hall, G. M., & Lister, D. (1976). Porcine malignant hyperthermia. I: Metabolic and physiological changes. *British Journal of Anaesthesia, 48,* 297–304.

Mackrill, J. J. (1998). Possible regulation of the skeletal muscle ryanodine receptor by a polyubiquitin binding subunit of the 26S proteasome. *Biochemical and Biophysical Communications, 245,* 428–429.

MacLennan, D. H., Duff, C., Zorzato, F., Fujii, J., Phillips, M., Korneluk, R. G., . . . Worton, R. G. (1990). Ryanodine receptor gene is a candidate for predisposition to malignant hyperthermia. *Nature, 343,* 559–561.

MacLennan, D. H., & Zvaritch, E. (2011). Mechanistic models for muscle diseases and disorders originating in the sarcoplasmic reticulum. *Biochemia et Biophysica Acta, 1813,* 948–964.

Maisel, A. S., Harris, T., Rearden, C. A., & Michel, M. C. (1990). ⊠-adrenergic receptors in lymphocyte subsets after exercise. Alterations in normal individuals and patients with congestive heart failure. *Circulation, 82,* 2003–2010.

Marks, A. R. (2002). Clinical implications of cardiac ryanodine receptor/calcium release channel mutations linked to sudden cardiac death. *Circulation, 106,* 8–10.

McCarthy, T. V., Healy, J. M. S., Heffron, J. J. A., Lehane, M., Deufel, T., Lehmann-Horn, F., . . . Johnson, K. (1990). Localization of the malignant hyperthermia susceptibility locus to human chromosome 19q12-13.2. *Nature, 343*, 562–564.

McKinney, L. C., Butler, T., Mullen, S. P., & Klein, M. G. (2006). Characterization of ryanodine receptor-mediated calcium release in human B cells: Relevance to diagnostic testing for malignant hyperthermia. *Anesthesiology, 104*, 1191–1201.

Moulds, R. F. W. (1975). Malignant hyperthermia. *Lancet, 305*(7908), 681.

Muldoon, S., Deuster, P., Brandom, B., & Bunger, R. (2004). Is there a link between malignant hyperthermia and exertional heat illness? *Exercise and Sports Science Reviews, 32*, 174–179.

Nelson, T. E. (2003). Malignant hyperthermia: A pharmacogenetic disease of Ca^{++} regulating proteins. *Current Molecular Medicine*, 2, 347–369.

Nelson, T. E., & Flewellen, E. H. (1983). Current concepts: The malignant hyperthermia syndrome. *The New England Journal of Medicine, 309*(7), 416–418.

Nishio, H., Sato, T., Fukunishi, S., Tamura, A., Iwata, M., Tsuboi, K., & Suzuki, K. (2009). Identification of malignant hyperthermia-susceptible ryanodine receptor type 1 gene (RYR1) mutations in a child who died in a car after exposure to a high environmental temperature. *Leg Med (Tokyo), 11*, 142–3.

Perry, S. M., Muldoon, S. M., Bunger, R., & Kasper, C. E. (2012). Catecholamine augmented RyR1 calcium release in malignant hyperthermia susceptible B-lymphocytes: A dissertation (Unpublished doctoral dissertation). Uniformed Services University, Bethesda, Maryland.

Redwine, L., Jenkins, F., & Baum, A. (1996). Relation between β-adrenergic receptor density and lymphocyte proliferation associated with acute stress. *International Journal of Behavioral Medicine, 3*(4), 337–353.

Ricci, A., Bronzetti, E., Conterno, A., Greco, S., Mulatero, P., Schena, M., . . . Amenta, F. (1999). Alpha1-adrenergic receptor subtypes in human peripheral blood lymphocytes. *Hypertension, 33*, 708–712.

Ryan, J. F., & Tedeschi, L. G. (1997). Sudden unexplained death in a patient with a family history of malignant hyperthermia. *Journal of Clinical Anesthesia, 9*, 66–68.

Sambuughin, N., Sei, Y., Gallagher, K. L., Wyre, H. W., Madsen, D., Nelson, T. E., . . . Muldoon, S. (2001). Screening of the ryanodine receptor gene and identification of novel mutations. *Anesthesiology, 95*(3), 594–599.

Sei, Y., Brandom, B. W., Bina, S., Hosoi, E., Gallagher, K. L., Wyre, H. W., . . . Muldoon, S. (2002). Patients with malignant hyperthermia demonstrate an altered calcium control mechanism in B lymphocytes. *Anesthesiology, 97*, 1052–1058.

Sei, Y., Gallagher, K. L., & Daly, J. W. (2001). Multiple effects of caffeine on Ca^{++} release and influx in human B lymphocytes. *Cell Calcium, 29*(3), 149–160.

Short, C. E., Paddleford, R. R., McGrath, C. J., & Williams, C. H. (1976). Pre-anesthetic evaluation and management of malignant hyperthermia in the pig experimental model. *Anesthesia and Analgesia, 55*(5), 643–653.

Stanec, A., & Stefano, G. (1984). Cyclic AMP in normal and malignant hyperpyrexia susceptible individuals following exercise. *British Journal of Anaesthesiology. 56*, 1243–1246.

Tobin, J. R., Challa, V. R., Nelson, T. E., & Sambuughin, N. (2001). Malignant hyperthermia and apparent heat stroke. *Journal of the American Medical Association, 286*(2), 168–169.

Vukcevic, M., Broman, M., Islander, G., Bodelsson, M., Ranklev-Twetman, E., Müller, C. R., & Treves, S. (2010). Functional properties of RyR1 mutations identified in Swedish patients with malignant hyperthermia and central core disease. *Anesthesia & Analgesia, 111*(1), 185–90.

Wappler, F., Fiege, M., Steinfath, M., Agarwal, K., Scholz, J., Sign, S., . . . Schulte, J. (2001). Evidence for susceptibility to malignant hyperthermia in patients with exercise-induced rhabdomyolysis. *Anesthesiology, 94*, 95–100.

Williams, C. H. (Ed.). (1988). *Experimental malignant hyperthermia*. New York, NY: Springer-Verlag.

Williams, L. T., Snyderman, R., & Lefkowitz, R. J. (1976). Identification of beta-adrenergic receptors in human lymphocytes by (-) (3H) alprenolol binding. *The Journal of Clinical Investigation*, *57*, 149–155.

Willner, J. H., Cerri, C. G., & Wood, D. S. (1981). High skeletal muscle adenylate cyclase in malignant hyperthermia. *Journal of Clinical Investigations*, *68*, 1119–1124.

Willner, J. H., Cerri, C. J., & Wood, D. S. (1979). Malignant hyperthermia: Abnormal cyclic AMP metabolism in skeletal muscle. *Neurology*, *29*, 557.

Wingard, S. W. (1981). Familial stress syndrome. In F. R. Ellis (Ed.), Inherited *disease and anaesthesia* (pp. 201–209). Amsterdam: Elsevier North Holland Biomedical Press.

Yuen, B., Boncompagni, S., Feng, W., Yang, T., Lopez, J. R., Matthaei, K. I., . . . Pessah, I. N. (2012). Mice expressing T4826I-RYR1 are viable but exhibit sex and genotype-dependent susceptibility to malignant hyperthermia and muscle damage. *Federation of American Societies for Experimental Biology*, *26*(3), 1311–1322.

CHAPTER 8

Family Caregivers of Veterans

A Critical Review of the Empirical Literature and Recommendations for Future Research

Constance R. Uphold, Meggan Jordan, and Magaly Freytes

ABSTRACT

In recent years, research on caregiving has grown in both quality and quantity. Caregivers play an important role in supporting and promoting the health and recovery of injured, disabled, and ill family members in their care. Although researchers have made a substantial contribution to our understanding of family caregiving, less is known about family caregivers of U.S. Veterans. The purpose of this review is to identify and evaluate the research surrounding caregivers of U.S. Veterans, particularly two populations of Veterans: those who returned from the wars in Iraq and Afghanistan and those who had suffered a stroke. A search of the available literature from 1987 to present day resulted in a review of 18 publications on Operation Enduring Freedom/Operation Iraqi Freedom caregivers and 19 publications on caregivers of Veterans with stroke. We summarize empirical findings, critique the study methods, and provide our recommendations to improve the quality of care of Veterans and their caregivers.

http://dx.doi.org/10.1891/0739-6686.32.155

INTRODUCTION

Family caregivers play a critical role in our society by providing financial contributions, emotional support, and a substantial proportion of the physical care that helps maintain the well-being of our injured, chronically ill, and aged populations. These contributions, although often rewarding, are taxing and typically exert a toll on the caregivers' own health and well-being. Although all caregivers face challenges, caregivers of Veterans are unique because they must contend with the circumstances of war, deployment, severe injury, and greater health risks than the general population. Veteran care recipients also have lower incomes, higher rates of chronic disease, more comorbid conditions, and poorer health status than their counterparts. Unsurprisingly, caregivers of Veterans report a heightened impact of caregiving on their lives than caregivers in general (National Alliance for Caregiving, 2010).

Family caregiving for Veterans, once a silent, overlooked phenomenon, has entered the realm of public policy and debate with the 2009 Secretary of Veterans' Affairs strategic plan and the passage of the Caregivers and Omnibus Health Services Act of 2010 (National Alliance for Caregiving, 2010). Along with these initiatives, the Veterans Health Administration (VHA) has increased efforts to provide better support for family caregivers (Lynn, 2014). The VHA is the largest centralized health care system in the United States consisting of medical centers, ambulatory care and community-based outpatient clinics, Veterans centers, nursing homes, residential treatment programs, and comprehensive home-based care programs. In recent years, the VHA has undergone organizational restructuring, implemented performance measures targeted to improving quality of care, and the increased use of health information technology. Consequently, the numbers of Veterans served and the ratings of quality of care and customer satisfaction have improved (Congressional Budget Office, 2007). One of the greatest transformations in the VHA has been the implementation of the VHA patient-centered home model, now known as the *Patient Aligned Care Team* (PACT). In this model, the patient is the center of the health care team that includes family members, caregivers, and health care professionals. In addition, the VHA has implemented a comprehensive array of assistance and support services for family caregivers. These services include in-home care, respite care, education and training, financial support, a caregiver telephone support line, an interactive website, support groups, caregiver support coordinators, and a peer mentoring program (Johnson, 2013).

The importance of research that evaluates these new caregiving initiatives and investigates the experiences of caregivers of Veterans cannot be underestimated. In this review, we discuss the results, strengths, and limitations of prior research related to caregiving of Veterans. We focus this review on caregivers of Operation Enduring Freedom (OEF)/Operation Iraqi Freedom (OIF) Veterans and Veterans with stroke, respectively, because their similarities and differences allow for a broader view of Veteran caregiving research than a review focused on a single group. Whereas research on caregivers of OEF/OIF Veterans is a new and emerging area, studies on caregivers of Veterans with stroke have been ongoing for many years. Because of generational and sociodemographic differences between OEF/OIF Veterans and Veterans with stroke, the resources and values of the caregivers of these two populations vary considerably. On the other hand, caregivers of OEF/OIF Veterans and Veterans with stroke are often dealing with similar issues that result when a Veteran suffers a brain injury, whether it is because of war trauma or a cerebrovascular problem. Our goal is to summarize the empirical findings, critically review the studies, and provide recommendations for research to improve the quality of care of Veterans and their caregivers.

Methods

This is a critical review of research literature on caregivers of two Veteran populations: Veterans with stroke and OEF/OIF Veterans. We chose Veterans with stroke and OEF/OIF Veterans because they represent significant populations that use considerable health care resources in the U.S. Department of Veterans Affairs (VA). Articles were found by searching large bibliographic health science databases, PubMed and Cumulative Index to Nursing and Allied Health Literature (CINAHL). We searched the VA's Health Services Research and Development (HSR&D) database to identify VA-funded studies and ClinicalTrials.gov to identify completed intervention studies. We also manually selected articles based on our knowledge of experts in the field of stroke and OEF/OIF caregiving.

Articles were included for consideration if they included in the sample the following three criteria: (a) "caregiver," "spouse," or "family"; (b) informal care of persons at any stage of military service such as "National Guard," "active duty," "service member," or "Veteran"; and (c) caregivers of persons with stroke, traumatic brain injury (TBI), or posttraumatic stress disorder (PTSD). Studies that broadly focused on families were included if they specifically sampled OEF/OIF Veterans and their family members. Additional inclusion criteria for articles included English language studies of adults (18 years and older), empirical studies, implementation studies, trials, conference presentations, or critical literature reviews. We reviewed research published in the last 30 years; the final pool of articles from the databases spanned from 1987 to 2014. We imported articles into the EndNote Reference Library software for citation management; 105 of these articles make up the bulk of our bibliography.

Our preliminary search included the terms *caregivers* and *Veterans* using PubMed, CINAHL, Academic Search Premier, and Google Scholar. This search produced a large pool of citations, so we decided to narrow our search terms.

A final set of searches was performed in PubMed and CINAHL using three search strategies. The first search strategy yielded 44 citations from the terms "caregivers" OR "family" AND "Veterans" OR "military" AND "stroke." The second search strategy yielded 125 citations using the terms "caregivers" OR "family" AND "Veterans" OR "military" AND "PTSD" OR "TBI." The final search strategy yielded 32 citations using the terms "caregivers" OR "family" AND "Veterans" OR "military" AND "OEF/OIF." We searched *M*edical *S*ubject *H*eading (MeSH) terms in the PubMed database and searched keyword terms in the CINAHL database.

FAMILY CAREGIVERS OF OEF/OIF VETERANS

Background

Since the war in Afghanistan began in 2001, more than 2 million men and women have been deployed in OIF/OEF (Tanielian et al., 2013). OEF and OIF together make up the longest sustained U.S. military operation in American history and have created the largest cohort of Veterans from an all-volunteer military (National Research Council, 2010). For many of the men and women who served during this period, returning home is a period of stress and turmoil (Sayers, Farrow, Ross, & Oslin, 2009). This stress occurs in the context of how the United States deploys its troops. The conflicts in Iraq and Afghanistan have seen a higher proportion of the armed forces deployed overseas. As a result, this is the first time in U.S. history that members of the National Guard and Reserve units have faced the hazards of the combat zone (National Research Council, 2010). Likewise, service members have endured multiple deployments that have been longer and with shorter time at home between deployments (Hosek, Kavanagh, & Laura, 2006). Fortunately, advances in both medical technology and body armor have led to increased survival rates and lower casualties during these deployments (Okie, 2005; Warden, 2006). At the same time, the injuries that do occur are multiple and severe in nature, requiring long-term caregiving support (Tanielian et al., 2013). These unique characteristics and circumstances impose a new set of changes and challenges that negatively impact not only the care receiver but also their family caregivers who bear the brunt of the Veterans' conditions.

Research has shown that family caregivers of Veterans from the recent conflicts differ from caregivers in the general population. Demographically, these caregivers are typically younger and more likely than civilian caregivers to live with the person for whom they care (National Alliance for Caregiving, 2010). Unlike caregivers from previous eras (World War I, World War II, Korea, or Vietnam), most OEF/OIF caregivers are individuals with young children (Tanielian et al., 2013). Spouses represent most OEF/OIF Veteran caregivers, and about 1 in 4 is apparent. These demographics and the unique circumstances such as multiple deployments, type of combat injury, and the military institution itself create a special group—what some have called *OEF/OIF caregivers* (Tanielian et al., 2013). OEF/OIF caregivers are unique because they grapple with having a Veteran with invisible wounds of war such as PTSD and severe physical injuries such as TBI; lack of coordination between health care systems (Department of Defense [DoD], VA, private providers); and the need for providing continuous care throughout the day and across the life span (Tanielian et al., 2013). As a result, more OEF/OIF caregivers report higher ratings of emotional stress than caregivers nationally (National Alliance for Caregiving, 2010).

Our review centers on two "signature injuries" of the Iraq and Afghanistan wars, TBI and PTSD (Warden, 2006). These injuries affect about 30% of service members from the recent conflicts (Tanielian & Jaycox, 2008). PTSD and TBI have also been described as "invisible wounds" because they are concealed by Veterans themselves or unseen by those untrained or ill equipped to detect them (Waddell & Orr, 2013). We will attempt to differentiate between these two conditions while also describing how they overlap. Military TBI occurs as a direct result of changes in atmospheric pressure, objects put in motion by the blast, or by individuals themselves hitting something like the inside of a military vehicle (Warden, 2006). The DoD notes that most TBI in military personnel is mild in severity (Sayer, 2012; U.S. Department of Defense, Defense and Veterans Brain Injury Center, 2014). Veterans with TBI of any severity level, however, exhibit postconcussive symptoms such as memory, concentration, and attention deficits; irritability, anxiety, and depression; and fatigue, disordered sleep, headache, and dizziness (American Congress of Rehabilitation Medicine, 1993; Sayer, 2012).

PTSD is an anxiety disorder resulting from exposure to traumatic events. A person may reexperience the traumatic event; avoid people, places, or feelings that remind them of the event; or feel "on edge" (Force Health Protection & Readiness Policy and Programs, 2014). Although persons with PTSD are unable to forget a traumatic memory, those with a TBI are unable to recall the traumatic event. That said, PTSD and TBI share a subset of symptoms, and the extent to which these disorders are distinct is a subject of debate (Hoge et al., 2008). In addition, research findings offer an inconclusive picture about the prevalence of these two seemingly different conditions (King, 2008; Klein, Caspi, & Gil, 2003). Reports indicate that the rate of PTSD and other psychiatric disorders among Iraq and Afghanistan Veterans is similar to the rate of TBI and that about 33%–44% of those with mild TBI may also have PTSD and/or depression (Hoge et al., 2008; Sayers et al., 2009; Tanielian & Jaycox, 2008). Unfortunately, the exact incidence and prevalence of deployment-related TBI is difficult to detect because of misdiagnosis or lack of immediate medical attention

(Sayers et al., 2009). What is most important and the focus of our review is the shared circumstances that PTSD and TBI caregivers face as a group. In light of the high prevalence of these injuries among the Veteran population and the cluster of behavioral, cognitive, and physical symptoms associated with them, researchers seek to understand how these conditions affect the lives of Veterans and their caregivers.

Results of Research Strategy

We conducted two searches in our section: one on OEF/OIF PTSD/TBI Veterans and caregivers and another on OEF/OIF Veterans and families. We integrate these studies in our writing because in the literature it is not always clear the difference between families and caregivers. Our review of the literature on caregivers of injured (PTSD and/or TBI) OEF/OIF Veterans includes 18 reports, articles, abstracts, and ongoing trials related to this population. Table 8.1 describes the results of our search by study design. We reviewed 5 comparative cross-sectional studies, 2 cross-sectional studies, 3 qualitative studies, 1 prospective cohort study, 1 critical literature review, 2 intervention studies, and 4 implementation science studies. Most research on caregivers of OEF/OIF Veterans falls into three broad themes: research that seeks to understand (a) the needs and experiences of OEF/OIF caregivers, and (b) risk and protective factors for family relationship strain after war trauma, and (c) emerging evidence-based interventions, and (d) implementation research. These themes are not discrete and overlap to the extent that researchers often address two or more themes within the same study. In the following paragraphs, we evaluate research documenting the impact of the OEF/OIF conflicts on caregivers and family relationships. Then we describe emerging interventions and implementation science studies that aim to help caregivers, Veterans, and families as a whole.

Needs and Experiences of Caregivers of OEF/OIF Veterans

Some of the first studies on OEF/OIF caregivers attempted to understand caregiver needs and problems. Basic caregiver concepts such as demographic characteristics, time spent on care, stress, mental health, and service needs were investigated using quantitative, qualitative, and mixed methods approaches. One study, called the Family and Caregiver Experiences Survey explored the needs and health impact of caregiving for OEF/OIF Veterans with TBI/PTSD. The goal of Griffin et al.'s research was to identify caregiver needs but also create a focused policy agenda on how to address them (Griffin, Friedemann-Sánchez, Hall, Phelan, & van Ryn, 2009; Griffin et al., 2012). Caregivers were asked about their care and support needs after their Veteran's acute rehabilitation and beyond (anywhere from 3 months to several years postinjury). The study involved a national, cross-sectional sample of 564 caregivers of U.S. service members

TABLE 8.1
OEF/OIF Families and Caregivers Studies

Author/Year/Title	Methods	Major Findings
Critical Literature Reviews		
Friedmann-Sanchez et al. (2012) "Communicating Information to Families of Polytrauma Patients: A Narrative Literature Review"	**Inclusion criteria:** TBI family caregivers information or educational needs; caregiver-provider communication strategies; communication content; or timing of receipt and delivery of information	A common theme across all research was caregivers' need for a clear understanding of a loved one's physical and cognitive condition. Polytrauma rehabilitation providers need more information on what families need to know, ways to deliver info, and when to deliver it.
Cross-Sectional Studies		
"National Alliance for Caregiving (2010) Caregivers of Veterans—Serving on the Homefront"	**Sample:** Self-identified family caregivers who provide care to a veteran whose injury, illness, or condition is related to military service ($n = 462$); 44% of sample were OEF/OIF caregivers **Approach:** Online survey **Main variables:** Caregiver and veteran characteristics; care activities and burden; mental and physical impact of caregiving; support service use; impact of caregiving on work; impact on caregiver's marriage	Findings illustrate the unique needs of caregivers of veterans in general and OEF/OIF caregivers in particular. General findings indicate that veteran care is a woman's issue and that caregivers of veterans have a greater care burden than caregivers of nonveterans.

(Continued)

TABLE 8.1
OEF/OIF Families and Caregivers Studies (Continued)

Author/Year/Title	Methods	Major Findings
Eaton et al. (2008) "Prevalence of Mental Health Problems, Treatment Need, and Barriers to Care Among Primary Care-Seeking Spouses of Military Service Members Involved in Iraq and Afghanistan Deployments"	**Sample:** Convenience sample of spouses of husbands deployed to Iraq or Afghanistan ($n = 940$) **Approach:** Paper survey at primary care clinic visits on a military base **Main variables:** Mental health status; alcohol or family problems; barriers to mental health care; care utilization rates	Spouses were more likely to seek care for mental health problems and were less concerned with stigma than were soldiers.
Comparative Cross-Sectional Studies		
Carlson et al. (2012) "Caregiver Reports of Subsequent Injuries Among Veterans With Traumatic Brain Injury After Discharge From Inpatient Polytrauma Rehabilitation Programs"	**Sample:** Caregivers of veterans discharged from VA Polytrauma Rehabilitation Centers (PRC) from 2001 to 2009 ($n = 564$) **Approach:** Cross-sectional mailed survey **Main variables:** Accidents/injuries after discharge from PRC; patient demographics, TBI severity level, injury type, health status postdischarge, caregiver mental and physical health were independent variables	Authors reported that a third of the veteran sample incurred injury after discharge (falls, car accidents). Caregiver physical and mental health were associated with patients' odds of subsequent injury.

Griffin et al. (2014) "Resources and Coping Strategies Among Caregivers of Operation Iraqi Freedom (OIF) and Operation Enduring Freedom (OEF) Veterans with Polytrauma and Traumatic Brain Injury"	**Sample:** Caregivers of veterans discharged from VA Polytrauma Rehabilitation Centers from 2001 to 2009 ($n = 564$) **Approach:** Cross-sectional mailed survey **Main variables:** Caregiver social support and loneliness; care relationship; family, financial, and internal resources; care relationship was the independent variable (spousal or parental)	Spouses had fewer social and family resources than parents. Parents had higher incomes and better family functioning but less access to health insurance than spouses. Spousal caregivers lacked many resources that could help them manage stress from caregiving.
Block et al. (2014) "Assessment of Veteran and Caregiver Knowledge About Mild Traumatic Brain Injury in a VA Medical Center"	**Sample:** Veterans ($n = 100$) and friends/family caregivers ($n = 50$) **Approach:** Cross-sectional survey **Main variables:** General brain injury knowledge	This study was one of the first to assess veterans' knowledge of consequences of mild TBI. The authors found areas of need within TBI education for veterans and their family members.
Renshaw et al. (2008) "Psychological Symptoms and Marital Satisfaction in Spouses of Operation Iraqi Freedom Veterans: Relationships with Spouses' Perceptions of Veterans' Experiences and Symptoms"	**Sample:** Partner dyads from the National Guard and Reserve ($n = 49$) **Approach:** Survey questionnaires 3 months after soldiers returned from Iraq **Main variables:** PTSD checklist; depression; combat exposure, spouse perception, relationship satisfaction	It is possible to assess spouse's perceptions of soldier's combat exposure, PTSD symptoms, and depressive symptoms. These perceptions were more strongly related to the spouse's own psychological and marital functioning than the soldier's own self-report.
Caska & Renshaw (2011) "Perceived Burden in Spouses of National Guard/Reserve Service Members Deployed During Operation Enduring and Iraqi Freedom"	**Sample:** Partner dyads from the National Guard and Reserve ($n = 130$) **Approach:** Cross-sectional survey completed in person during a marriage education workshop **Main variables:** Spouses perceived burden	Spousal perceptions of burden are significantly associated with partners' symptom severity.

(Continued)

TABLE 8.1
OEF/OIF Families and Caregivers Studies (Continued)

Author/Year/Title	Methods	Major Findings
Qualitative Studies		
Hayes et al. (2010) "Identification of Domains and Measures for Assessment Battery to Examine Well-Being of Spouses of OIF/OEF Veterans With PTSD"	**Sample:** Expert panel and qualitative interviews with caregivers of veterans with PTSD (n = 7) **Approach:** Focus groups and expert panel teleconferences **Main variables:** Caregiver burden, health status, mental health, marital/parental conflict, social support, quality of life, and role reversal	Findings suggest that spouses of OEF/OIF veterans experience considerable difficulty in handling all the demands placed on them (i.e., wife, care partner, employee, mother) and that any spousal assessment instruments should include the full spectrum of these demands. Spouses strongly recommended that an instrument to assess veteran–child relations be included.
Freytes et al. (2013) "The Impact of War on Puerto Rican Families: Challenges and Strengthened Family Relationships"	**Sample:** PR OEF/OIF veterans (n = 8) and family members (n = 8) **Approach:** Two focus groups were conducted—one with veterans and one with family members **Main variable:** Family functioning	Veterans and family members reported both negative and positive impacts of war on family functioning. Negative impact included changes in the deployed veterans, shifts in relationships, the veteran's difficulty transitioning to civilian life, lack of shared experiences, and lack of recognition of hard work and sacrifices. Positive impact included strengthened family relationships and renewed appreciation for family.

Hannold et al. (2011) "Unmet Health Services Needs Experienced by Puerto Rican OEF/OIF Veterans and Families Post Deployment"	**Sample:** PR OEF/OIF veterans (n = 8) and family members (n = 8) **Approach:** Two focus groups were conducted—one with veterans and one with family members **Main variable:** Postdeployment health services needs	Veterans reported unmet health services needs including psychological evaluations, mental health services, support groups, medical evaluations, and pain treatment. Family members reported a need for family support groups.
Prospective Cohort Studies		
McNulty (2013) "Adaptability and Resiliency of Military Families During Reunification: Results of a Longitudinal Study"	**Sample:** Spouses of Army active duty and Army reserve members (n = 455) **Approach:** Spouses interviewed 3 months before and 3, 6, and 12 months after reunification using quantitative and qualitative methods **Main variables:** Family adaptability, resilience, well-being; spouses self-reported stress, anxiety, and psychological health	Spouses who were younger and had children living at home were at greatest risk for poor family resiliency and adaptation. Ten percent of the couples in the sample divorced over the course of the study.
Intervention Studies		
Fischer et al. (2013) "Outcomes of Participation in the REACH Multifamily Group Program for Veterans with PTSD and Their Families"	**Sample:** Veterans with PTSD (n = 100) and family members (n = 96) **Approach:** Longitudinal evaluation of 9-month REACH program; participants completed self-report measures four times throughout the program **Main variables:** Relationship distress, satisfaction, social support, symptom status, quality of life	Family members showed statistically significant improvements on most measures. Study results suggest that multifamily group psychoeducation is useful in treatment of PTSD, leading to increases in targeted PTSD knowledge and skills, as well as improving family functioning and symptom status for both veterans and family members.

(Continued)

TABLE 8.1
OEF/OIF Families and Caregivers Studies (Continued)

Author/Year/Title	Methods	Major Findings
Sautter et al. (2011) "A Couple-Based Approach to the Reduction of PTSD Avoidance Symptoms: Preliminary Findings"	**Sample:** Veterans with PTSD and their partners ($n = 6$) **Approach:** Nonexperimental design testing for a reduction in PTSD symptoms after 10 sessions of Strategic Approach Therapy (SAT) **Main variables:** Reductions in clinician-rated and self-reported PTSD	Data from this preliminary study support the hypothesis that SAT is associated with significant reductions in PTSD symptoms like avoidance and emotional numbing, in addition to reducing overall PTSD severity.
Dissemination and Implementation Science Studies		
Uphold et al. (2008) "Community Reintegration and Puerto Rican OEF/OIF Veterans and Families"	**Sample:** Two focus groups—one with OEF/OIF veterans ($n = 19$) and another with providers from the VA and from veteran service organizations ($n = 12$) **Approach:** A CBPR approach was used to guide this project. It consisted of three main components: (a) analysis of existing educational materials and findings from a previous study, (b) formative evaluation using focus groups to pilot test 12 fact sheets and identify best dissemination and implementation strategies, and (c) revisions to the fact sheets. **Main variables:** Postdeployment needs of OEF/OIF veterans and families and dissemination strategies	Twelve culturally relevant fact sheets were specifically developed for PR OEF/OIF veterans and families to facilitate their postdeployment readjustment. Study participants underscore the importance of developing educational materials specifically for the PR population, written in PR Spanish, with culturally relevant pictures and graphics.

Uphold et al. (2010) "Improving Community Reintegration of OEF/OIF Veterans and Families Living in Puerto Rico Through Printed and Web-Based Education"	**Sample:** Focus groups—one with OEF/OIF veterans ($n = 9$) and one with providers ($n = 11$) to evaluate the effectiveness of the booklet **Approach:** A CBPR approach was used to guide this project. It consisted of three main components: (a) using findings from a previous study to package fact sheets into a booklet format; (b) collaboration with partners to disseminate booklet throughout various efforts; and (c) summative evaluation consisting of telephone interviews with partners, a focus group with veterans, and a short survey. **Main variables:** Dissemination; providers' and veteran's perceptions about the PR booklet; booklet's effectiveness	An educational booklet for PR OEF/OIF veterans and their families that included 13 fact sheets, a resource list, information about My Health*e*Vet, and a personal health record. Almost 14,000 guides were disseminated.

(Continued)

TABLE 8.1
OEF/OIF Families and Caregivers Studies (Continued)

Author/Year/Title	Methods	Major Findings
Uphold et al. (2012) "Unmet Needs of OEF/OIF/OND Veterans and Their Families Living in the U.S. Virgin Islands"	**Sample:** Four focus groups—two with OEF/OIF veterans (n = 33) and the two with providers from the VA and from veteran service organizations (n = 11) **Approach:** A CBPR approach was used to guide this project. There were two main components: (a) a formative evaluation consisting of a focus group with veterans and another one with providers to identify the needs of the USVI population and best dissemination strategies and (b) a summative evaluation consisting of a focus group with veterans and another one with providers to determine the effectiveness of booklet and dissemination strategies **Main variables:** Postdeployment needs of OEF/OIF veterans and families; dissemination; providers' and veteran's perceptions about the USVI booklet; booklet's effectiveness	An educational booklet for USVI OEF/OIF veterans and their families that included 18 fact sheets, a resource list, information about My Health*e*Vet, a personal health record, and information for veterans' employers. Nine-hundred fifty guides were disseminated.
Straits-Troster et al. (2013) "Multifamily Group Treatment for Veterans With Traumatic Brain Injury: What is the Value to Participants?"	**Sample:** Three focus groups with OEF/OIF veterans with TBI (n = 8) and family members (n = 8) **Approach:** Focus groups with veterans and their family members to discuss their perceptions about a multifamily psychoeducation intervention **Main variables:** Problems before and during the intervention; helpful aspects of the intervention; and intervention improvements	Findings supported the feasibility and acceptability of multifamily group treatment for TBI and identified areas of improvement for the intervention and recommendations for implementation.

Note. CBPR = Community-based participatory research; PTSD = posttraumatic stress disorder; PR = Puerto Rican; REACH = Reaching Out to Educate and Assist Caring, Healthy Families; TBI = traumatic brain injury; USVI = U.S. Virgin Islands; VA = U.S. Department of Veterans Affairs.

discharged from four VA Polytrauma Rehabilitation Centers (Minneapolis, Palo Alto, Richmond, and Tampa) from 2001 to 2009 (Griffin, 2009). Veterans with multiple, severe wounds enter these Centers for specialized, intense rehabilitation care. The first pool of participants completed a mailed survey; 16 caregivers were then purposively sampled for in-depth interviews. Griffin et al. found that most of these caregivers were female and parents who worked more than 8 hr a day on a task related to the Veteran's care, such as managing emotions, keeping track of medical expenses, and navigating the health system (Carlson et al., 2012; Griffin et al., 2012). The good news from this survey was that one-third of family members reported that the survivor no longer required care. The strength of Griffin et al.'s work is improved knowledge on the kinds of care required, the characteristics of the OEF/OIF caregiver population, and the challenges of rehabilitation in the short and long term. The weaknesses include omitting secondary caregiver perspectives, a reliance on caregivers' proxy reports on the Veterans' injury, and lack of follow-up. The investigators intended to create a cohort of caregivers that could be followed longitudinally postrehabilitation, but they are currently limited to cross-sectional findings.

To contextualize the research on needs and barriers, researchers have also compared the needs of caregivers with those of nonveteran caregivers. One national study, "Caregivers of Veterans: Serving on the Homefront" (National Alliance for Caregiving, 2010), surveyed two groups of caregivers: 462 Veteran caregivers and 1,307 caregivers of adults nationally. Forty-four percent of the former group was OEF/OIF caregivers. The latter group participated in an online survey, and these results were compared to an existing dataset from the National Alliance for Caregiving. Focus groups and telephone interviews were conducted to guide development of the online survey questionnaire, but surveys were not psychometrically tested. Because the researchers examined OEF/OIF caregiver needs, findings bolster Griffin et al.'s (2009) conclusions about higher levels of care burden and stress among this group. Veteran caregivers compared to non-veteran caregivers had poor outcomes on various indicators (length in caregiving role, daily time spent caregiving, sleep deprivation, and healthy behavior). The top challenges facing the Veteran caregivers included not knowing what to expect with the Veteran's condition, not being aware of VA services that could help, not knowing how to address PTSD or mental illness, and difficulty getting through bureaucracies to receive services. This study was simply a descriptive account of caregiving that did not test any measures of association and only reported simple frequencies and proportions. Although the study was important for highlighting the problems of OEF/OIF caregivers as a special caregiving group, it is difficult to draw firm conclusions about differences between caregiving populations from two separate datasets.

Subsequent research on OEF/OIF caregiver needs during rehabilitation has emerged since Griffin et al.'s (2009) study, albeit with much less rigor and fewer national samples. For example, researchers have examined family needs during the rehabilitation process. Wilder Schaaf et al.'s (2013) study, involving a survey of 44 family members at a single VA Polytrauma Rehabilitation Center, found a need for instrumental and emotional support for the caregiver during and after rehabilitation. Although they rated providers highly on delivering injury-related information, caregivers had few extended family or friends who understood what they were going through. The investigators cautioned against further conclusions in light of their small sample size. Along similar lines, but with a different Veteran population, Hannold, Freytes, and Uphold (2011) conducted 16 interviews (8 Veterans and 8 family members residing in Puerto Rico) to examine the perceptions of unmet health services needs among native Puerto Rican (PR) OEF/OIF Veterans and families postdeployment. Veterans' unmet health services needs included psychological evaluations, mental health services, support groups, medical evaluations, and pain treatment. Family members reported a need for family support groups. Similar to others, the team found that denial and stigma had a negative impact on Veterans' willingness to seek mental health treatment. Although a strength of this study is its focus on a neglected population, study findings may not be comparable to other cases and contexts because the sample only included Veterans and family members from a small geographic area in Puerto Rico.

The need for TBI education has also been a focus of researchers who argue that raising awareness of mild TBI among service members would improve TBI identification and management. Block et al. (2014) assessed knowledge about mild TBI from a convenience sample of 100 unexposed Veterans and 50 caregivers using a 60-item questionnaire examining TBI symptoms and misconceptions. The Veteran and caregiver groups demonstrated equal levels of TBI knowledge, but both groups had difficulties identifying true TBI symptoms. Although Wilder Schaff et al. (2013) and Block et al.'s (2014) findings make useful contributions to the literature, they appear to lack a cohesive research or policy agenda that is present in Griffin et al.'s (2009, 2012) work. It is also difficult to draw firm conclusions about Veteran caregiver experience from studies with small, regional sample sizes.

Eaton and colleagues (2008) conducted one of the first studies on the prevalence of mental health problems and needs among a group of OEF/OIF spouses seeking primary care at a large U.S. military base in 2003. Spouses were recruited from the primary care clinics that serve soldiers, spouses, and children. The authors note that mental health services for spouses were not available at this base clinic but outsourced to professionals in the wider community. The survey focused on past symptoms of depression and anxiety, health care use, and barriers to mental health services. Nine hundred and forty spouses completed the survey, and the majority had husbands who were deployed to the Middle East. The sample was not representative of the population of military spouses but likely representative of primary care–seeking spouses involved in the particular combat deployments at the time. About 20% of the sample reported that stress and emotional problems were having a significant effect on their lives, which was, the authors note, about the same rate for soldiers returning from combat. Many spouses reported practical reasons for not seeking mental health care, such as difficulty taking time off work or affordability of services. However, if they did seek mental health care, they used their primary care physician on the military base. Unfortunately, the authors neither assessed the adequacy of mental health services that these primary care physicians provided, nor did important follow-up to see if mental health status changed when soldiers returned home.

Hayes and colleagues (2010) conducted a needs assessment of OEF/OIF caregivers of Veterans with PTSD to develop an assessment battery for assessing spousal well-being. They gathered input on needs using two methods: an expert panel featuring members knowledgeable about war, trauma, and families; and two focus groups with seven spouses of OEF/OIF Veterans with PTSD at a Midwest VA Medical Center. The expert panel discussed, reviewed, and rated the instruments for assessing caregiver burden during teleconference meetings. The panel created a battery of instruments to share with Veteran spouses in the focus group. Focus groups discussed ongoing issues related to care and the panel's caregiver instruments. Spousal caregivers reported that some of their biggest challenges were finding personal time, juggling multiple roles (wife, care partner, employee, mother), receiving social support from in-laws, and shielding children from the emotional trauma of a parent's PTSD. Spouses also questioned their ability to provide a lifetime of support and wondered how long they could continue providing it. Based on caregiver responses, Hayes and her team selected the most valid and reliable assessment tools for screening caregivers on their well-being and unmet needs. In addition to the small sample size, the study was also limited by lack of implementation. Hayes et al. intended to test the instruments in practice for VA outreach and mental health service use, but they, like many other researchers on needs of this population, did not take this crucial next step.

Risk and Protective Factors for Family Relationship Strain

A second theme uncovered in our review of the literature was the disruption of family relationships, particularly the negative impact on the spousal caregiver. For example, family trauma researchers used multiple regression or longitudinal data analyses to test the associations between combat exposure, mental health problems, family functioning, and intimate relationships in the OEF/OIF population. Family resiliency, or why certain families adapt well to stress while others do not, is a particularly salient line of inquiry among researchers concerned with family functioning. Researchers from various disciplines have documented the psychological consequences of PTSD symptoms in OEF/OIF Veterans (e.g., impaired decision making, irritability, memory loss, sleep problems, or intrusive traumatic memories). These symptoms appear to exacerbate family stress, burden, poor psychological adjustment in Veteran partners, and poor caregiver mental health (Gewirtz, Erbes, Polusny, Forgatch, & Degarmo, 2011; Milliken, Auchterlonie, & Hoge, 2007; Price & Stevens, 2014; Taft, Walling, Howard, & Monson, 2011).

Caregivers, usually referred to as *intimate partners* in this literature, find that their partner has become a different person after returning home from the war. This fact is important because couple conflict can dissolve the primary support system that the Veteran needs to recover—the family. Thus, couple interaction and adaptation to injury and trauma is an area of concern for researchers. Renshaw, Rodrigues, and Jones (2008) investigated caregiver burden among spouses of returning OEF/OIF National Guard soldiers with PTSD. In their first study, Renshaw et al. sampled 49 partner dyads from a National Guard unit that was deployed to Iraq for 1 year. The authors did not report how couples were approached for participation. Couples were asked to rate their relationship satisfaction, combat exposure, and spousal perceptions of husband's symptoms and experiences. The study explored how spouses react to the presence of PTSD among partners returning from war. For example, wives reported more relationship strain if they believed their husbands had low levels of combat exposure but high PTSD symptoms. In other words, perceptions of combat experiences and differences in illness attribution appeared to play a role in marital discord. This study was limited by its focus on National Guard soldiers who only had one deployment, its small sample size, and no assessment of spousal psychological trauma. Caska and Renshaw (2011) then assessed spouses' perceived burden of caring for their husbands (National Guard/Reserve members) who reported PTSD symptoms. There were 130 spouses/partners included in the study. The authors did not report statistics on the number of deployments within their sample. Their main finding was that spousal perceptions of burden were significantly associated with partners' symptom severity. However, service members' symptoms accounted for less than 10% of the variance in spousal burden and the authors did not examine extraneous factors. Renshaw and colleagues' (2008) work is important for examining the role spousal characteristics might play in perceived burden associated with PTSD caregiving, but their studies relied on small samples of all male service members, self-reports, and cross-sectional designs.

Along the same lines, Freytes, Hannold, Resende, Wing, and Uphold (2013) examined the impact of war on PR Veterans and their families. They conducted in-depth interviews with returning OEF/OIF Veterans residing in Puerto Rico (n= 8) and family members (n = 8). The Veterans and family members included in this study were not related to one another. The team used the constant comparative method to code the data. They uncovered two broad categories: challenges associated with postdeployment family reintegration and the positive aftermath of war on the family. The first category included five themes: (a) changes in the person who was deployed, (b) shifts in relationships, (c) the Veteran's difficulty transitioning to civilian life, (d) lack of shared experiences between Veteran and family members, and (e) lack of recognition of Veterans and family members' hard work and sacrifices. These themes show that Veterans and family members experienced added stress and challenges that hindered their family reintegration process. Conversely, the themes that emerged from the second category were: (a) strengthened family relationships and (b) renewed family appreciation. Like most studies we have discussed, this one also suffers from a non-representative small sample. However, unlike other studies, this examination provides a starting point for understanding the postdeployment process of a population that has not received much attention, PR Veterans and family members.

Although most research on OEF/OIF caregivers used cross-sectional designs, VA nurse researcher McNulty (2010, 2013) led the first national, longitudinal study on adaptability and resiliency of spouses before and after their husband's deployment, or what she calls "separation" and "reunification." She explored protective and risk factors for experiencing problems after deployment among 455 family members of OEF/OIF service members. Mailed surveys were administered and open-ended telephone interviews were conducted at 3 months before separation and 3, 6, and 12 months after reunification. About two-thirds of this sample consisted of spouses of active duty service members. Participants completed questionnaires assessing family adaptability, resilience, well-being, and the spouse's self-reported stress, anxiety, and mental health. Results showed "alarmingly high" levels of poor resiliency and adaptation before separation, suggesting that these families began the study with high level of family dysfunction. McNulty found that once the honeymoon phase of reunification ended, spouses dealt with increased stress that did not rise to the surface until many months later. Spouses confronted PTSD stigma, delays in diagnosis, and lack of proper treatment for service members when they returned home. The situation at home remained so chaotic and dysfunctional that 10% of the sample divorced during the study duration. McNulty's work is important because it is the first to analyze family problems over time, but the study suffered from two weaknesses. First, because of study attrition (more than half of participants did not complete all phases of the study), the spouses who needed the most help were not included in the sample. Second, causes or associations between risk factors and family outcomes were not clearly articulated or identified, nor was intimate partner violence explored. What is clear from McNulty's study is that families are struggling; how this knowledge has made a tangible impact on caregivers, family adjustment, and prevention of family dysfunction is less clear.

Emerging Evidence-Based Interventions for OEF/OIF Family Caregivers

Research questions within military family policy have shifted within the last 10 years (Flynn, 2014). At the height of the wars in Iraq and Afghanistan, the central question was "What is the impact of deployments on service members and families?" The research described in the previous section is an outgrowth of that question. Currently, the focus has shifted to "What is the impact of interventions and programs on service members and families?" (Flynn, 2014). Interventions that specifically target families of patients with TBI and PTSD are far fewer than for other conditions, such as dementia (Griffin et al., 2014). This does not mean that few programs exist. In fact, the immediacy of family needs at the height of the Iraq and Afghanistan conflicts led to a surge of programming without the means to measure participant outcomes or demonstrate effectiveness (Flynn, 2014). Now that the pace of deployment has slowed, more researchers are subjecting these programs to rigorous scientific scrutiny. Van Houtven, Voils, and Weinberger (2011) suggest that all caregiver interventions should measure a common set of outcomes to facilitate cross-time and cross-study comparisons of effectiveness. They recommend that caregiver interventions assess for quality and quantity of caregiving activities, health care use by the caregiver, and economic status of the family unit. These factors would not only help us understand how well the intervention worked for caregivers but would also explore metrics beyond caregiver burden and the Veteran's health status.

Here we describe interventions to help OEF/OIF Veterans and their families resolve the difficulties they confront postdeployment. Only a handful of researchers have completed interventions and published their results. Sautter, Armelie, Glynn, and Wielt (2011) applied strategic approach therapy (SAT) to target the avoidance/numbing symptoms of PTSD. This therapy uses empathetic communication training to help couples improve their ability to cope with trauma-related anxiety. Findings from six Veteran couples who completed the intervention include significant improvements in these symptoms according to patient, partner, and clinician ratings. Fischer and her team tested Reaching Out to Educate and Assist Caring, Healthy Families (REACH; Fischer, Sherman, Han, & Owen, 2013). REACH is a 9-month, three-phase clinical program for Veterans and their families that employs single- and multi-family sessions. One hundred Veterans with PTSD and 96 family members participated in the program. Results indicated significant improvements over time for Veterans and family members on measures such as empowerment, family problem solving, relationship satisfaction, and social support. Although this publication reports results from a sample of Vietnam Veterans, multifamily group programs are currently being tested for OEF/OIF Veterans with PTSD and their family members. Other intervention studies are ongoing and have not yet reported results. Through our search of ClinicalTrials.gov found, we found several interventions involving topics such as caregiver skills training, family stress and resiliency, improvements to non-VA services for caregivers, and couples therapy.

Implementing Research on OEF/OIF Family Caregivers Into Practice

Dissemination and implementation studies contribute and expand on the knowledge about the impact of interventions and programs. Dissemination research examines how information about interventions or programs is created, packaged, transmitted, and interpreted among stakeholder groups. Implementation is "the use of strategies to adopt and integrate evidence-based health interventions and change practice patterns within specific settings" (Schillinger, 2010). We found four dissemination/implementation studies that focused on OEF/OIF Veterans and families.

Recognizing how culture can shape the postdeployment experience, Uphold and her team conducted three studies on the postdeployment needs of families of Veterans from Puerto Rico (Uphold, Bober, Wing, & Freytes, 2008; Uphold, Freytes, et al., 2010) and the U.S. Virgin Islands (USVI; Uphold, Midolo, et al., 2012). Despite the high numbers of PR and USVI service members who have served in previous and current conflicts, these Veterans have been largely overlooked in both research and professional practice. Community-based participatory research (CBPR) methods were used to identify the unique postdeployment educational needs and preferences of OEF/OIF Veterans and families and develop materials that specifically met their needs.

In the first study, "Education Materials for Puerto Rican Veterans and Their Families," the team reviewed literature and analyzed existing education materials on postdeployment readjustment. They used findings from this analysis of available material and from a previous project to identify the needs of PR OEF/OIF Veterans and families. They developed 12 culturally relevant fact sheets addressing the pre-identified needs. The fact sheets were written in PR Spanish and included PR symbols such as the national flag and the coqui (small frog).

Social marketing techniques, such as consistent branding, eye-catching graphics, and bullets to emphasize main points, were also employed. They conducted two focus groups to pilot test the fact sheets and identify dissemination strategies; one with OEF/OIF Veterans ($n = 19$) and the other one with providers from the VA and from Veteran service organizations ($n = 12$). Findings were used to make modifications to the materials and determine effective dissemination methods. Study findings revealed that both providers and Veterans felt strongly about the importance of educational materials developed specifically for the PR population and written in PR Spanish. Particularly, they liked that the fact sheets unequivocally target PR Veterans and families (i.e., PR flag symbols/colors, coqui). Findings also revealed that the most effective dissemination strategies for this population included disseminating printed materials at the VA hospital, Veterans' service organizations, or events for Veteran and families, as well as promoting the educational materials via traditional media outlets (i.e., radio and television).

The team conducted a second study entitled, "Dissemination Evaluation of Educational Materials for Puerto Rican OIF/OEF Veterans and Families." They used findings from the previous study to make final revisions to the fact sheets and packaged all the education materials in a tabulated booklet format that included 13 fact sheets, a resource list, information about My Health*e*Vet, the VA's online personal health record, and a convenient one-page personal record. Dissemination efforts included disseminating booklets at VA facilities, military and Veteran service organizations, Veteran outreach events, and online via the VA Caribbean Healthcare System's (CHS) website. They used the Re-AIM framework (King, Glasgow, & Leeman-Castillo, 2010) to evaluate the effectiveness of the dissemination efforts. To accomplish this, they tracked the number of booklets disseminated, the dissemination approaches used (i.e., a provider at a clinic, an outreach event, etc.), and kept notes on dissemination barriers and facilitators. Almost 14,000 booklets were disseminated. Events geared to Veterans and families were the most effective for disseminating the booklet.

Using similar methods as in the two aforementioned studies, the team conducted a third study, "Printed and Web-Based OEF/OIF Culturally-Relevant Family Education" to address the needs of OEF/OIF Veterans and their families in another area of the Caribbean—the USVI. The USVI includes three islands—St. Croix, St. Thomas, and St. John. Because the USVI is geographically isolated, it is often overlooked and is one of the most underserved areas in the VA health care system. Collaborating with both VA and non-VA partners (e.g., Veterans' service organizations, government officials), the team created a booklet that specifically addressed the unique needs of this population. From the formative evaluation that included interviews with partners in the USVI and across the VA and two focus groups—one with Veterans (n = 9) and one with providers (n = 7)—they identified 18 topics for the booklet. They found that in the USVI, like in the U.S. mainland, there is high stigma associated with mental illness. Other issues included domestic violence, high unemployment, and the use of substances as a coping mechanism. A notable finding was that because of the small size of the USVI, anonymity is difficult, and therefore, many Veterans choose not to enroll for and access services. Other unique issues in the USVI included a lack of services and poor customer service issues in the two small VA clinics, the challenge of traveling via airplanes to the main medical center in Puerto Rico to receive many needed services, financial concerns, and the perception that the care in Puerto Rico was not culturally relevant to Veterans and families from the USVI. The team promoted the booklets through media coverage including several stories published in the local newspapers and appearances by members of the team in popular radio shows. Nine hundred fifty booklets were disseminated to Veterans and their families at Veteran Service Organizations and National Guard events and through professionals in the VA and the University of the Virgin Islands. The booklet was also available online on the VA CHS website. Focus groups—one with Veterans (n = 24) and one with providers (n = 4)—revealed an overwhelming positive response about the book. Veterans and family members liked the information, and some were motivated to enroll for services.

Perhaps the biggest strength about the work completed by the Uphold team was its focus on a neglected subpopulation of Veterans and families. The team found that using the CBPR approach was key to raising awareness of this overlooked population and to the overall success of this line of study. The main limitation of these studies was a small sample size.

The last implementation study, "Multifamily Group Treatment for Veterans with Traumatic Brain Injury: What is the Value to Participants?" conducted by Straits-Troster and associates (2013) explored the feasibility, acceptability, and helpfulness of implementing a multifamily group for OEF/OIF Veterans with TBI and their families that was conducted at two VA medical centers (Bronx, New York, and Durham, North Carolina). In two focus groups with Veterans (n = 8) and family members (n = 8), program participants reported that they benefitted from the discussions and the information received from the psychoeducation group. Findings supported the feasibility and acceptability of multifamily group treatment for TBI. To improve the effectiveness of the program and increase adoption and participation, Veterans and family members recommended providing opportunities for them to discuss issues specific to each group, and allow more than one family member to enroll in the program (Straits-Troster et al., 2013). This study shows the importance of conducting early program evaluations to detect emergent implementation issues. Study authors caution about the generalizability of their findings in light of the small, all-Army Veteran sample from a small area in the eastern U.S.

These studies show the need for cognizant inclusion of a dissemination and implementation plan in the development and evaluation of clinical interventions. Successful translation of research findings into practice requires early identification of factors that hinder or facilitate not only the intended outcomes of the intervention but also its adoption, implementation, and sustainability. The PR and USVI studies highlighted the need for interventions that are tailored to its intended population and the positive impact of the CBPR approach in the adoption and dissemination of the booklet. The multifamily group treatment study demonstrated how findings can inform improvements at different levels of the intervention.

Recommendations for Future Research on OEF/OIF Caregivers and Families

Broadly speaking, research on the burden of care for OEF/OIF caregivers is an important emerging area of study. Multiple publications have used cross-sectional observational designs to investigate the needs and problems surrounding care for a Veteran or service member with TBI and/or PTSD. Researchers have found that caregivers are strained by the constant vigilance required for managing behavioral symptoms and the advocacy skills needed to navigate VA resources and care. Thanks to these researchers, we have a better understanding of how Veteran injuries drive unique caregiver needs. Surveying this literature, we observe that caregiver needs and barriers are fairly well documented, and we have a clearer picture of the care load and service gaps that family members confront. This knowledge was sorely lacking at the beginning of the OEF/OIF conflicts. Similarly, research focusing on the factors that mediate the relationship between PTSD, depression, war atrocities, caregiver burden, and family dysfunction is also building toward a critical mass.

Despite these strengths, we have several suggestions for researchers who embark on a study of OEF/OIF caregivers. First, implementing findings into practice appears to be a weak point for OEF/OIF caregiver research. Translating existing knowledge into meaningful change on the systemic level should be the next step for this field. Second, we have several methodological considerations. Researchers should opt for fewer cross-sectional study designs in favor of prospective, longitudinal designs that can capture changes in caregiver outcomes. Future researchers should also investigate the strengths and weaknesses of VA programs for OEF/OIF caregivers and how new programs address needs and barriers to services. In addition, the symposium on military family research (Willerton, MacDermid Wadsworth, & Riggs, 2011) recommends using analytic techniques that effectively examine families as systems, as opposed to focusing only on individuals or dyads. Third, we encountered a challenge in reviewing studies on family caregiving and OEF/OIF Veterans with PTSD. This body of literature does not examine "caregivers" by themselves; the focus is instead on "family members," "spouses," and/or Veterans. Collapsing family members and caregivers makes sense from a family systems perspective, but it also creates ambiguity about the daily care tasks and emotion work that usually fall to one person (e.g., the primary caregiver). We recommend more research documenting the "care tasks," which spouses do for both the family and the Veteran with PTSD. Fourth, research on caregivers of Vietnam Veterans with PTSD (Calhoun, Beckham, & Bosworth, 2002; Manguno-Mire et al., 2007) could be linked to the current struggles that OEF/OIF families confront. Integrating the PTSD experience across different generations of Veterans could focus more on the similarities between all military families. Finally, researchers should work together to guarantee a shared vision for the outcomes of their research. With a few exceptions, most studies reviewed here lack of a coherent research agenda, vision, or goal for how findings should be used. Such agendas are always useful for developing future directions for research, practice, and policy.

FAMILY CAREGIVERS OF VETERAN WITH STROKE

Background

Whereas research on OEF/OIF caregivers is a new, emerging area of study, research on caregivers of stroke survivors has been ongoing for many years. There is a breadth of stroke caregiving research that has used quantitative, qualitative, and mixed methods approaches and included observational studies and clinical trials. Most of the published work, however, has not differentiated between caregiving of Veterans versus nonveterans. Thus, our knowledge of differences in sociodemographic characteristics, type of care provided, and experiences between caregivers of Veterans with stroke versus caregivers of nonveterans with stroke is limited. In addition, there is little information on how caregivers of Veterans with stroke navigate or function within the unique and large, integrated VA health care system.

Caregivers of Veterans with stroke have many of the same challenges as caregivers of Veterans with TBI/PTSD and polytrauma. Both caregiver populations face abrupt changes in their roles because of the Veterans' sudden and unexpected brain and physical injuries. Likewise, both populations are forced to deal with multiple physical, social, and mental issues that accompany brain injuries (e.g., speech problems, cognitive decline, poor motor functioning). Unlike caregivers of Veterans with other conditions (e.g., dementia, cancer, heart disease) who usually have inevitable downhill course, caregivers of Veterans with stroke and caregivers of OEF/OIF Veterans are frequently caring for family members who have high potential for rehabilitation and recovery.

On the other hand, there are notable differences between caregivers of Veterans with stroke and caregivers of OEF/OIF Veterans. For example, these two groups have experiential and generational differences. Compared to caregivers of OEF/OIF Veterans, caregivers of Veterans with stroke are usually older and are managing the health of Veterans from the World War II, Korea, and Vietnam eras who have more concomitant chronic diseases, including heart disease, diabetes, and dementia. In addition, the social lives of these groups differ because the caregivers of Veterans with stroke as oppposed to OEF/OIF caregivers are more likely to be retired and have grown, adult children and grandchildren who are available to share in the caregiving responsibilities. And because women did not join the military in a significant numbers until the 1970s, caregivers of Veterans with stroke, in contrast to caregivers of OEF/OIF Veterans, are almost exclusively women.

Characteristics of Strokes and Stroke Caregiving in the General Population

Stroke is the fourth leading cause of death and the major cause of serious, long-term disability in the United States (Miller et al., 2010; Rogers et al., 2012). An alarming fact is that every 40 seconds, an individual in the United States has a stroke (Rogers et al., 2012). In the VA health care system, there were approximately 6,000 admissions or acute ischemic stroke in 2007 (Rogers et al., 2012).

Between 25% and 74% of stroke survivors have residual deficits and require some assistance, whereas other survivors are completely dependent on others for meeting their needs of daily living (Dewey et al., 2002). Family caregivers are the major sources of support for stroke survivors. Unlike other chronic diseases, strokes occur suddenly and caregivers have little time to prepare and adjust to their new roles (Greenwood, Mackenzie, Cloud, & Wilson, 2008). In addition, strokes are often accompanied by functional limitations, cognitive impairments, speech difficulties, swallowing deficits, and urinary incontinence. As a result of these abrupt changes, family caregivers have high rates of depression (Anderson,

Linto, & Stewart-Wynne, 1995; Berg, Palomäki, Lönnqvist, Lehtihalmes, & Kaste, 2005), burden (McCullagh, Brigstocke, Donaldson, & Kalra, 2005), and poor quality of life (Van Puymbroeck & Rittman, 2005). In particular, the first months post-hospital discharge has been identified as the most stressful time because this is when caregivers recognize the full impact of the stroke survivors' disabilities (Bakas et al., 2009; Grant, Weaver, Elliott, Bartolucci, & Newman Giger, 2004). Consequently, national practice guidelines (Miller et al., 2010; The Management of Stroke Rehabilitation Working Group, 2010) urge providers to educate and support *both* stroke survivors and their family caregivers posthospitalization.

VA nurse researcher, Dr. Karen Saban and colleagues, conducted a critical literature review of family caregivers of stroke survivors in the general population (Saban, Sherwood, DeVon, & Hynes, 2010). Using Ovid MEDLINE, PsycINFO, and Ovid Nursing Database for the period of July 1999 through June 2009, the authors found 24 articles. Articles were reviewed if they included measures of stress and physical health or health-related quality of life among adults who were caregiving for an adult who had suffered a stroke. The review found that there were inconsistencies in the instruments and variables studied and that less than half of the studies used a theoretical framework. The authors emphasized the need for additional longitudinal studies to pinpoint time points when caregivers are most vulnerable and in need of intensive interventions and care.

Results of Search Strategy

Although there is a plethora of publications on stroke caregiving in the general population, our review found only 19 publications regarding stroke caregiving in the Veteran population. The designs and methodological approaches were varied, but most researchers used quantitative methods and comparative cross-sectional or prospective designs (see Table 8.2). Most of the publications reported findings that were part of or obtained from three larger, funded VA projects. These large VA projects are described in the next three paragraphs.

The first project was a screening program conducted by VA researcher, Dr. Leslie Gonzalez-Rothi and implemented in the VA Gainesville Brain Research Rehabilitation Research Center. This project was not a research study but rather a program to identify caregivers and stroke patients who were potential candidates for future rehabilitation investigations. In this project, the majority but not all of the stroke patients, was receiving care in a VA facility. Patients were assessed for cognitive and physical functioning with a battery of neuropsychological and activities of daily living instruments and their caregivers completed an array of self-report questionnaires. Tiegs et al. (2006) and Perrin, Heesacker, Stidham, Rittman, and Gonzalez-Rothi's (2008) manuscripts were based on findings from this large project.

TABLE 8.2
Stroke Studies

Author/Year/Title	Methods	Major Findings
Cross-Sectional Studies		
Lutz et al. (2007) "Care Coordination/Home-Telehealth for Veterans With Stroke and Their Caregivers: Addressing an Unmet Need"	**Sample:** Veterans with stroke and spousal/partner caregivers ($n = 22$) **Approach:** In-depth qualitative interviews with participants in their homes **Main variables:** Postdischarge needs of veterans with strokes and their caregivers	One theme was that veterans and caregivers used multiple strategies to manage the residual effects of stroke, such as exercise to improve functional abilities. The second theme was that both veterans and caregivers had shifts in their roles and responsibilities.
Comparative Cross-Sectional Studies		
Tiegs et al. (2006)[a] "Coping by Stroke Caregivers: Sex Similarities and Differences"	**Sample:** Stroke patients ($n = 199$) and caregivers ($n = 175$) **Approach:** Stroke patients were assessed for depression and caregivers completed self-report instruments **Main variables:** Depression of stroke patients; caregivers' depression, sense of competence, and sense of coherence	No significant differences were found in stroke survivors' depression based on the gender of the caregiver. Compared to females, male caregivers had less depression and burden.

Perrin et al. (2008)[a] "Structural Equation Modeling of the Relationship Between Caregiver Psychosocial Variables and Functioning of Individuals With Stroke"	**Sample:** Dyads of stroke patients and their caregiver dyads (n = 135) **Approach:** Veterans underwent an extensive battery of neuropsychological assessments and caregivers completed a packet of printed scales **Main variables:** Stroke survivors' depression, language, recovery, and stroke impact; caregivers' depression, sense of competence, sense of coherence	Psychosocial functioning of caregivers of stroke patients was associated with the stroke survivors' levels of everyday functioning.
Uphold et al. (2007)[b] "Predictors of Positive Aspects of Caregiving and Depression Among Informal Caregivers of Stroke Survivors"	**Sample:** Caregiver/veteran dyads (n = 100) **Approach:** Telephone interviews were conducted. **Main variables:** Caregivers' positive aspects of caregiving, depression, social support, and health promoting behaviors	Being a spouse and higher social support were predictors of caregivers' better perceptions of positive aspects of caregiving. Older age, higher social support, and more frequent health promoting behaviors were predictive amongst caregivers' lower depressive symptoms.
Hinojosa & Rittman (2009)[b] "Association Between Health Education Needs and Stroke Caregiver Injury"	**Sample:** Caregiver/veteran dyads (n = 276) **Approach:** Telephone interviews at one time point were conducted. **Main variables:** Caregivers' information/education needs and injury state	Caregivers with increased education needs were about twice as likely to have injuries related to activities they performed in their caregiving roles.

(Continued)

TABLE 8.2
Stroke Studies (Continued)

Author/Year/Title	Methods	Major Findings
Hayes et al. (2009)[b] "The Prevalence of Injury for Stroke Caregivers and Associated Risk Factors"	**Sample:** Caregiver/veteran dyads (n = 275) **Approach:** Telephone interviews were conducted at one time point. **Main variables:** Caregivers' depressive and burden; veterans' health and functioning	Caregivers of stroke patients who experienced higher burden and/or depression were more likely to have an increased risk for injury.
Rittman et al. (2009)[b] "Subjective Sleep, Burden, Depression and General Health Among Caregivers of Veterans Poststroke"	**Sample:** Caregiver/veteran dyads (n = 276) **Approach:** Telephone interviews were conducted **Main variables:** Caregivers' depressive, burden, health, and subjective sleep	Poorer sleep experience of caregivers was associated with greater burden and depression and poorer health.
Prospective Cohort Studies		
Chumbler et al. (2004)[c] "The Sense of Coherence, Burden, and Depressive Symptoms in Informal Caregiver During the First Month After Stroke"	**Sample:** Caregiver/veteran dyads (n = 104) **Approach:** In-person interviews with caregivers 1 month after their veterans' discharge from medical center were conducted **Main variables:** Caregivers' sense of coherence (coping), sense of competence (burden), and depressive symptoms	Caregiver sense of coherence (coping) was associated with fewer depressive symptoms.

Van Puymbroeck & Rittman (2005)[c] "Quality-of-Life Predictors of Caregivers at 1 and 6 Months Poststroke: Results of a Path Analyses"	**Sample:** Dyads of veterans and caregivers (n = 127); analysis was conducted with a subsample (n = 92) **Approach:** In-person interviews were conducted with veterans and caregivers. **Main variables:** Veterans' functional status; caregivers sense of coherence (e.g., coping), depression, sense of competence (e.g., burden); and quality of life	The most influential factor predicting caregivers' quality of life at both 1 and 6 months poststroke was caregivers' sense of coherence or coping.
Hinojosa & Rittman (2007)[c] "Stroke Caregiver Informational Needs: Comparison of Mainland and Puerto Rican Caregivers"	**Sample:** Caregivers (n = 120) **Approach:** In-person interviews were conducted at baseline (1 month after discharge to home). **Main variables:** Caregivers' information/education needs	Compared to mainland caregivers, Puerto Rican caregivers had greater information needs.
Chumbler et al. (2008)[c] "Association in Sense of Coherence and Depression in Caregivers of Survivors With Stroke Across 2 Years"	**Sample:** Caregiver/veteran dyads (n = 115) **Approach:** In-person interviews at five time points over 2 years were conducted. **Major variables:** Caregivers sense of coherence (coping) and depressive symptoms	Stronger sense of coherence (coping) was associated with lower levels of caregiver depression 2 years following a stroke.
Hinojosa, Zsembick, et al. (2009)[c] "Patterns of Informal Care Among Puerto Rican, African American and White Stroke Survivors"	**Sample:** Caregivers/veteran dyads (n = 118) **Approach:** In-person interviews at 6 and 12 months postdischarge were conducted. **Major variables:** Size of caregiving networks, primary caregiver relationship and co-residency	Puerto Rican (PR) caregiving networks were larger and more PR caregivers were in co-residency with their stroke survivors than White and African American caregivers. PR caregiving networks were more likely to change in size over a 12-month time period through both contraction and expansion.

(Continued)

TABLE 8.2
Stroke Studies (Continued)

Author/Year/Title	Methods	Major Findings
Hinojosa, Rittman, & Hinojosa (2009)[c] "Informal Caregivers and Racial/Ethnic Variation in Health Service Use of Stroke Caregivers"	**Sample:** Caregivers (n = 125) **Approach:** In-person interviews were conducted with caregivers at four time points over 12 months and veterans' health records were reviewed. **Main variables:** Veterans' health service use, functional status, instrumental activities of daily living; caregivers' daily time spent on tasks and help received from others	African American and PRs were less likely to receive in-patient therapy services. Compared to Whites, PRs were less likely to be admitted to the hospital and more likely to use outpatient services. Living with their caregivers was associated with higher likelihood of outpatient service use.
Hinojosa, Rittman, Hinojosa, & Rodriguez (2009)[c] "Racial/Ethnic Variation in Recovery of Motor Function in Stroke Survivors: Role of Informal Caregivers"	**Sample:** Caregivers (n = 125) **Approach:** In-person interviews were conducted with caregivers at five time points over 24 months and veterans' health records were reviewed **Main variables:** Veterans' health service use, functional status, instrumental activities of daily living; caregivers' daily time spent on tasks and help received from others	No racial/ethnic differences were found in the veterans' recovery of motor function. PR caregivers provided more care and had larger caregiver networks than Whites and African Americans.
Perrin et al. (2009)[c] "Identifying At-Risk, Ethnically Diverse Stroke Caregivers for Counseling: A Longitudinal Study of Mental Health"	**Sample:** Caregivers/veteran dyads (n = 124) **Approach:** In-person interviews were conducted at 1, 6, and 12 months postdischarge. **Main variables:** Veterans' functioning; caregivers' sense of coherence (coping), burden, and mental health	At 1 month after discharge, care recipients' (veterans') low daily functioning, caregivers' low sense of coherence, high burden, and caregiver high depressive symptoms were the best predictors of poor caregiver mental health at 11 months postdischarge.

Perrin, Heesacker, et al. (2010)[c] "Caregiver Mental Health and Racial/Ethnic Disparities in Stroke: Implications for Culturally Sensitive Intervention"	**Sample:** Caregivers/veteran dyads ($n = 124$) **Approach:** In-person interviews at 1, 6, and 12 months postdischarge were conducted. **Main variables:** Veterans' functional independence and performance of instrumental activities of daily living; caregivers depressive symptoms, sense of competence (burden), and sense of coherence (coping)	There were no statistically significant differences in mental health between Puerto Rican, African American, and White caregivers. Over time, in dyads with an African American or White caregiver, caregiver mental health and functioning of stroke survivors were related.
Intervention Studies		
Lutz et al. (2009)[c] "Testing a Home-Telehealth Programme for US Veterans Recovering From Stroke and Their Family Caregivers"	**Sample:** Veterans ($n = 18$) and caregivers ($n = 14$) **Approach:** A nonrandomized open trial using mixed methods was conducted to evaluate the use of a stroke-specific, home telehealth program that used in-home messaging devices to communicate with Veterans and caregivers. **Main variables:** Stroke survivors' depression, physical impairment, and falls; caregivers' burden	The results confirmed that the home telehealth program was a feasible approach for assessing the health and well-being of veterans poststroke. The caregivers stated that the program was beneficial and provided a sense of security that they could receive professional help if needed.
Perrin, Johnston, et al. (2010)[c] "A Culturally Sensitive Transition Assistance Program for Stroke Caregivers: Examining Caregiver Mental Health Stroke Rehabilitation"	**Sample:** Caregiver/veteran dyads ($n = 61$) **Approach:** In-person interviews were conducted with dyads randomized to an intervention or control group. **Main variables:** Caregivers' strain, depression, and program satisfaction	Caregivers in the intervention group had lower depression than caregivers in the control group at the 3-month follow-up.

(Continued)

TABLE 8.2
Stroke Studies (Continued)

Author/Year/Title	Methods	Major Findings
Dissemination and Implementation Science Studies		
Uphold et al. (2010)[c] "Culturally-Sensitive, Senior-Friendly Health Information for Caregivers of Veterans With Stroke"	**Sample:** Three focus groups with health care providers (n = 32) at three sites (Gainesville, Florida; San Juan, Puerto Rico; Milwaukee, Wisconsin); in-person interviews with caregivers (n = 42) from the three sites; usability testing with health care providers (n = 8) and caregivers (n = 7) **Approach:** This implementation study had five components: (a) creation of a draft stroke caregiver website, (b) formative evaluation of the website through focus groups with health care providers and in-person interviews with caregivers, (c) usability testing of the website with health care providers and caregivers, (d) social marketing campaign to promote the website, and (e) Webtrends analysis and Google search to determine website usage. **Main variables:** Health care providers and caregivers' perceptions about the websites' appearance, content, readability and navigability; website usage	A low-literacy, culturally sensitive, senior-friendly website written in English and Spanish languages was created to improve the quality of lives of caregivers of stroke patients and to offer health care providers a resource for patient education materials. A Google search found that the website was in the number 1 position for resources of caregivers of stroke patients.

Note. VA = U.S. Department of Veteran Affairs.
[a]These manuscripts were generated from Dr. Gonzalez-Rothi's Screening Program at the VA Brain Rehabilitation Research Center.
[b]These manuscripts were generated from Dr. Rittman's VA Project, "Informal Caregivers of Veterans Post Stroke."
[c]These manuscripts were generated from Dr. Rittman's VA Project "Culturally Sensitive Models of Stroke Recover and Caregiving After Discharge Home."

Most of the remaining publications were generated from two projects conducted by VA nurse researcher, Dr. Maude Rittman. In one study, "Informal Caregivers of Veterans Post Stroke," telephone interviews were conducted with both Veterans and their caregivers to learn about their experiences following a stroke. A major strength of this project was the large sample of 276 Veteran/caregiver dyads who were recruited from four geographically diverse regions of the VA health care system. Whereas most previous caregiver studies have focused solely on negative outcomes, such as depression and burden, this study also collected data on positive aspects of caregiving and caregivers' desire to institutionalize their loved ones. Four studies evolved from this project and are listed in Table 8.2.

In the second project conducted by Dr. Rittman, "Culturally Sensitive Models of Stroke Recovery and Caregiving After Discharge Home," 125 Veteran/caregiver dyads receiving services at VA medical centers were interviewed. Research assistants of the same ethnicity of the Veterans collected data during home visits at 1, 6, 12, 18, and 24 months following the Veterans' discharge to home. Main variables in the project were caregivers' sense of competence or coping, sense of coherence or burden, depression, general health, and hours and type of caregiving activities. A major strength of the project was the diverse sample that included caregivers from different geographic regions (i.e., South Georgia, Florida, Puerto Rico, USVI) and racial/ethnic groups (White, African American, Latino). Unfortunately, even though culturally relevant, rich qualitative data were collected, none of the publications reported these findings. Further, extensive longitudinal data were collected, but the authors did not report which time points over the 2-year period following discharge were the most stressful and vulnerable times for Veterans and stroke caregivers. Nonetheless, the project is a first step in bringing awareness to a neglected area in the general stroke caregiving literature: the importance of culture in the lives of stroke caregivers. See Table 8.2 to find the nine publications that evolved from this project.

In the remaining sections, we organize individual publications into five thematic areas: (a) needs and experiences of caregivers of Veterans with poststroke, (b) factors that predict Veteran outcomes (i.e., health care use, functioning, and quality of life), (c) factors that predict caregiver outcomes (e.g., depression, burden, quality of life), (d) racial/ethnic variations in stroke caregiving, and (e) interventions and programs to educate and support caregivers using experimental designs or implementation science methods.

Needs and Experiences of Caregivers of Veterans Poststroke

Surprisingly, we found only one study in this thematic area. In a cross-sectional, qualitative study, Lutz, Chumbler, and Roland (2007) interviewed 10 spousal/partner caregivers and 12 Veterans in their homes following discharge from a hospital or rehabilitation facility. Using grounded dimensional analysis, two themes emerged from the data: (a) assessing and managing residual effects of stroke and (b) shifting roles and responsibilities. With the support of their caregivers, Veterans used self-determination strategies, leisure activities, and exercise to improve their functional abilities. Both Veterans and caregivers expressed the overwhelming realization that the stroke changed all aspects of their lives. Tasks that were previously done by the Veteran, such as yard work, handling finances, and maintaining the home, became the responsibility of the caregiver. Caregivers expressed that these added responsibilities left them physically and mentally exhausted. Although the qualitative, analytic methods used in this study were strong, the findings generated little new information on stroke caregiving.

Factors That Predict Veteran With Stroke Outcomes

In the general population, evidence is accumulating that caregivers play a critically important role in helping survivors recover poststroke (Miller et al., 2010). Research has shown that caregiver depression, stress, and burden can worsen stroke survivors' quality of life, recovery from injuries, and overall functioning (Carnwath & Johnson, 1987; King, Shade-Zeldow, Carlson, Feldman, & Philip, 2002; Tsouna-Hadjis, Vemmos, Zakopoulos, & Stamatelopoulos, 2000). Caregiving burden was even found to be the main reason for institutionalization of stroke survivors (Han & Haley, 1999).

Similar to literature on stroke caregiving in general, many researchers have focused specifically on caregivers of Veterans and investigated how caregiving impacts the Veterans' lives. One article (Hinojosa, Rittman, & Hinojosa, 2009) found relationships between the type and quantity of in-home caregiving and Veterans' health service use. Veterans whose caregivers provided more care, co-resided in the same household, and received more outside help had higher outpatient service use. Strengths of this publication were the use of Andersen's Behavioral Model of Health Services Use (Andersen, 1995) and a strong analytical plan that controlled for caregivers' and Veterans' predisposing, enabling, and need factors. Unfortunately, the sample size of 135 caregiver/Veteran dyads was too small for a study whose goal was to describe the patterns of health service use across the large VA health care system.

Two studies (Perrin et al., 2008; Tiegs et al., 2006) that used data collected from 135 caregiver/dyads in Gonzalez-Rothi's screening project investigated the relationship between caregiver factors and functioning of individuals with stroke. Tiegs et al. (2006) found that caregivers' gender was unrelated to survivors' depression with stroke. Perrin et al. (2008) concluded that lower quality of caregiving impeded the recovery of persons with stroke. These two publications are the only known reports that used a predominantly Veteran population to uncover the importance of caregiver factors in promoting the recovery of persons with stroke. On the other hand, the findings in these publications must be interpreted cautiously as multiple, unmeasured and uncontrolled variables (e.g., Veterans' cognitive functioning and health care use; caregivers' physical health) could have confounded the relationships between caregiver factors and Veteran functioning.

Factors That Predict Caregiver Outcomes

Most publications within the Veteran population are similar to those in the general stroke caregiving population in terms of theoretical models, designs, and variables. For example, previous studies on caregivers of both Veterans with stroke and nonveterans with stroke have investigated the influence of patient characteristics (e.g., age, physical health, depression) and caregivers characteristics (e.g., education, income, burden) on different mental health or quality of life outcomes in caregivers.

Tiegs et al. (2006) explored differences in how men and women handled the demands of providing care to stroke survivors. Although the investigators found no differences between men and women in amount and types of caregiving, there were notable gender-related differences. For example, male caregivers had less depression, burden, and better coping abilities than their female counterparts.

In four publications, a theoretical model developed by Dr. Rittman was evaluated. This model predicted that stroke survivor/Veteran characteristics (e.g., functional status, income) and caregiver characteristics (e.g., relationship to Veteran, coping or sense of coherence) were associated with caregiver mental health (e.g., burden, depression, quality of life). Although the authors of these publications studied caregivers at different time points, included slightly different dependent and independent variables, and analyzed the data with various statistical tests, the results across the studies were essentially similar. For example, researchers studied caregivers 1 month after discharge (Chumbler, Rittman, Van Puymbroeck, Vogel, & Qin, 2004), 6 months after discharge (Van Puymbroeck & Rittman, 2005), 12 months after discharge (Perrin, Heesacker, Hinojosa, Uthe, & Rittman, 2009), and 2 years after discharge (Chumbler, Rittman, & Wu, 2008). Regardless of which independent variables were controlled, a common finding across time was that a sense of coherence or coping was associated with better caregiver mental health or quality of life outcomes. Although it is noteworthy that these researchers analyzed longitudinal data, the main finding that coping predicts mental health variables has already been well established.

Along slightly different lines, Rittman, Hinojosa, and Findley (2009) explored caregivers' subjective sleep experience. Although not surprising, caregivers' negative sleep experience were associated with greater burden and depression and poorer health. Other studies focused on caregiver injury. One study

(Hinojosa & Rittman, 2009) found that caregivers with increased educational needs were most likely to have injuries. Another study (Hayes, Chapman, Young, & Rittman, 2009) revealed that caregivers' injuries interfered with their abilities to manage their Veterans' care and that these injuries were more likely to occur if the caregiver had higher levels of burden and depression. Although findings in these studies are to be expected, the outcome variables (i.e., sleep, injuries) in these studies have been relatively overlooked in prior research.

Similarly, Uphold, Van Puymbroeck, Sberna, and Young (2007) investigated another outcome variable, positive aspects of caregiving, that has not been previously well studied. Most previous research has conceptualized stroke caregiving as a negative, stressful experience. This publication, however, revealed that 22% of the studied caregivers had extremely positive caregiving experiences. Further, the study found that even though a large number of caregivers were at risk for clinical depression, they simultaneously held positive perceptions of caregiving.

Overall, except for inclusion of new variables, such as injury and positive aspects of caregiving, the publications discussed in this section are not groundbreaking and add minimally to the body of research on stroke caregiving. Nonetheless, these studies are important in increasing awareness of which predictive factors are important to assess and modify, if possible, to improve caregiver outcomes.

Racial/Ethnic Variations in Stroke Caregiving

It is well known that African Americans and Latinos have higher incidence of stroke, greater stroke mortality, and greater physical impairment poststroke than Whites (Horner, Swanson, Bosworth, & Matchar, 2003; McGruder, Malarcher, Antoine, Greenlund, & Croft, 2004). In addition, it is established that race and culture have a great impact on family structure, family norms, and family stress management (Dilworth-Anderson et al., 2005).

Recognizing the important role culture plays in enhancing the skills of caregivers of stroke patients, Hinojosa and Rittman (2007) explored the information needs of different race/ethnic groups of caregivers. This publication revealed that caregivers living in PR perceived a greater need for information than those caregivers living in the mainland United States. A supplemental finding was that caregivers received most of their information from doctors, the VHA, and the Internet.

Three publications examined the racial/ethnic variations in outcomes of Veterans with stroke and their caregivers. One publication (Hinojosa, Rittman, & Hinojosa, 2009) reported on differences in health care use between three race/ethnic groups (i.e., Whites, African Americans, and Puerto Ricans [PRs]). Whites were most likely to use inpatient therapy services, whereas PRs were most likely to use outpatient services and least likely to have hospital admissions. A publication written by Hinojosa and associates reported on differences in Veterans' motor function and found that PRs had greater impairments and African Americans had fewer impairments than Whites (Hinojosa, Rittman, Hinojosa, et al., 2009). Another publication (Perrin et al., 2009; Perrin, Heesacker, Uthe, & Rittman, 2010) reported that PR caregivers had the poorest mental health outcomes compared to the other two race/ethnic groups, but these differences were not statistically significant.

The most informative publication described informal caregiver networks of Whites, African Americans, and PRs and how these networks changed over a course of 12 months. PR networks were larger than the other groups and PR caregivers more commonly lived in the same households as their stroke care recipients. Compared to Whites and African Americans, PR networks were more likely to contract and expand over time. The authors surmised that these network changes may be because PRs are more mobile than individuals in other race/ethnic groups and often relocate to the mainland United States.

Publications within this section reveal that race/ethnicity does indeed impact on Veteran and caregiver outcomes. Furthermore, the publications highlight the importance of cultural awareness when designing studies on stroke caregiving. Unfortunately, however, these publications report only quantitative findings and thus do not provide a full picture of the rich variations in caregiving experiences that are likely to exist among different race/ethnic groups.

Interventions and Dissemination and Implementation Studies

Although multiple, effective interventions have been tested in the general stroke population (Brereton, Carroll, & Barnston, 2007; Lui, Ross, & Thompson, 2005; Visser-Meily et al., 2006), there has been little research evaluating interventions and programs to improve the lives of caregivers in the Veteran population. Lutz, Chumbler, Lyles, Hoffman, and Kobb (2009) conducted a feasibility study to determine the usability and acceptability of a home telehealth device. This device attached to a landline telephone and allowed care coordinators (i.e., registered nurses) and caregivers to communicate through text messages and enabled care coordinators to send educational information. Fourteen caregivers participated in the 14-day trial and were able to successfully answer questions and receive information via the technology. Qualitative interviews with a subsample of six caregivers found that caregivers thought the program was beneficial, provided helpful education, and provided a sense of security that a health care provider could be easily reached when needed.

In a clinical demonstration program, "Transition Assistance Program (TAP)," Perrin, Johnston, et al. (2010) pilot tested an intervention that included culturally sensitive caregiver skill development, education, and supportive problem solving using videophone technology. Sixty-one participant caregivers at two sites (Puerto Rico and Texas) received four videophone calls over a 6-week period. Exploratory analyses found a treatment effect of lowering caregiver strain. Caregivers in the intervention group also had lower depression than caregivers in the control group at the 3-month follow-up. Caregivers gave high satisfaction ratings of the program.

Although the importance of implementing research findings into clinical practice has been established, Uphold and associates (Uphold, Findley, et al., 2010) is the only known research team to have evaluated a Veteran caregiver program using implementation science methods. Recognizing that there is a solid body of evidence and clinical guidelines that emphasize the importance of caregiver education, Uphold et al. collaborated with VA partners (VA My Health*e*Vet, VA Coordination Office, VA National Center for Health Promotion and Disease Prevention) and non-VA partners (American Stroke Association) to develop a draft of a Spanish- and English-language, evidence-based RESCUE website. The website's purpose was to improve caregivers' knowledge and skills and to serve as a patient education resource for health care providers. RESCUE stands for "Resources and Education for Stroke Caregivers' Understanding and Empowerment." To evaluate the draft website, three focus groups with health care providers at three sites (Gainesville, Florida; San Juan, Puerto Rico; Milwaukee, Wisconsin) and 42 face-to-face, qualitative interviews with informal caregivers (n = 22 in Gainesville; n =13 in San Juan; n = 7 in Wisconsin) were conducted. Based on feedback from the focus groups and interviews, the RESCUE website was revised to include 45 fact sheets, a list of resources, newsletters, self-management tools, caregiver testimonials, and a glossary of terms with phonetic spelling. The investigative team then conducted usability evaluation with "think aloud" cognitive testing with a sample of 8 providers (3 English-speaking and 5 Spanish-speaking) and 7 female, informal stroke caregivers (4 English-speaking and 3 Spanish-speaking) to improve the website navigability. A multipronged promotional campaign that included newsletters, booths at health fairs, announcements of VA/VHA Facebook and Twitter, professional and community presentations, and publications in professional and lay journals was implemented to increase awareness of the website. Summative evaluation findings from qualitative telephone interviews with 18 VA health care providers confirmed that the RESCUE website fulfilled an important niche in the VA for an easy-to-read and comprehensive website for stroke caregivers. Using Webtrends analysis, the investigative team found that there were 218,529 views of the RESCUE web pages between October 2010 and December 2012. This project illustrates how implementation science and health marketing techniques can be used to translate research evidence into practice. The project addressed a need for a culturally relevant and low-literate website for both health care providers and stroke caregivers. A limitation was that only one minority cultural group (i.e., Latinos living in Puerto Rico) was studied. Another shortcoming was that the project did not evaluate whether the information on the RESCUE website affected caregivers' knowledge and skills.

Additional implementation projects and clinical trials are needed to rigorously evaluate caregiver programs and initiatives. Nonetheless, the projects in this section illustrate how online education and newer technologies, such as structured telehealth programs and videophones, can potentially enhance in-home stroke caregiving. As the VHA continues to strengthen its care coordinator program, additional studies will be needed to evaluate the costs and benefits of different interventions and technologies.

Recommendations for Future Research on Caregivers of Veterans With Stroke

Most reviewed publications failed to capture the unique experiences of family members who specifically care for Veterans. For example, few researchers compared differences between caregivers of Veterans and caregivers of nonveterans. Likewise, we found no study that investigated how caregivers use and navigate the unique VHA health care system. Most publications used quantitative methods and cross-sectional comparative or prospective cohort designs. Researchers found that caregiver factors (e.g., sociodemographics, coping, burden) predict Veteran outcomes (e.g., functioning) and caregiver outcomes (e.g., depression, quality of life). Although these publications draw attention to the important role of caregivers of Veterans, they add little to what is already known about stroke caregiving in general. Notable exceptions are the publications generated from Dr. Rittman's project, "Cultural Sensitivity Models of Stroke Recovery and Caregiving . . . " in which researchers explored the differences between caregivers of White, African American, and Latino race/ethnicities.

Based on our review, we have several recommendations for future research. We found only one qualitative study (Lutz et al., 2009) related to stroke caregiving of Veterans. However, because this study generated limited new information on caregivers' needs and stressors, we recommend that future researchers use qualitative and mixed methods to study more complex and novel caregiver issues.

Similarly, we suggest additional longitudinal studies be conducted. A new direction would be to explore how caregiving tasks, needs, and outcomes change over time. Such studies would uncover when caregivers are most vulnerable and what types of interventions would be most beneficial at particular points in time. Another recommendation is to conduct studies that evaluate and test caregiver programs and interventions using experimental designs and implementation science methods. There is evidence from the general stroke literature that effective caregiver interventions are available. Now is the time to replicate these projects in the Veteran population and/or evaluate how best to translate these interventions into clinical practice.

In recent years, the VHA has invested significant resources to transform the health care system by implementing programs that are Veteran- and family-centric. Although these programs have focused on the predominantly younger OEF/OIF caregiver population, the VA Office of Geriatrics and Extended Care has funded numerous clinical demonstration projects under its noninstitutional and long-term care program. Because most of these projects are in their infancy state, now would be an ideal time to gather baseline information and evaluate the programs as they evolve over time.

SUMMARY

A growing body of science has found that caregivers of family members make enormous contributions caring for our nation's injured, disabled, and chronically ill Veterans. Caregiving has been studied from various perspectives and health states, but most research literature examines the burden of care on family members. Fewer studies have shed light on the Veteran caregiver experience, whether positive or negative. Thus, we undertook a review of the existing literature on caregivers of Veterans to assess the "state of the science" for this unique population.

In this review, we limited our search of the literature to caregivers of Veterans, and more specifically to two specific populations of Veterans—OEF/OIF Veterans and Veterans with stroke. Regardless of which population studied, caregiving was characterized as burdensome and stressful. Likewise, both groups of caregivers tended to sacrifice their own well-being to assist their ill or injured family member.

We know little, however, about how caregiving of Veterans changes over time and at which time points caregivers are most vulnerable. There is limited research that examines how caregivers of Veterans interact and navigate the health care system; how new technologies, such as smartphones and telehealth, impact caregiver outcomes; and how barriers and facilitators affect caregivers' experience in accessing and using services both within and outside the VA health care system. We also need more research that examines caregiver preparedness, reluctance to care, barriers to respite, and the positive and negative impacts of caregiving across the life span.

To address these overlooked areas, we have several recommendations for future research. More qualitative and mixed methods approaches are suggested to obtain rich data that captures the complexity of the caregiving experience.

Case-control studies that compare caregivers of Veterans with caregivers of non-Veterans would help identify the unique needs of these two groups and guide future-targeted interventions and programs. Lastly, it is time to move beyond descriptive and correlational studies toward a robust evaluation of caregiver interventions and programs.

DISCLAIMER

The views expressed in this chapter are those of the authors and do not necessarily reflect the official policy or position of the Department of Veterans Affairs.

REFERENCES

American Congress of Rehabilitation Medicine. (1993). Definition of mild traumatic brain injury. *Journal of Head Trauma Rehabilitation*, *8*(3), 86–87. https://www.acrm.org/pdf/TBIDef_English_Oct2010.pdf

Andersen, R. M. (1995). Revisiting the behavioral model and access to medical care: Does it matter? *Journal of Health and Social Behavior*, *36*, 1–10.

Anderson, C. S., Linto, J., & Stewart-Wynne, E. G. (1995). A population-based assessment of the impact and burden of caregiving for long-term stroke survivors. *Stroke*, *26*(5), 843–849.

Bakas, T., Farran, C. J., Austin, J. K., Given, B. A., Johnson, E. A., & Williams, L. S. (2009). Stroke caregiver outcomes from the Telephone Assessment and Skill-Building Kit (TASK). *Topics in Stroke Rehabilitation*, *16*(2), 105–121. http://dx.doi.org/10.1310/tsr1602-105

Berg, A., Palomäki, H., Lönnqvist, J., Lehtihalmes, M., & Kaste, M. (2005). Depression among caregivers of stroke survivors. *Stroke*, *36*(3), 639–643. http://dx.doi.org/10.1161/01.STR.0000155690.04697.c0

Block, C., Fabrizio, K., Bagley, B., Hannah, J., Camp, S., Mindingall, N., . . . Lokken, K. (2014). Assessment of Veteran and caregiver knowledge about mild traumatic brain injury in a VA medical center. *The Journal of Head Trauma Rehabilitation*, *29*(1), 76–88. http://dx.doi.org/10.1097/HTR.0b013e3182886d78

Brereton, L., Carroll, C., & Barnston, S. (2007). Interventions for adult family carers of people who have had a stroke: A systematic review. *Clinical Rehabilitation*, *21*(10), 867–884. http://dx.doi.org/10.1177/0269215507078313

Calhoun, P. S., Beckham, J. C., & Bosworth, H. B. (2002). Caregiver burden and psychological distress in partners of Veterans with chronic posttraumatic stress disorder. *Journal of Traumatic Stress*, *15*(3), 205–212. http://dx.doi.org/10.1023/A:1015251210928

Carlson, K. F., Meis, L. A., Jensen, A. C., Simon, A. B., Gravely, A. A., Taylor, B. C., . . . Griffin, J. M. (2012). Caregiver reports of subsequent injuries among Veterans with traumatic brain injury after discharge from inpatient polytrauma rehabilitation programs. *The Journal of Head Trauma Rehabilitation*, *27*(1), 14–25. http://dx.doi.org/10.1097/HTR.0b013e318236bd86

Carnwath, T. C., & Johnson, D. A. (1987). Psych morbidity among spouses of patients with stroke. *British Medical Journal*, *294*, 409–411.

Caska, C. M., & Renshaw, K. D. (2011). Perceived burden in spouses of National Guard/Reserve service members deployed during Operations Enduring and Iraqi Freedom. *Journal of Anxiety Disorders*, *25*(3), 346–351. http://dx.doi.org/10.1016/j.janxdis.2010.10.008

Chumbler, N. R., Rittman, M., Van Puymbroeck, M., Vogel, W. B., & Qin, H. (2004). The sense of coherence, burden, and depressive symptoms in informal caregivers during the first month after stroke. *International Journal of Geriatric Psychiatry, 19*(10), 944–953. http://dx.doi.org/10.1002/gps.1187

Chumbler, N. R., Rittman, M. R., & Wu, S. S. (2008). Associations in sense of coherence and depression in caregivers of stroke survivors across 2 years. *Journal of Behavioral Health Services and Research, 35*(2), 226–234. http://dx.doi.org/10.1007/s11414-007-9083-1

Congressional Budget Office. (2007). *The health care system for Veterans: An interim report*. Washington, DC: Congress of the United States. Retrieved from http://www.cbo.gov/sites/default/files/cbofiles/ftpdocs/88xx/doc8892/12-21-va_healthcare.pdf

Dewey, H. M., Thrift, A. G., Mihalopoulos, C., Carter, R., Macdonell, R. A. L., McNeil, J. J., & Donnan, G. A. (2002). Informal care for stroke survivors: Results from the North East Melbourne Stroke Incidence Study (NEMESIS). *Stroke, 33*(4), 1028–1033. http://dx.doi.org/10.1161/01.str.0000013067.24300.b0

Dilworth-Anderson, P., Brummett, B. H., Goodwin, P., Williams, S. W., Williams, R. B., & Siegler, I. C. (2005). Effect of race on cultural justifications for caregiving. *The Journals of Gerontology Series B: Psychological Sciences and Social Sciences, 60*(5), S257–S262.

Eaton, K. M., Hoge, C. W., Messer, S. C., Whitt, A. A., Cabrera, O. A., McGurk, D., . . . Castro, C. A. (2008). Prevalence of mental health problems, treatment need, and barriers to care among primary care-seeking spouses of military service members involved in Iraq and Afghanistan deployments. *Military Medicine, 173*(11), 1051–1056.

Fischer, E. P., Sherman, M. D., Han, X., & Owen, R. R., Jr. (2013). Outcomes of participation in the REACH multifamily group program for Veterans with PTSD and their families. *Professional Psychology: Research and Practice, 44*(3), 127–134. http://dx.doi.org/10.1037/a0032024

Flynn, C. A. (2014). Evolution of a research agenda for military families. In S. MacDermid Wadsworth & D. S. Riggs (Eds.), *Military deployment and its consequences for families* (pp. 79–84). New York, NY: Springer Science+Business Media.

Force Health Protection & Readiness Policy and Programs. (2014). *TBI & PTSD quick facts*. Retrieved from http://fhp.osd.mil/image/outreach/quick_white.pdf

Freytes, I. M., Hannold, E. M., Resende, R., Wing, K., & Uphold, C. R. (2013). The impact of war on Puerto Rican families: Challenges and strengthened family relationships. *Community Mental Health Journal, 49*(4), 466–476. http://dx.doi.org/10.1007/s10597-012-9486-1

Friedmann-Sanchez, G., Griffin, J. M., Rettmann, N. A., Rittman, M., & Partin, M. R. (2012). Communicating information to families of polytrauma patients: A narrative literature review. *Rehabilitation Nursing, 33*(5), 206–214.

Gewirtz, A. H., Erbes, C. R., Polusny, M. A., Forgatch, M. S., & Degarmo, D. S. (2011). Helping military families through the deployment process: Strategies to support parenting. *Professional Psychology: Research and Practice, 42*(1), 56–62. http://dx.doi.org/10.1037/a0022345

Grant, J. S., Weaver, M., Elliott, T. R., Bartolucci, A. R., & Newman Giger, J. (2004). Sociodemographic, physical and psychosocial factors associated with depressive behaviour in family caregivers of stroke survivors in the acute care phase. *Brain Injury, 18*(8), 797–809. http://dx.doi.org/10.1080/02699050410001671766

Greenwood, N., Mackenzie, A., Cloud, G. C., & Wilson, N. (2008). Informal carers of stroke survivors—Factors influencing carers: A systematic review of quantitative studies. *Disability and Rehabilitation, 30*(18), 1329–1349.

Griffin, J. M. (2009, December). *Family and caregiver experiences with polytrauma: Preliminary findings from the FACES study*. Paper presented at the Second Annual Trauma Spectrum Disorders Conference, Bethesda, MD.

Griffin, J., Friedemann-Sánchez, G., Carlson, K., Jensen, A., Gravely, A., Taylor, B., . . . Houtven, C. (2014). Resources and coping strategies among caregivers of Operation Iraqi Freedom (OIF)

and Operation Enduring Freedom (OEF) Veterans with polytrauma and traumatic brain injury. In S. MacDermid Wadsworth & D. S. Riggs (Eds.), *Military deployment and its consequences for families* (pp. 259–280). New York, NY: Springer.

Griffin, J. M., Friedemann-Sanchez, G., Hall, C., Phelan, S., & van Ryn, M. (2009). Families of patients with polytrauma: Understanding the evidence and charting a new research agenda. *Journal of Rehabilitation Research and Development*, *46*(6), 879–892.

Griffin, J. M., Friedemann-Sanchez, G., Jensen, A. C., Taylor, B. C., Gravely, A., Clothier, B., . . . van Ryn, M. (2012). The invisible side of war: Families caring for US service members with traumatic brain injuries and polytrauma. *The Journal of Head Trauma Rehabilitation*, *27*(1), 3–13. http://dx.doi.org/10.1097/HTR.0b013e3182274260

Han, B., & Haley, W. E. (1999). Family caregiving for patients with stroke. Review and analysis. *Stroke*, *30*(7), 1478–1485.

Hannold, E. M., Freytes, I. M., & Uphold, C. R. (2011). Unmet health services needs experienced by Puerto Rican OEF/OIF Veterans and families post deployment. *Military Medicine*, *176*(4), 381–388.

Hayes, J., Chapman, P., Young, L. J., & Rittman, M. (2009). The prevalence of injury for stroke caregivers and associated risk factors. *Topics in Stroke Rehabilitation*, *16*(4), 300–307. http://dx.doi.org/10.1310/tsr1604-300

Hayes, J., Wakefield, B., Andresen, E. M., Scherrer, J., Traylor, L., Wiegmann, P., . . . Desouza, C. (2010). Identification of domains and measures for assessment battery to examine well-being of spouses of OIF/OEF Veterans with PTSD. *Journal of Rehabilitation Research and Development*, *47*(9), 825–840.

Hinojosa, M. S., & Rittman, M. (2007). Stroke caregiver information needs: Comparison of mainland and Puerto Rican caregivers. *Journal of Rehabilitation Research and Development*, *44*(5), 649–658.

Hinojosa, M. S., & Rittman, M. (2009). Association between health education needs and stroke caregiver injury. *Journal of Aging and Health*, *21*(7), 1040–1058. http://dx.doi.org/10.1177/0898264309344321

Hinojosa, M. S., Rittman, M., & Hinojosa, R. (2009). Informal caregivers and racial/ethnic variation in health service use of stroke survivors. *Journal of Rehabilitation Research and Development*, *46*(2), 233–241.

Hinojosa, M. S., Rittman, M., Hinojosa, R., & Rodriguez, W. (2009). Racial/ethnic variation in recovery of motor function in stroke survivors: Role of informal caregivers. *Journal of Rehabilitation Research and Development*, *46*(2), 223–232.

Hinojosa, M. S., Zsembick, B., & Rittman, M. (2009). Patterns of informal care among Puerto Rican, African American, and white stroke survivors. *Ethnicity and Health, 14*(5), 1–16.

Hoge, C. W., McGurk, D., Thomas, J. L., Cox, A. L., Engel, C. C., & Castro, C. A. (2008). Mild traumatic brain injury in U.S. soldiers returning from Iraq. *The New England Journal of Medicine*, *358*(5), 453–463. http://dx.doi.org/10.1056/NEJMoa072972

Horner, R. D., Swanson, J. W., Bosworth, H. B., & Matchar, D. B. (2003). Effects of race and poverty on the process and outcome of inpatient rehabilitation services among stroke patients. *Stroke*, *34*(4), 1027–1031. http://dx.doi.org/10.1161/01.str.0000060028.60365.5d

Hosek, J., Kavanagh, J., & Laura, L. M. (2006). *How deployments affect service members* (Report No. MG-432-RC). Santa Monica, CA: RAND. Retrieved from http://www.rand.org/content/rand/pubs/monographs/MG432.html

Johnson, N. J. (2013, April). *Assistance and support services for family caregivers*. Paper presented at the VA National Caregiver Support Program, Teleconference.

King, D. K., Glasgow, R. E., & Leeman-Castillo, B. (2010). Reaiming RE-AIM: Using the model to plan, implement, and evaluate the effects of environmental change approaches to enhancing population health. *American Journal of Public Health*, *100*(11), 2076–2084. http://dx.doi.org/10.2105/ajph.2009.190959

King, N. S. (2008). PTSD and traumatic brain injury: Folklore and fact? *Brain Injury*, *22*(1), 1–5. http://dx.doi.org/10.1080/02699050701829696

King, R. B., Shade-Zeldow, Y., Carlson, C. E., Feldman, J. L., & Philip, M. (2002). Adaptation to stroke: A longitudinal study of depressive symptoms, physical health, and coping process. *Topics in Stroke Rehabilitation*, *9*(1), 46–66.

Klein, E., Caspi, Y., & Gil, S. (2003). The relation between memory of the traumatic event and PTSD: Evidence from studies of traumatic brain injury. *The Canadian Journal of Psychiatry*, *48*(1), 28–33.

Lui, M. H., Ross, F. M., & Thompson, D. R. (2005). Supporting family caregivers in stroke care: A review of the evidence for problem solving. *Stroke*, *36*(11), 2514–2522. http://dx.doi.org/10.1161/01.str.0000185743.41231.85

Lutz, B. J., Chumbler, N. R., Lyles, T., Hoffman, N., & Kobb, R. (2009). Testing a home-telehealth programme for US Veterans recovering from stroke and their family caregivers. *Disability and Rehabilitation*, *31*(5), 402–409. http://dx.doi.org/10.1080/09638280802069558

Lutz, B. J., Chumbler, N. R., & Roland, K. (2007). Care coordination/home-telehealth for Veterans with stroke and their caregivers: Addressing an unmet need. *Topics in Stroke Rehabilitation*, *14*(2), 32–42. http://dx.doi.org/10.1310/tsr1402-32

Lynn, J. (2014). Strategies to ease the burden of family caregivers. *Journal of the American Medical Association*, *311*(10), 1021–1022. http://dx.doi.org/10.1001/jama.2014.1769

Manguno-Mire, G., Sautter, F., Lyons, J., Myers, L., Perry, D., Sherman, M., . . . Sullivan, G. (2007). Psychological distress and burden among female partners of combat Veterans with PTSD. *Journal of Nervous and Mental Disease*, *195*(2), 144–151. http://dx.doi.org/10.1097/01.nmd.0000254755.53549.69

McCullagh, E., Brigstocke, G., Donaldson, N., & Kalra, L. (2005). Determinants of caregiving burden and quality of life in caregivers of stroke patients. *Stroke*, *36*(10), 2181–2186. http://dx.doi.org/10.1161/01.str.0000181755.23914.53

McGruder, H. F., Malarcher, A. M., Antoine, T. L., Greenlund, K. J., & Croft, J. B. (2004). Racial and ethnic disparities in cardiovascular risk factors among stroke survivors: United States 1999 to 2001. *Stroke*, *35*(7), 1557–1561. http://dx.doi.org/10.1161/01.str.0000130427.84114.50

McNulty, P. A. (2010). Adaptability and resiliency of army families during reunification: Initial results of a longitudinal study. *Federal Practitioner*, *27*(3), 18–27.

McNulty, P. A. (2013). Adaptability and resiliency of military families during reunification: Results of a longitudinal study. *Federal Practitioner*, *30*(8), 14–22.

Miller, E. L., Murray, L., Richards, L., Zorowitz, R. D., Bakas, T., Clark, P., & Billinger, S. A. (2010). Comprehensive overview of nursing and interdisciplinary rehabilitation care of the stroke patient: A scientific statement from the American Heart Association. *Stroke*, *41*(10), 2402–2448. http://dx.doi.org/10.1161/STR.0b013e3181e7512b

Milliken, C. S., Auchterlonie, J. L., & Hoge, C. W. (2007). Longitudinal assessment of mental health problems among active and reserve component soldiers returning from the Iraq war. *Journal of the American Medical Association*, *298*(18), 2141–2148. http://dx.doi.org/10.1001/jama.298.18.2141

National Alliance for Caregiving. (2010). *Caregivers of Veterans—Serving on the homefront*. Retrieved from http://www.caregiving.org/data/2010_Caregivers_of_Veterans_FULLREPORT_WEB_FINAL.pdf

National Research Council. (2010). *Returning home from Iraq and Afghanistan: Preliminary assessment of readjustment needs of Veterans, service members, and their families*. Retrieved from http://www.nap.edu/openbook.php?record_id=12812

Okie, S. (2005). Traumatic brain injury in the war zone. *New England Journal of Medicine*, *352*(20), 2043–2047. http://dx.doi.org/10.1056/NEJMp058102

Perrin, P. B., Heesacker, M., Hinojosa, M. S., Uthe, C. E., & Rittman, M. R. (2009). Identifying at-risk, ethnically diverse stroke caregivers for counseling: A longitudinal study of mental health. *Rehabilitation Psychology*, *54*(2), 138–149. http://dx.doi.org/10.1037/a0015964

Perrin, P. B., Heesacker, M., Stidham, B. S., Rittman, M. R., & Gonzalez-Rothi, L. J. (2008). Structural equation modeling of the relationship between caregiver psychosocial variables and functioning of individuals with stroke. *Rehabilitation Psychology*, *53*(1), 54–62. http://dx.doi.org/10.1037/0090-5550.53.1.54

Perrin, P. B., Heesacker, M., Uthe, C. E., & Rittman, M. R. (2010). Caregiver mental health and racial/ethnic disparities in stroke: Implications for culturally sensitive interventions. *Rehabilitation Psychology*, *55*(4), 372–382. http://dx.doi.org/10.1037/a0021486

Perrin, P. B., Johnston, A., Vogel, B., Heesacker, M., Vega-Trujillo, M., Anderson, J., & Rittman, M. (2010). A culturally sensitive Transition Assistance Program for stroke caregivers: Examining caregiver mental health and stroke rehabilitation. *Journal of Rehabilitation Research and Development*, *47*(7), 605–617.

Price, J. L., & Stevens, S. P. (2014). *Partners of Veterans with PTSD: Research findings*. Retrieved from http://www.ptsd.va.gov/professional/treatment/family/partners_of_vets_research_findings.asp

Renshaw, K. D., Rodrigues, C. S., & Jones, D. H. (2008). Psychological symptoms and marital satisfaction in spouses of Operation Iraqi Freedom Veterans: Relationships with spouses' perceptions of Veterans' experiences and symptoms. *Journal of Family Psychology*, *22*(4), 586–594. http://dx.doi.org/10.1037/0893-3200.22.3.586

Rittman, M., Hinojosa, M. S., & Findley, K. (2009). Subjective sleep, burden, depression, and general health among caregivers of Veterans poststroke. *Journal of Neuroscience Nursing*, *41*(1), 39–52.

Rogers, V. L., Go, A. S., Lloyd-Jones, D. M., Benjamin, E. J., Berry, J. D., Borden, W. B., . . . Turner, M. B. (2012). Heart disease and stroke statistics—2012 update: A report from the American Heart Association. *Circulation*, *125*(1), e2–e220. http://dx.doi.org/10.1161/CIR.0b013e31823ac046

Saban, K. L., Sherwood, P. R., DeVon, H. A., & Hynes, D. M. (2010). Measures of psychological stress and physical health in family caregivers of stroke survivors: A literature review. *Journal of Neuroscience Nursing*, *42*(3), 128–138.

Sautter, F. J., Armelie, A. P., Glynn, S. M., & Wielt, D. B. (2011). The development of a couple-based treatment for PTSD in returning Veterans. *Professional Psychology: Research and Practice*, *42*(1), 63–69. http://dx.doi.org/10.1037/a0022323

Sayer, N. A. (2012). Traumatic brain injury and its neuropsychiatric sequelae in war Veterans. *Annual Review of Medicine*, *63*, 405–419. http://dx.doi.org/10.1146/annurev-med-061610-154046

Sayers, S. L., Farrow, V. A., Ross, J., & Oslin, D. W. (2009). Family problems among recently returned military Veterans referred for a mental health evaluation. *The Journal of Clinical Psychiatry*, *70*(2), 163–170.

Schillinger, D. (2010). An introduction to effectiveness, dissemination and implementation research. In P. Fleisher & E. Goldstein (Eds.), *UCSF Clinical and Translational Science Institute (CTSI) resource manuals and guides to community-engaged research*. San Francisco, CA: Clinical Translational Science Institute Community Engagement Program, University of California. Retrieved from http://accelerate.ucsf.edu/files/CE/edi_introguide.pdf

Straits-Troster, K., Gierisch, J. M., Strauss, J. L., Dyck, D. G., Dixon, L. B., Norell, D., & Perlick, D. A. (2013). Multifamily group treatment for Veterans with traumatic brain injury: What is the value to participants? *Psychiatric Services*, *64*(6), 541–546. http://dx.doi.org/10.1176/appi.ps.001632012

Taft, C., Walling, S., Howard, J., & Monson, C. (2011). Trauma, PTSD, and partner violence in military families. In S. M. Wadsworth & D. Riggs (Eds.), *Risk and resilience in U.S. military families* (pp. 195–212): New York, NY: Springer Publishing.

Tanielian, T., & Jaycox, L. H. (2008). *Invisible wounds of war: Psychological and cognitive injuries, their consequences, and services to assist recovery* (Report No. MG-720-CCF). Santa Monica, CA: RAND. Retrieved from http://www.rand.org/content/dam/rand/pubs/monographs/2008/RAND_MG720.pdf

Tanielian, T., Rajeev, R., Michael, P. F., Carra, S. S., Racine, S. H., & Margaret, C. H. (2013). *Military caregivers: Cornerstones of support for our nation's wounded, ill, and injured Veterans* (Report

No.RR-244-TEDF). Santa Monica, CA: RAND. Retrieved from http://www.rand.org/content/rand/pubs/research_reports/RR244.html

The Management of Stroke Rehabilitation Working Group. (2010). *VA/DoD clinical practice guideline: Management of stroke rehabilitation*. Retrieved from http://www.healthquality.va.gov/guidelines/Rehab/stroke/stroke_full_221.pdf

Tiegs, T. J., Heesacker, M., Ketterson, T. U., Pekich, D. G., Rittman, M. R., Rosenbek, J. C., . . . Gonzalez-Rothi, L. J. (2006). Coping by stroke caregivers: Sex similarities and differences. *Topics in Stroke Rehabilitation, 13*(1), 52–62. http://dx.doi.org/10.1310/cjvw-wcpk-2fcv-369p

Tsouna-Hadjis, E., Vemmos, K. N., Zakopoulos, N., & Stamatelopoulos, S. (2000). First-stroke recovery process: The role of family social support. *Archives of Physical Medicine and Rehabilitation, 81*(7), 881–887. http://dx.doi.org/10.1053/apmr.2000.4435

Uphold, C. R., Bober, J., Wing, K., & Freytes, M. (2008). *Community reintegration and Puerto Rican OEF/OIF Veterans and families*. Paper presented at the Poster session at the 2008 QUERI National Meeting, Phoenix, AZ.

Uphold, C. R., Findley, K., Wing, K., Freytes, I. M., Knauff, L., Shorr, R. I., . . . Beyth, R. J. (2010). Culturally-sensitive, senior-friendly health information for caregivers of Veterans with stroke. *Federal Practitioner, 27*(9), 33–36.

Uphold, C. R., Freytes, I. M., Knauff, L., Wing, K., Anderson, S., & Easey, K. (2010). *Improving community reintegration of OEF/OIF Veterans and families living in Puerto Rico through printed and web-based education*. Poster session presented at the Research in the Southeast—RFPs to Outcomes: Translating Research to Practice Conference, Orlando, FL.

Uphold, C. R., Midolo, J. P., Freytes, I. M., del Valle, L. E., Wing, K. L., Knauff, L., & Findley, K. (2012). *Unmet needs of OEF/OIF/OND Veterans and their families living in the U.S. Virgin Islands*. Paper presented at the VA Health Services Research and Development Annual Meeting, Washington, DC.

Uphold, C. R., Van Puymbroeck, M., Sberna, M., & Young, L. (2007). Predictors of positive aspects of caregiving and depression among informal caregivers of stroke survivors. *Poster abstract from Journal of American Geriatrics Society, 55*(4), S1–S146, Abstract D151, S215.

U.S. Department of Defense, Defense and Veterans Brain Injury Center. (2014). *DoD worldwide numbers for TBI*. Retrieved from http://dvbic.dcoe.mil/dod-worldwide-numbers-tbi

Van Houtven, C. H., Voils, C. I., & Weinberger, M. (2011). An organizing framework for informal caregiver interventions: Detailing caregiving activities and caregiver and care recipient outcomes to optimize evaluation efforts. *BMC Geriatrics, 11*, 1–18. Retrieved from http://www.biomedcentral.com/1471-2318/1411/1477

Van Puymbroeck, M., & Rittman, M. R. (2005). Quality-of-life predictors for caregivers at 1 and 6 months poststroke: Results of path analyses. *Journal of Rehabilitation Research and Development, 42*(6), 747–760.

Visser-Meily, A., Post, M., Gorter, J. W., Berlekom, S. B., Van Den Bos, T., & Lindeman, E. (2006). Rehabilitation of stroke patients needs a family-centred approach. *Disability and Rehabilitation, 28*(24), 1557–1561. http://dx.doi.org/10.1080/09638280600648215

Waddell, M. C., & Orr, K. K. (2013). *Wounded warrior, wounded home: Hope and healing for families living with PTSD and TBI*. Grand Rapids, MI: Baker Books.

Warden, D. (2006). Military TBI during the Iraq and Afghanistan wars. *Journal of Head Trauma Rehabilitation, 21*(5), 398–402.

Wilder Schaaf, K. P., Kreutzer, J. S., Danish, S. J., Pickett, T. C., Rybarczyk, B. D., & Nichols, M. G. (2013). Evaluating the needs of military and Veterans' families in a polytrauma setting. *Rehabilitation Psychology, 58*(1), 106–110. http://dx.doi.org/10.1037/a0031693

Willerton, E., MacDermid Wadsworth, S., & Riggs, D. (2011). Introduction: Military families under stress: What we know and what we need to know. In S. MacDermid Wadsworth & D. Riggs (Eds.), *Risk and resilience in U.S. military families* (pp. 1–20). New York, NY: Springer.

CHAPTER 9

Prehospital Tourniquets

Review, Recommendations, and Future Research

Paul C. Lewis

ABSTRACT

The tourniquet is a simple device that has been used since the Middle Ages. Although different variations have been designed throughout its history, the simplicity of design has remained. The history of tourniquets follows two distinct paths—the operating room and the prehospital setting. From the earliest recorded history, tourniquets have been used for surgical procedures which were originally to amputate war-ravaged limbs and then to create a bloodless field for routine limb surgery. This history has continued uninterrupted since the early 1900s with continued research to foster advances in knowledge. The history of tourniquets in the prehospital setting, however, has not progressed as smoothly. The debate regarding the use of a tourniquet to save a life from excessive limb hemorrhage began in the 1600s, and continues to this day. This chapter will explore the prehospital use of tourniquets, which may shed some light on where this debate originated. The current state of the knowledge regarding tourniquets will then be discussed with a focus on prehospital use, using the operating room literature when needed to fill knowledge gaps. The chapter will conclude with recommendations for prehospital tourniquet use and some areas for future research. Tourniquets are used for operative procedures

http://dx.doi.org/10.1891/0739-6686.32.203

within accepted clinical guidelines throughout the world as the standard of care. Current science supports a similar stance for the use of prehospital tourniquets within clinical guidelines.

INTRODUCTION

In this age of remarkable medical technological advancements, one life-saving device remains essentially unchanged and just as effective as when it was introduced in the 16th century. A simple and intuitive design, tourniquets have had their proponents, and detractors, since they were first introduced. The use of a tourniquet for limb trauma has been a source of debate from its earliest days on through to the present day. Although use of the tourniquet is not without risk, much of the historical discussion places the blame on tourniquets for what are actually shortfalls within the medical system. This chapter will explore the history of tourniquets and then discuss the current state of knowledge regarding their use. As tourniquets have been an accepted tool within the confines of the operating room since the beginning of the 20th century, this chapter will instead focus on tourniquet use in the prehospital trauma setting.

GENERAL HISTORY OF TOURNIQUETS

The history of tourniquet use dates back to the Middle Ages. Among the first records of tourniquet use was in the 6th century BC for treatment of snake bites (Kragh, Swan, Smith, Mabry, & Blackbourne, 2012). Tourniquets were next reported as being used by the Romans and interestingly, may be the origin of the great tourniquet debate. The functioning of the circulatory system was poorly understood by Roman medical practitioners, and therefore, the treatment of hemorrhage often led to incorrect conclusions (Kragh et al., 2012). The understanding at the time was that a tourniquet worsened bleeding "in the same way, if you tie a rope around a skin bag and tighten it, if that bag has a leak, it will of course squirt out its contents" (Majno, 1975).

The recent history of tourniquet use begins with more clarity in the 1600s. Most early writings of tourniquet use as well as tourniquet improvements were accomplished during times of war and focused primarily on controlling bleeding during amputation surgery instead of hemorrhage control. In 1517, a German surgeon named Hans Von Gersdorff published a book on trauma surgery entitled *Feldtbuch der Wundtartzney*, which included one of the first depictions of a tourniquet being used while performing an amputation (Gersdorff, 1967). In the mid-1500s, French surgeons were considered among the best educated surgeons of the time and are responsible for a relative rapid evolution of tourniquets in surgery. In 1564, Ambriose Pare, a well-known French war surgeon who is often credited with major advances in amputation surgery, described the use of "a strong cord around the limb above the amputation site, to hold the muscles retracted from the skin, to limit bleeding, and reduce sensation" (Mabry, 2006). This practice was soon modified by another French surgeon named Guy de Chauliac who recommended putting a "tight band above and below the site of amputation to reduce pain and minimize bleeding by compressing the soft tissues against the bone" (Welling, Burris, Hutton, Minken, & Rich, 2006). A final innovation was introduced by a third French surgeon, Leonardo Botallo, by recommending using three tight bands around the limb and performing the amputation between the lower two (Wangensteen & Wangensteen, 1978).

The windlass style tourniquet was introduced by a German physician in the late 1500s, but there is some debate whether to credit the innovation to Wilhelm Fabry (Mabry, 2006) or Fabricius Hildanus, often referred to as the father of German surgery (Welling, McKay, Rasmussen, & Rich, 2012). The tourniquet was updated in a 17th-century surgical text called *Armamentarium Chirurgicum* by a renowned German physician named Johannes Scultetus. This illustrated text included a catalogue of many surgical instruments of the day, but most notably, a picture of a screw compressor tourniquet (Schultheiss & Jonas, 1998). The screw concept was adapted in 1718 by a French surgeon, John Louis Petit, who is also credited with naming the tourniquet from the French word *tourner*, which means "to turn" (Wangensteen & Wangensteen, 1978). Petit (1718) modified the tourniquet described by Scultetus to include a mechanical screw and padded leather to both control tension and make it more comfortable. The most significant innovation with this design was that the tourniquet required no assistant to hold tension and could be quickly released if needed (Klenerman, 1962). This tourniquet design would remain essentially unchanged for the next hundred years until the latter part of the 19th century. Tourniquets were still primarily used only for surgical amputations as there is no evidence that the Petit tourniquet was used for any purpose other than emergency and elective limb surgery (Kragh et al., 2012). A contemporary of Petit, Henry Le Dran (1749), a French military surgeon, recommended the Petit tourniquet as standard equipment for military surgery because he considered it as invaluable in controlling bleeding while performing amputations. Le Dran (1749) also noted the Petit tourniquet was a more efficient use of resource because the surgeon required fewer assistants during ligation of amputated vessels.

The final advances in tourniquet development were specifically surgical in nature and beginning to separate from its wartime roots. In 1864, Joseph Lister was the first to describe the use of a bloodless field for a routine, nontraumatic hand amputation as well as the benefit of raising the limb prior to applying a tourniquet. Lister noted that " . . . when the hand was raised to the utmost degree and kept so for a few minutes and then . . . a common tourniquet was applied . . . I had practically a bloodless field to operate on . . . " (Klenerman, 2003). Johann Friedrich August von Esmarch, a professor of surgery at Kiel, expressed concern over the amount of blood remaining in the amputated limb. He introduced the Esmarch's bandage, which is a flat rubber bandage that was used to empty the limb of blood prior to amputation (Klenerman, 2003). Coincidentally, the Esmarch bandage was also the first tourniquet with which nerve palsies were reported if it was applied too tightly (Klenerman, 2003). The final tourniquet innovation came in 1904 when Harvey Cushing introduced the pneumatic tourniquet. Cushing had abandoned the rubber tourniquet because of the newly recognized danger of nerve palsy as well as the relative difficulty of applying and removing the rubber tourniquet during surgery (Klenerman, 2003). He took his inspiration from the newly introduced pneumatic blood pressure cuff. By the mid-1900s, the use of the pneumatic tourniquet in extremity surgery was considered routine (Doyle & Taillac, 2008). Since the introduction of the pneumatic tourniquet, there have been technological advances in the design but it remains essentially unchanged and is used in the operating room every day across the world as the standard of care for establishing a bloodless operating field.

MILITARY HISTORY OF TOURNIQUETS

One of the first recorded uses of a tourniquet for hemorrhage control on a battlefield was during the Siege of Besancon in 1674. Etienne Morel, a French Army surgeon stated "Since the blood vessels were compressed by the pressure of the band and bled very little, they could be sutured without undue haste" (Laffin, 1999). Morel described a tourniquet in which a belt was passed through a block of wood and then a stick was used in the belt loop to twist the tourniquet tight (referred to as a *block tourniquet*; Laffin, 1999; Schwartz, 1958). This windlass-type tourniquet was an adaptation of the first windlass introduced in the late 1500s by either Wilhelm Fabry or Fabricius Hildanus and would be improved upon about 30 years later by Petit.

During the Crimean War (1853–1856), a noted British surgeon named George MacLeod (1862) is credited with contemplating preventable battlefield deaths among those that did not make it to medical care. His conclusion, however, was that tourniquets "are of little use on the battlefield" because even though "many sink from haemorrhage, still, it would be impossible . . . to rescue them in time, the nature of the wounds . . . causing death very rapidly" (MacLeod, 1862).

The American Civil War (1861–1865) quickly found the American medical system overwhelmed by the sheer number of casualties. The Battle of Shiloh experienced more casualties than in all previous American wars combined and about equal to the number seen in the Battle of Waterloo (Mabry, 2006). At the outset of the war, there were no trauma surgeons and no formal military medical training (Richey, 2007). The combination of sheer number of casualties with inexperienced trauma surgeons resulted in significantly delayed evacuation times from the battlefield. This perpetuated the tourniquet debate as the delay in evacuation often resulted in the need for an amputation caused by the limb being ischemic for too many hours (Mabry, 2006). In 1862, Jonathan Letterman, the Medical Director of the Army of the Potomac, implemented a novel integrated medical treatment and evacuation system (Richey, 2007). Unfortunately, the system would not be fully recognized until World War I when the prolonged evacuation times were again an issue.

Interestingly, the premier surgeons from the Union and the Confederacy took opposite stances on the use of tourniquets. In 1861, a Union academic surgeon, S.D. Gross, published *A Manuel of Military Surgery*. In this manual, he stated:

> When the wound is severe, or involving a large artery or vein . . . the bleeding may prove fatal in a few minutes unless immediate assistance is rendered. . . . It is not necessary that the common soldier carry a Petit's tourniquet but every soldier must put into his pocket a stick of wood, six inches long, and a handkerchief or piece of roller, with a thick compress, and be advised how, where and when they are used. (Gross, 1861)

Dr. Gross would later support the use of a simple strap and buckle tourniquet, which would subsequently be distributed to a great number of Civil War troops. Unfortunately, a high complication rate became readily apparent caused by both misuse as well as delay from hours to days before casualties could be evaluated. This led to many required amputations that may have been otherwise avoided (Mabry, 2006). Within the same year, as Gross recommended the use of tourniquets, the story began to change. After the Battle of Bull Run in 1861, with more than 2,000 injured, a physician wrote he was informed by the Brigade surgeon that "the use of the field tourniquet was so frequently followed by mortification and loss of limb, that he had come to the conclusion it was far safer to leave the wound to nature, without any attempts to arrest the flow of blood than depend upon the common army tourniquet" (Longmore, 1895). Recognizing that delayed evacuation was a major issue, an attempt was made to alleviate the limb ischemic time by providing for collateral circulation after a tourniquet was applied. Two such devices were the Dupuytren's compressor and the Lambert field tourniquet. Each was an attempt to put pressure only over the affected artery but allow collateral circulation to avoid gangrene with extended use. The Lambert field tourniquet was subsequently endorsed and issued to Union soldiers. The Dupuytren's compressor was quickly abandoned and replaced with the Petit tourniquet because of its ability to stay in place. However, this did not solve the complications associated with prolonged tourniquet use, and by 1864, very little support remained for any tourniquet use on the battlefield for the North or the South. Julian Chisolm, Confederate Surgeon General seemed to chastise his Union counterpart when he stated:

> The field tourniquet, in former days, was so much in vogue that it was considered indispensable on the battlefield, and was, therefore, carried in large numbers . . . Now they are nearly discarded from field service, and recent experience, based upon the carelessness with which they are used, recommends their abolition from the field as doing more harm than good to the wounded. (Chisolm, 1861)

Interestingly, during this period, the tourniquet discussion was also being followed by England. Sir Thomas Longmore, who was at the time the Professor of Military Surgery, commented " . . . to many uneducated and excited men this [gunshot wound] bleeding would at once be interpreted as showing the need for a tourniquet: evils . . . would result . . . thus a simple wound be converted into a relatively grave one" (Longmore, 1895). Surprisingly, he would later advocate for distribution of tourniquets among all trained "bearers and attendants" (Longmore, 1895). The Confederacy Surgeon General Julian Chisholm strongly disagreed with the recommendation stating, "Unless hemorrhage is very violent, threatening immediate destruction of life, the tourniquet is rarely required. The finger pressure of an intelligent assistant is better than any tourniquet made" (Chisolm, 1861).

Despite the discussion regarding the pros and cons of tourniquet use among the surgeons, little documentation exists which provides any actual data on the complication rate from battlefield tourniquet use (Richey, 2007). It is stated in the *Medical and Surgical History of the War of the Rebellion* that "early in the war it was recommended that each soldier should have in his possession some simple form of tourniquet . . . how far they were of use is not known, as no cases are recorded of life being saved by them; but it is probable that they were used little, and it is very doubtful if, in the confusion and excitement of battle, they could have been applied with any efficacy" (Otis & Huntington, 1883).

World War I (1914–1918) saw the introduction of the battlefield medic, which moved the initial medical care for casualties to the front lines. However, trauma and surgical papers of the time were still being written by surgeons at the terminal end of the casualty pipeline and the resultant viewpoint on the use of tourniquets continued to be viewed negatively. Major Blackwood from the Royal Army Medical Corps Journal plainly stated he was "inclined to think that tourniquets are an invention of the Evil One" (Blackwood, 2001). In 1918, the U.S.

government reprinted the British book entitled *Injuries and Diseases of War*. The manual stated, “the systematic use of elastic tourniquet cannot be too severely condemned. The employment of it . . . usually indicates the person using it is quite ignorant both of how to stop bleeding properly and also of the danger to life and limb by the tourniquet” (Great Britain Army Medical Services, 1918). The French surgeon Tuffier (1915) concurred stating, “As soon as a tourniquet is seen in an ambulance it should be taken away.”

There were a few instances of surgeons who began to acknowledge the tourniquet may have a place in prehospital care. An Austrian surgeon named Lorenz Böhler identified the tourniquet as a very useful tool and recognized that one of the reasons people die after reaching medical care was failure to apply a clamp or tourniquet when hemorrhage was not arrested by compression (Kragh et al., 2012). However, because of the continued misuse, he later withdrew his support stating, “when in 1914 the number of amputations necessary because of the improper application of tourniquets increased rapidly, I suggested . . . this practice be discontinued. The injurious effects of improperly applied tourniquets then disappeared” (Böhler, 1956). This was also the first time prehospital guidelines were identified. In the *Handbook for the Medical Soldier*, Tuttle (1927) wrote four rules for tourniquet use which still apply today: (a) never cover up a tourniquet; (b) write the word tourniquet clearly on the medical card; (c) if the injured man is conscious, instruct him to tell every medical officer he has a tourniquet in place; (d) and remember, if the tourniquet is left on for more than 6 hr, the limb will die.

As World War II approached, an influential United Kingdom physician named Reginald Watson-Jones (1955) published instructional courses on orthopedic casualty care. In the courses, he recommended abolishing the first aid tourniquets stating “more limbs have been lost by the use of tourniquets than have been saved.” However, as war broke out, the tourniquet was still used by soldiers on the battlefield, unfortunately with similar problems seen in previous wars. Nothing seemed to be remembered from the complications of previous wars with it being noted of this war “soldiers—whether medical or nonmedical—regularly misused tourniquets. They applied them unnecessarily; left them unloosened for too long; and occasionally evacuated patients with tourniquets concealed . . .” (Cosmas & Cowdrey, 1992). This continued misuse led the United States’ 7th Army surgeon to issue guidance to clarify tourniquet use. The guidance clarified three key aspects—the sole indication for a tourniquet is “active spurting hemorrhage from a major artery”; proper documentation and notification are essential; and once in place, a tourniquet should only be removed by a medical officer (Cosmas & Cowdrey, 1992; Richey, 2007). Medical instructions of the time also included the caution that any tourniquet placed during evacuation would likely require amputation (U.S. Surgeon General's Office, 1944). In 1941, Hamilton Bailey edited a book entitled *Surgery of Modern Warfare* in which an entire chapter was devoted to tourniquets. In it, he set forth three indications for tourniquet use: (a) control of primary arterial bleeding; (b) reactionary and secondary bleeding (placing a loose tourniquet in case a stump begins to bleed during evacuation); and (c) create a bloodless surgical field (Bailey, 1941). Importantly, Bailey also reinforced the dangers of tourniquets, which were either too tight, causing skin damage and other complications, or too loose, which would lead to excessive bleeding. The importance of documentation was also reiterated. His own views on the battlefield use of tourniquets were cautious when he stated tourniquets should be "regarded with respect because of the damage it may cause, and with reverence because of the lives it undoubtedly saves" (Bailey, 1941). In 1945, an article was written by Wolff and Adkins (1945) which focused on series of 200 service members who had a tourniquet applied. In the article, they were very critical of the army's current strap and buckle tourniquet as being ineffective and causing skin damage. They also described tourniquet times of more than 6 hr with no negative consequences under certain conditions. They were strong advocates for the tourniquet and stated not finding a single case of gangrene directly attributable to use of a tourniquet as well as no incidence of thromboembolic events, skin damage, or nerve damage postoperatively.

Little information exists regarding tourniquet use during the Korean War and the Vietnam War, although there is no question tourniquets continued to be used. Dr. Carl Hughes (1954), an army surgeon deployed to Korea, conducted a review of 79 major extremity vascular injuries and reported 47% of them arrived with a tourniquet in place applied from 40 min to 14 hr (average 4 hr). He did not, however, discuss any outcomes from the use of tourniquets. Vietnam War also saw the use of tourniquets and even improvised tourniquets were considered commonplace (Richey, 2007). Most accounts are anecdotal, however, and little actionable information exists. One analysis of casualties was able to estimate that approximately 7.4% or 2,590 might have been saved with more liberal use of tourniquets (Maughon, 1970).

The recent conflicts of Iraq and Afghanistan have seen the first clear focus on tourniquet use in the combat environment. The recorded use of tourniquets in these conflicts has increased 20-fold since they were introduced in 2006 as standard issue items (Brodie et al., 2009). The U.S. Forces deployed a team named the *Deployed Combat Casualty Research Team* to collect real-time trauma data, one of which was specifically tracking tourniquet use on injured service members as they arrived at the deployed military hospital. Increased survival was seen for many markers with the use of a tourniquet. Overall, the mortality rate from limb exsanguination on the battlefield dropped from 7.4% seen in the

Vietnam War to only 2% in the current conflicts (Kragh et al., 2009). Compared to those military members who did not have a tourniquet applied when it was indicated, survival was dramatically increased with the use of prehospital tourniquets (0% vs. 87%; Kragh et al., 2009). Increased survival was also seen if the tourniquet was placed prehospitally rather than in the emergency room (89% vs. 78% respectively; Kragh, Littrel, et al., 2011) and placed before signs of shock were evident on assessment (96% vs. 4%; Kragh, Littrel, et al., 2011). Misuse of tourniquets was a major concern in previous wars. Data from this conflict shows between 2% (16/651; Kragh, Littrel, et al., 2011) and 18% (12/52; Beekley et al., 2008) of injured service members had tourniquets applied when they were not indicated. However, there does not appear to have been any associated morbidity among those with inappropriate tourniquets applied (Beekley et al., 2008). The overall morbidity associated with tourniquet use has been found to be quite low. Nerve palsy was found to occur in 0.2% (Kragh, O'Neill, et al., 2011) to 1.7% (Kragh et al., 2009) of the cases with the predominance occurring in the arm (Kragh, O'Neill, et al., 2011) and with tourniquets applied in a prehospital setting (Kragh, O'Neill, et al., 2011). The nerve palsies all resolved between 3 and 47 days (Beekley et al., 2008; Kragh, O'Neill, et al., 2011). No other complications were found to be associated with tourniquet use. These included no evidence of thrombolic events (Kragh et al., 2008), no increased rate of fasciotomies based on length of tourniquet application time (Kragh et al., 2008), and no amputations due solely to tourniquet use (Kragh, O'Neill, et al., 2011; Kragh et al., 2008).

Tourniquets have had a very unique place in military medical papers. It has been love–hate relationships throughout history with each war having surgeons take opposite stances on the safety and efficacy of tourniquets on a battlefield. Unfortunately, many of the past decisions have been made on poor information. A clear picture of the risks and benefits of tourniquet use were difficult to determine because of poor education on proper use, difficult casualty evacuation in previous wars, and limited record keeping on the use and outcomes of tourniquets. Therefore, the use of tourniquets was very confusing and surgeons' recommendations were contradictory. The dichotomy of perspective from surgeons can be summed up best in an article written in 1962 by Dr. L. Klenerman (1962). When discussing the use of a pneumatic tourniquet for surgery, he states, "The pneumatic tourniquet is the instrument of choice . . . " and "Because of the care taken and the widespread use of the pneumatic cuff, complications from the use of the 'bloodless method' are now rare." However, when he discusses the use of the same tourniquet while rendering first aid, he states, "There is no place for the tourniquet as a first-aid measure for acute haemorrhage. Watson-James pointed out that more limbs have been lost by the use of the tourniquet than have been saved" (Klenerman, 1962). It is ironic that this same discussion continues to this day. Operating room tourniquets are considered standard of care around the country, but any use of the tourniquet outside the hospital is still met with resistance.

Given the new information of the most recent conflicts, as well as many other excellent papers written on the use of tourniquets, this chapter will now provide an overview of what is currently known about tourniquets.

TOURNIQUET APPLICATION

Tourniquet research in the operating room has steadily progressed throughout the 21st century. Prehospital tourniquet research has been sporadic and disjointed, likely because of the difficulty conducting research in that setting. Although this chapter will focus on prehospital use, operating room research will be referenced to fill knowledge gaps in the realm of prehospital tourniquet use. This section of the chapter will look at the current research regarding (a) when to apply a tourniquet, (b) where to apply it, (c) the type to use and how tight it should be, and (d) how long a tourniquet can be left in place.

When to Apply a Tourniquet

There has been much discussion on when is the correct time to apply a tourniquet in the prehospital setting. At its most basic level, a decision to apply a tourniquet must meet three criteria: (a) significant and active arterial bleeding; (b) the patient is at risk for exsanguination and; (c) there is sufficient limb remaining on which a tourniquet can be applied (Lewis, 2013). Although Criteria 3 can be challenged with atypical tourniquets, such as a Petit-type, currently being explored for high groin injuries (Kheirabadi et al., 2013; Kotwal et al., 2013), Criteria 1 and 2 are clear and necessary. The indication for tourniquets is clearly reserved for instances of active arterial bleeding with imminent risk of exsanguination. This is clearly the "why" of applying a tourniquet which is indisputable (Table 9.1). Unfortunately, this well-defined indication is often accompanied by the caveat of "when other options fail." This is perhaps the gravest lack of perspective and respect for the judgment of the professionals who administer prehospital care. Direct pressure, elevation, and compression dressings are

TABLE 9.1

"Why": Defining the Need for a Tourniquet

- Extreme life-threatening limb hemorrhage
- Limb bleeding not controlled by direct pressure

always the optimal treatment for noncritical wounds. However, when the initial assessment of a wound leads to the conclusion that the patient has (a) significant arterial bleeding and (b) is in imminent danger of exsanguination, these initial options are no longer the best option. Time and clotting are required to bring bleeding under control with pressure and elevation; all the while, more blood is continuing to be lost. Applying a tourniquet will immediately stem the flow of blood and significantly limit blood loss. The simple difference between applying the tourniquet before signs of hypovolemic shock appear may mean the difference between life and death (Kragh et al., 2009).

The discussion of tourniquet application often becomes cloudy because the "why" is confused with the "when." There are many situations when a tourniquet can be applied as an assistive device to help manage a casualty. Although the patient should still be perceived to meet the "why" criteria, the threshold for tourniquet use may be lower in certain situations in which the patient needs to be quickly moved or evacuated before a clear determination if the first two requirements have truly been met. These situations range from entrapment, to an overwhelming number of casualties, and to a hostile environment (Table 9.2). It is during these types of situations where tourniquet use becomes a tool for emergency medical personnel to use in order to achieve the best predicted outcomes. Although application is still predicated on the primary requirements for tourniquet use, judgment and clinical expertise must also be applied to allow tourniquets to be applied before a complete assessment is accomplished. It is in these

TABLE 9.2

"When": Determining the Occasion to Apply a Tourniquet

1. Mass casualty incident with major limb hemorrhage and limited resources (Doyle & Taillac, 2008; Lee et al., 2007)
2. Point of significant hemorrhage not accessible because of victim entrapment (Lee et al., 2007)
3. Significant extremity hemorrhage with any of (Doyle & Taillac, 2008)
   a. Need for airway/breathing management
   b. Evidence of hypovolemic shock
   c. Need for other emergent interventions
4. Bleeding from multiple sources
5. Impaled object in extremity with ongoing bleeding (Doyle & Taillac, 2008)
6. In unsafe environment such as gunfire, risk of explosion, or industrial accident (Doyle & Taillac, 2008; Lee et al., 2007; Lewis, 2013; Walters & Mabry, 2005)
7. To prevent hypovolemic shock (Kragh et al., 2009)
8. Rural or wilderness incidents with limited resources and delayed or unconventional transportation to definitive care (Lee et al., 2007)

"when" scenarios that current prehospital emergency medical use of tourniquets is often questioned. Applying a tourniquet as the first line of treatment is contrary to current emergency medical treatment teachings. Emergency medical technicians (EMTs) are taught to use direct pressure, elevation, and pressure points to control massive extremity bleeding. However, significant hemorrhage during the conflicts in Iraq and Afghanistan resulted in a paradigm shift for the primary assessment. The new Army mnemonic became MARCH (Massive bleeding, Airway, Respirations, Circulation, Head Injury), in recognition that massive hemorrhage is the primary treatable threat to survival on the battlefield (Sebesta, 2006). Because of this shift, the military subsequently adopted a first-use policy of "when in doubt, apply a tourniquet" for any significant extremity bleeding. Although it is understood that a military environment differs in significant ways from a civilian environment, there is growing support for first-use among civilian prehospital providers (Doyle & Taillac, 2008; Richey, 2007). It is important to note here that historically, most complications from a tourniquet arose as a result of delayed evacuation (Welling et al., 2006). The modern medical evacuation in both military and civilian trauma care renders this a much less significant concern in all but a few select scenarios.

Where to Apply a Tourniquet

Placement of a tourniquet is important for two considerations. The first consideration is the tourniquet must be placed to have the best opportunity to stop the hemorrhage for which it is being applied. The second consideration is to place the tourniquet to minimize any potential complications. Traditional instruction on tourniquet application for a traumatic injury has been to apply the tourniquet as distal on the limb as possible and as close to the source of the arterial hemorrhage as possible. Where a more precise measurement is required, a tourniquet should be applied approximately 5 cm proximal to the source of the arterial bleeding or traumatic amputation (Lakstein et al., 2003). Although the recommendation of applying a tourniquet as distal as possible makes intuitive sense (treat the wound), the question may be asked if this recommendation is a remnant of prior war experience, which warned any tissue distal to the tourniquet must be considered "lost" (*Basic Medical Specialist Manual 91B*, 1975). This distal application is contrary to the current recommendation by the Association of periOperative Registered Nurses (AORN), which states tourniquets should be placed over the widest part of the limb to minimize the chance for complications ("Pneumatic Tourniquets, Application and Use," 2011). Rationale for avoiding distal limb application also relates to the relative noncompressible nature of the tissue between the two bones in the lower half of both upper and lower extremities. However, tourniquet application to the most proximal and widest portion of the limb does not seem to be supported by the prehospital literature. Application of distal extremity tourniquets in the military literature did not show significant difficulties with hemorrhage control and found generally low complication rates (Swan, Wright, Barbagiovanni, Swan, & Swan, 2009). Military literature also finds thigh application is often less effective when compared to lower leg application (73% vs. 100% respectively; Kragh et al., 2008) when using a windlass tourniquet likely because of the increased compression necessary to sufficiently compress the tissue in the larger thigh (Calkins, Snow, Costello, & Bentley, 2000). In regard to the upper extremities, both surgical and military literature suggest that the complication rate may actually be higher with the use of a tourniquet over the wider upper arm compared to the lower arm (Kragh et al., 2008).

It should not be surprising that there appear to be discrepancies between operating room use and prehospital use of tourniquets. There are some fundamental differences in tourniquet research between the operating room and the prehospital setting to include issues such as the reason for application, the acuity of the patient, stability of the environment, and the technology available to monitor patient status. Given this research on tourniquet use, especially research recently conducted in a combat environment, a change in practice does not appear warranted. Prehospital tourniquets should continue to be applied as distal as possible on the injured limb to control excessive arterial bleeding.

Type and Tightness of the Tourniquet

The primary concern when considering the type of tourniquet requires a choice of a tourniquet, which will consistently and predictably stop the flow of blood while exposing the patient to as little risk of additional injury as possible. Choosing a type of tourniquet which stops the flow of blood is relatively easy as many different tourniquet designs have been shown to be effective in stopping the blood flow, including commercially available pneumatic or windlass designs and even improvised tourniquets (Calkins et al., 2000; Lakstein et al., 2003; Savage, Pannell, Payne, O'Leary, & Tien, 2013; Swan et al., 2009; Wall et al., 2013). In choosing a tourniquet, avoiding additional injury becomes the real concern and this discussion revolves around one issue—width. In general, tourniquets may cause long-term morbidity by two mechanisms—ischemia and compression. Tissue ischemia is unavoidable because the sole intent of applying a tourniquet is to arrest the flow of blood to a limb, and as stated earlier, many methods seem equally helpful in achieving this result. Tissue ischemia will be discussed in more detail later in this chapter. So the discussion returns to compression. Ideally, the tourniquet should exert just enough pressure to occlude the underlying arterial blood flow while distributing the compressive force across the tissue. This is important because it has been determined that nerve damage associated with tourniquet use is caused by sheer forces on the underlying nerves during compression and not because of tissue ischemia or muscle damage (Gilliatt, Ochoa, Rudge, & Neary, 1974; Ochoa, Danta, Fowler, & Gilliatt, 1971; Ochoa, Fowler, & Gilliatt, 1972). Thus, by distributing the force over a wider area, the sheer forces, or pressure gradients, can be decreased as seen in the figure by McEwen and Casey (2009; Figure 9.1). The wider tourniquet has an additional benefit of also decreasing the overall pressure necessary to occlude the underlying arterial blood flow. A study by Crenshaw, Hargens, Gershuni, and Rydevik (1988) measured fluid tissue pressures at four levels in both upper and lower extremities using a cadaver model. It was found that wider cuffs provided a broader area of tissue compression at all depths and transmitted a greater percentage of the tourniquet cuff pressure to the deeper tissues.

Increased width does present some limitations such as the increased width also means an increased amount of tissue that must be compressed, which in turn greatly increases the effort required to produce sufficient tension (Walters & Mabry, 2005). Another limitation is the tendency for wider strap tourniquets to bow or roll at the edges, thus functionally becoming narrower and transmitting

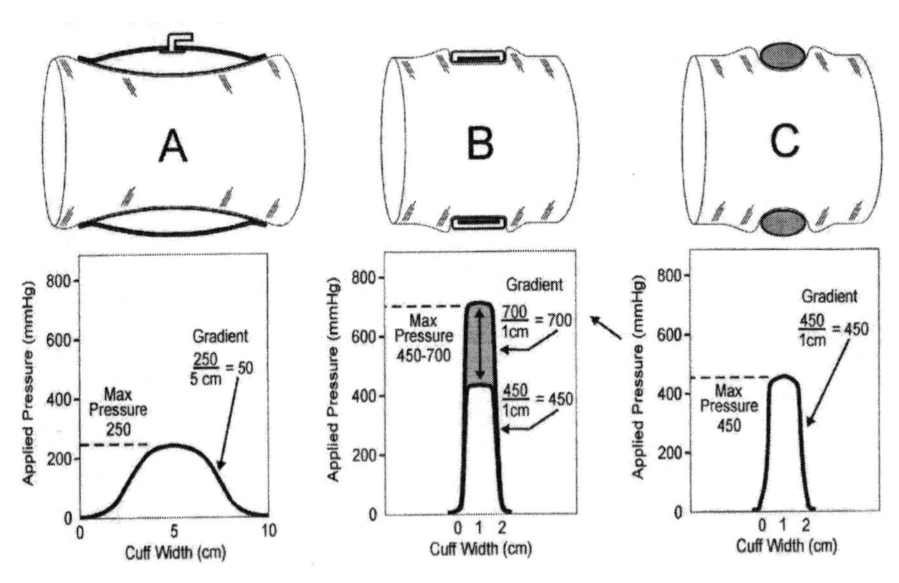

FIGURE 9.1 Applied pressures and pressure gradients of three different tourniquets. Used with permission by Dr. James McEwen. McEwen, J. A., & Casey, V. (2009, May). *Measurement of hazardous pressure levels and gradients produced on human limbs by non-pneumatic tourniquets*. Paper presented at the Proceedings of the 32nd Conference of the Canadian Medical & Biological Engineering Society, Calgary, Canada.

higher pressures to the center of the tourniquet (McLaren & Rorabeck, 1985). And finally, wider tourniquets may simply not fit properly on shorter or amputated limbs. The science does not specify an ideal width. For pneumatic tourniquets, the general rule of thumb which is applied to the sphygmomanometer cuff can be used—as wide as can comfortably fit on the limb while still allowing sufficient room to put it into position without overlapping a joint. For the windlass tourniquet, there is some indication that using two side by side may decrease compressive sequela, possibly because of the two acting similar to one wider tourniquet (Kragh, O'Neill, et al., 2011). In the unpredictable prehospital setting, however, the location of the limb injury will ultimately dictate what size the tourniquet can be to adequately fit the space available.

The discussion to this point has been on what type of tourniquet limits the tissue pressure but not on what is acceptable tissue pressure. For this, the operating room literature supplies an answer with discussion of the limb occlusion pressure (LOP). LOP is defined as "the minimum pressure required, at a specific time by a specific tourniquet cuff applied to a specific patient's limb at a specific location, to stop the flow of arterial blood into the limb distal to the cuff" (Noordin, McEwen, Kragh, Eisen, & Masri, 2009). LOP takes into account the anatomical and physiological characteristics of the patient's limb, the characteristics of the tourniquet being used as well as the systolic blood pressure (Noordin et al., 2009; Oragui, Parsons, White, Longo, & Khan, 2011). As has been alluded to in an earlier discussion, LOP is directly correlated with the width of a tourniquet (Walters & Mabry, 2005), and can be plotted as a predictable parabolic curve, with narrower cuffs requiring higher occlusive pressures and wider cuffs requiring lower occlusive pressure (Noordin et al., 2009; Figure 9.2). Knowing this relationship, a formula was created to determine predicted occlusion pressures (Graham, Breault, McEwen, & McGraw, 1993):

$$\text{Predicted occlusion pressure} = (\text{limb circumference/tourniquet width}) \times 16.67 + 67$$

The LOP can also be determined by gradually inflating the tourniquet to determine the least pressure necessary at which the distal pulse is no longer present using a Doppler stethoscope (McEwen, Kelly, Jardanowski, & Inkpen, 2002; Oragui et al., 2011). The AORN provides guidelines for adding a safety margin of increased pressure above the LOP to insure a continued bloodless field during surgery. This process has since been automated in the operating room with a device which constantly measures the LOP and alarms if the pressure is incorrect. Research has shown that using this methodology results in a significantly lower occlusion pressure, and therefore decreased risk of neurological injury, when compared to a standard pressure used on all patients (Olivecrona, Lapidus, & Benson, 2013; Younger, McEwen, & Inkpen, 2004).

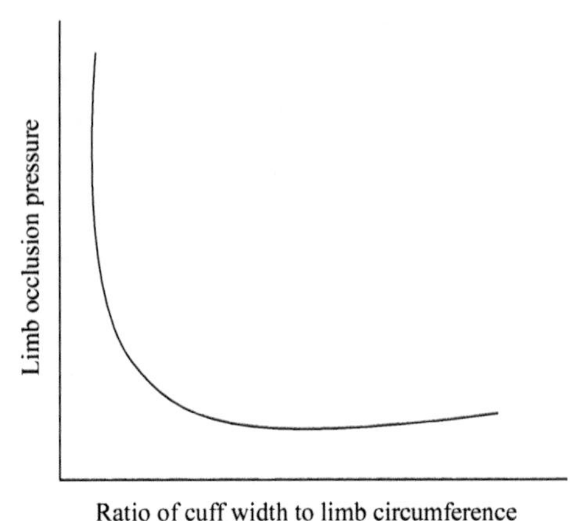

FIGURE 9.2 Limb occlusion pressure versus tourniquet width to limb circumference ratio.

Using the LOP is considered standard of care in the operating room. However, that standard is difficult to apply in the prehospital setting because the situations that warrant the use of a tourniquet usually mean the distal pulses may already be absent because of either significant proximal arterial bleeding or possibly an amputated limb. Pneumatic tourniquets have also been avoided in both the military and civilian prehospital settings because of concerns with the size, weight, ruggedness, and potential failure of the bladder (Walters & Mabry, 2005); however, no research was found that evaluated these concerns. The narrow windlass tourniquets are convenient, compact, light, easily carried, and with less risk of catastrophic failure when used by military or civilian medics. But as was shown in Figure 9.1, these narrower tourniquets also result in much higher compressive forces after application and therefore represent a higher risk for morbidity. The research is clear that wider pneumatic tourniquets minimize possible morbidity after tourniquet application. Pneumatic tourniquets have been designed and marketed for the prehospital setting and, given the preponderance of research on pneumatic tourniquets, may actually be superior to the current windlass-type tourniquet (Taylor, Vater, & Parker, 2011).

Length of Application

This is the most controversial and, simultaneously, the least disputed topic relating to tourniquets. Tourniquet time is defined as the total time during which arterial flow beyond the instrument can be safely interrupted (Doyle & Taillac, 2008). Experts and clinicians agree on three points: (a) There is no completely safe tourniquet time, (b) longer tourniquet times are associated with increasing likelihood of morbidity, and (c) 2 hr is the accepted tourniquet time with minimal risk for subsequent morbidity. These points are built on a consensus referred to as a "useful guideline" (Wakai, Winter, Street, & Redmond, 2001) and should "suffice" (Fitzgibbons, Digiovanni, Hares, & Akelman, 2012) because of variance in the animal models as well as the inability to ethically conduct prospective human research, which extends beyond the current gold standard of 2 hr duration for tourniquet time. The preponderance of what is known about human use tourniquet time depends almost exclusively on hemodynamically stable operating room cases and recent combat-related military research. When examining any tourniquet time beyond this accepted 2-hr window depends on three sources: animal studies, anecdotal operating room data from prolonged surgeries, and a new source of data from the Iraq and Afghanistan conflicts.

A review of the animal research by Fitzgibbons et al. (2012) evaluated outcomes with variable tourniquet time from 1 to 5 hr. Although there were minor changes before 2 hr, such as elevated creatinine phosphokinase (Chiu, Wang, & Blumenthal, 1976) and endothelial alterations (Bushell, Klenerman, Davies, Grierson, & Jackson, 1996), after 2 hr, the complications became more significant with nerve changes (Nitz & Matulionis 1982), neuromuscular deficits (Jacobson, Pedowitz, Oyama, Tryon, & Gershuni, 1994), weakness (Chiu et al., 1976), and some local tissue necrosis (Pedowitz, 1991). The studies that evaluated tourniquets for 3–5 hr found cellular degeneration (Heppenstall, Scott, Sapega, Park, & Chance, 1986), nerve palsies (Mohler, Pedowitz, Myers, et al., 1999), and necrotic muscle fibers (Patterson & Klenerman, 1979). There were three monkey studies conducted. A study by Patterson and Klenerman (1979) found muscle compressed for 3 hr was histologically normal, whereas those compressed for 5 hr showed many necrotic fibers after 3 days. Another study by Patterson, Klenerman, Biswas, and Rhodes (1981) found at the 6-day interval decreased muscle tension in both the compressed and ischemic muscle at both the 3- and 5-hr marks with the latter being significantly degraded. The third study by Klenerman, Biswas, Hulands, and Rhodes (1980) found no nerve palsies after 5 hr.

The length of tourniquet time in the operating room is guided by the current standard of care with 120 min as the upper limit. This is partly supported by research which shows tissue nutrition appears to be depleted after 2–3 hr (Haljamäe & Enger, 1975; Santavirta, Höckerstedt, Niinikoski, 1978). Most surgeons extend total tourniquet time beyond these 2 hr by allowing a reperfusion period or a tourniquet-release period of between 5 and 30 min after each 120 min of inflation. But the literature is not clear on the benefits of this practice, with Noordin et al. (2009) stating, "There is no evidence to support the use of this technique . . . and time limits for subsequent ischemia are unknown," followed by Horlocker et al. (2006) who state tourniquet effects "were only somewhat attenuated by tourniquet deflation," who is in turn countered by Fitzgibbons et al. (2012) who states, "most studies support the use of a reperfusion interval." There is, however, general consensus that the risk of complications increases with increased tourniquet time (Hirota et al., 2001; Horlocker et al., 2006; Wakai, Winter, et al., 2001). Olivecrona et al. (2013) estimated a 20% increased risk for every 10 min of application time greater than 100 min. Horlocker et al. (2006) conducted a retrospective study of 1,001 cases of orthopedic surgeries, focusing on those which lasted more than 120 min. Of those, 759 were cases had uninterrupted tourniquet time (i.e., no reperfusion intervals) with a mean inflation interval of 135 min (range 120–216). This study found a 2.8 times increased risk for experiencing neurological dysfunction for every 30-min increment. Interestingly, in the univariate analysis, there were fewer occurrences of palsies among cases having no reperfusion intervals compared with those that used reperfusion intervals. These two studies are countered by Odinsson and Finsen (2006) who evaluated 63,484 Norwegian orthopedic surgeries using tourniquets. In this study, only 2 of the 18 complications seen were in patients who had greater than 120 min of tourniquet time (one was 130 min, the other was 180 min). There were two permanent neurological injuries of which only one occurred in the group with more than 120 min of tourniquet time. Although the consensus has been to accept the 2-hr limit for tourniquet application within the operating room, it remains unclear if that is yet based on consistent scientific results.

The final source of limited data for safe tourniquet times comes from military experience. A study conducted by Kragh et al. (2008) on combat-injured soldiers found no association in the incidence of pain and palsies between tourniquet times of 3–5 hr and those with tourniquet times less than 2 hr. A retrospective study by Lakstein et al. (2003) on Israeli Defense Forces did not specifically address tourniquet times more than 120 min, but did relate that 1 person out of 91 with tourniquets had a tourniquet time of 187 min and suffered bilateral peroneal and radial paralysis. It is not clear from the article if the tourniquet applied was commercially available or an improvised tourniquet.

As with the lower limit, there is a consensus that 6 hr of continuous application is the upper limit of tourniquet time after which medical amputation is recommended. However, even this time may not be hard and fast (Kragh, Baer, & Walters, 2007). It has been recognized since World War II that tourniquet times can be extended up to 8 hr by simply cooling the limb (Wolff & Adkins, 1945). There is evidence from an operating room study that limb cooling may decrease muscle damage during prolonged tourniquet time (Swanson, Livengood, & Sattel, 1991) and animal studies have shown that inducing limb hypothermia will reduce the incidence of neuropathy (Kelly, Creagh, Grace, & Bouchier-Hayes, 1992) and muscle damage (Irving & Noakes, 1985; Nakahara, 1984).

RELEASING THE TOURNIQUET

When a tourniquet has been applied in the prehospital setting, there are only two occasions when it can be released: to confirm continued bleeding and when definitive care is available. The practice employed by the operating room of using reperfusion periods to extend tourniquet time is not acceptable in the prehospital setting. Attempting reperfusion periods in a trauma patient defeats the purpose for which the tourniquet was applied and simply results in a controlled progressive exsanguination (Clifford, 2004). Releasing a tourniquet en route is acceptable only if the patient had a tourniquet placed before a complete assessment was conducted (e.g., the "when" dictated the placement before the terms of the "why" were completely assessed). Once the time is available and the paramedic or EMT has completed the patient assessment and determined the patient is stable, the tourniquet pressure may be slowly released for a "trial conversion" (Lee, Porter, & Hodgetts, 2007). If the bleeding has stopped or can be controlled with other methods, the tourniquet can be let down but should be left in place in case uncontrolled bleeding resumes during resuscitation. However, if when the tourniquet is released the bleeding remains uncontrolled, the tourniquet should be reapplied and left in place until definitive care is available (Walters & Mabry, 2005). There are certain situations when once a tourniquet has been placed, it should not be released at all until definitive care is available. These include amputation, inability to observe bleeding injury during rescue or transport, signs of shock, and if the tourniquet has been in place for greater than 6 hr (Richey, 2007; Walters & Mabry, 2005).

POTENTIAL COMPLICATIONS FROM TOURNIQUETS

In the prehospital setting, the tourniquet is a life-saving tool but it is not without potential risk of complications. The complications, however, must be put into perspective. Most research on tourniquet complications has been done in the operating room on elective surgeries. Therefore, at least theoretically, the risk–benefit ratio will always be weighted toward avoiding undue risk. In the prehospital setting, however, tourniquet use is not an elective procedure. It is applied for the principle purpose of saving a life. Therefore, the risk–benefit ratio must be weighted more toward the benefit side. To put it into context, tourniquets used in emergency situations have been shown to cause complications, but, in many cases, that is because the person lived to experience them.

For all the concern and admonitions against using tourniquets, the general complication rate is by all accounts quite low in both the operating room literature and the prehospital literature. Operating room studies that look at tourniquet use within the standard 120 min find complication rates which range from 0.07% (Middleton & Varian, 1974) to 0.15% (McEwen, 1981). A study by Middleton and Varian (1974) conducted in the 1970s found the rate of adverse events related to tourniquets to be about 1 in 5,000 in upper extremity tourniquets and about 1 in 13,000 for lower extremity tourniquets, which is consistent with other studies that have found that the upper limbs are more susceptible to tourniquet complications (Kam, Kavanagh, & Yoong, 2001). Studies that examined only nerve complications also found similarly low injury rates between 0.02% (Odinsson & Finsen, 2006) and 0.13% (Flatt, 1972). A study conducted by Horlocker et al. (2006) looked specifically at operations with tourniquet times greater than 120 min (mean 145 ± 25 min) and found a slightly higher 7.7% incidence of nerve injuries. However, 89% of the peroneal and 100% of the tibial palsies went on to a complete recovery. Indeed, it appears as if most palsies are reversible in about 2–6 months (Mohler, Pedowitz, Lopez, & Gershuni, 1999; Odinsson & Finsen, 2006).

There has been little research conducted in the prehospital setting but what is available is consistent with the operating room literature. A study by Lakstein et al. (2003) that looked at tourniquet use, including improvised tourniquets, among the Israeli Defense Forces found a 0.9% neurological complication rate. Research conducted during the Iraqi and Afghanistan conflicts found a slightly higher palsy rate of 1.7% (Kragh, O'Neill, et al., 2011). But even these were transient with all palsies tracked resolving within 3 days. Also consistent with the operating room literature, 82% of the palsies noted in the conflict zone were upper extremities. Interestingly, all the palsies in this study occurred when the single tourniquet was applied prehospital but no palsies were noted when two tourniquets were used side by side or if the pneumatic tourniquet was applied in the emergency room (Kragh, O'Neill, et al., 2011).

There are many complications that can result even with proper tourniquet application. However, with the exception of pain, all complications manifest once the tourniquet is released, and are therefore more of a concern for the emergency department than the paramedics and EMTs. In general, tourniquet complications can be divided into two categories: local and systemic (Table 9.3). The complication most discussed is compressive neurapraxia. As explained earlier, the sheering forces of the tourniquet cause nerve damage, which most often is transient but can be permanent. Choosing the correct tourniquet and rapid transport is the task paramedics and EMTs have to minimize the risk of compressive neurapraxia. A second possible local complication is compartment syndrome. Studies are not clear on whether this is more often because of the tourniquet or the wound for which the tourniquet was placed (Odinsson & Finsen, 2006), and often fasciotomies are conducted prophylactically without any evidence of

TABLE 9.3
Complications Associated With Tourniquet Use

Local		Systemic
Compressive neurapraxia Direct vascular injury Tissue and bone necrosis Compartment syndrome (Niven & Castle, 2010) Tissue infection Pain Decreased muscle power (Mohler, Pedowitz, Lopez, et al., 1999) Reperfusion injury (Lee et al., 2007)	General	Acid–base alterations (Wakai, Winter, et al., 2001) Myonephrotic syndrome (Noordin et al., 2009) Hypertension (Wakai, Winter, et al., 2001)[a] Lactic and respiratory acidosis (Wakai, Wang, et al., 2001) Elevated temperature (Akata, Kanna, Izumi, Kodama, & Takahashi, 1998) Cerebral infarction
	Circulatory	Deep vein thrombosis (Hernandez, Almeida, Favaro, & Sguizzato, 2012) Coagulopathy (Kohro et al., 1998) Shock (Wakai, Wang, et al., 2001) Arrhythmias secondary to hyperkalemia (Wakai, Wang, et al., 2001) Increased central venous pressure[a] Arterial hypertension[a]
	Respiratory	Pulmonary embolism (Hirota et al., 2001; Parmet et al., 1998)
	Renal	Acute renal failure from rhabdomyolysis (Richey, 2007)

[a]Likely specific only to operating room because of intentional limb exsanguination using Esmarch bandage before the tourniquet is applied.

compartment syndrome (Kragh et al., 2008). Although compartment syndrome seems to be a significant concern in the prehospital literature, an incidence rate could not be found.

Systemic complications are of more immediate concern to the emergency setting. When a tourniquet is released and perfusion resumes to the ischemic limb, toxic metabolites are flushed out and may lead to myonephropathic metabolic syndrome, which is characterized by metabolic acidosis, hyperkalemia, myoglobulinemia, and myoglobinuria (Haimovici, 1979). Myoglobinuria is a result of ischemic muscle damage with resultant rhabdomyolysis, which may lead to acute renal failure. Ischemic cells may also leak potassium into the interstitial spaces which when perfusion is restored, results in significant hyperkalemia and cardiac arrhythmias (Chaudry, Clemens, & Baue, 1981). Also, as a result of anaerobic respiration in the ischemic limb, once circulation is restored, an acid–base imbalance will likely occur. However, operating room research has found that this imbalance will normalize within 120 min after tourniquet release (Klenerman et al., 1980). No research was found that addressed acid–base imbalance in the emergency setting. Reperfusion may also trigger coagulopathies, such as thrombolytic activity through activation of the antithrombin III and protein C pathways (Noordin et al., 2009), or deep venous thrombosis (Parmet et al., 1998) with a significant risk for emboli (Hirota et al., 2001). The risk of thrombosis has been shown to be minimized with a single pretreatment dose of acetylsalicylic acid. However, the research did not look at any effects of taking the medication after the tourniquet was in place (Ojanen, Kaukinen, Seppälä, Kaukinen, & Vapaatalo, 2003). A final long-term syndrome which may occur is called the posttourniquet syndrome, which typically resolves within 3 weeks. It is relatively common and manifests as weakness, paresthesias, pallor, and stiffness to the affected limb (Kam et al., 2001).

CONCLUSIONS

Tourniquets have been used since before the time of the Roman Empire. Initially, the use of the tourniquet was clouded by poor understanding of blood circulation, as well as poor medical evacuation from the battlefield. At the beginning of the 20th century, tourniquets became an accepted device in the operating room but continued to receive mixed reviews from surgeons who were treating war injuries. Because of poor research abilities and poor outcome tracking, the history of the tourniquet was being strongly influenced by the negative anecdotal information published at the time. The justification for limiting the tourniquet to only an operative environment is becoming more difficult to support scientifically, but overcoming the past is often difficult. The misinformation persists. A study conducted in 2013 by Galante, Smith, Sena, Scherer, and Tharatt (2013) surveyed all emergency medical services (EMS) directors in California regarding the use of tourniquets. Of the respondents, 57% said tourniquets were used in their areas, whereas 86% felt tourniquets did have a role in civilian EMS. However, the top three identified barriers for not incorporating the tourniquet into standard EMS practice are (a) civilian wounding patterns are different than the military, (b) no proven benefit to tourniquets, and (c) tourniquets have potentially dangerous complications. Given events such as mass shootings and bombings among civilian settings, a case can be made that there are similarities between civilian and military injury patterns, but the difference only lies in the frequency of such events. The final two barriers are misinformation, which has persisted for more than a century.

Given what is known today, several statements regarding tourniquets can be made:

- Tourniquets have been shown to have a low complication rate when used in the operating room—a highly controlled environment with predictable "wounding." Tourniquets have also been shown to have a similarly low complication rate when used in a combat environment—a low control environment with catastrophic injuries. It is not unreasonable to expect civilian prehospital tourniquet complication rates to be somewhere between these two extremes.
- The 2-hr "safe" tourniquet time is based on operating room literature, which has a different risk/benefit consideration. There are indications that up to 3 hr or more may be possible, and inducing limb hypothermia may extend the time well beyond that.
- Tourniquets have been and will continue to be used in acute and emergency situations. EMS directors recognize the use of tourniquets, and civilians reflexively improvise them in times of need. Denying their use in emergency care is not based in science or common sense.
- Pneumatic tourniquets have been shown to be superior to either the windlass type or an improvised tourniquet because of the variable and excessive compression forces of the latter devices. In addition, using the concept of LOP results in significantly lower application pressures, which theoretically translates to lower complication risks.
- The literature on tourniquet placement is contradictory. Operating room recommends placing over the widest part of the limb. Prehospital recommendations are to place as close to the injury as possible. However, given the difficulty with arterial occlusion on thigh application of the windlass tourniquet, and recent data which shows successful applications with low complications on distal extremities, prehospital placement should continue to be as distal as possible.

RECOMMENDATIONS

It is time to reconsider the tourniquet as a useful tool for emergency situations. The use of the tourniquet should, first and foremost, meet the critical criteria of "why" to apply it—extreme life-threatening hemorrhage and bleeding that is not controlled with direct pressure. If a casualty meets these two initial assessment parameters, there should be no question that a tourniquet will effectively and quickly rectify the situation. However, there are also key "when" scenarios in which using a tourniquet should become a first-line tool. The military literature helps to show that patients who may develop symptoms of hypovolemic shock have a higher survival rate if a tourniquet is applied before symptoms appear. Also, a tourniquet should be considered as first line when care is being rendered in a dangerous environment or when the number of casualties exceeds the current medical support. In both of those situations, the necessity for the tourniquet can be reevaluated when time permits, but it provides that critical time until a full assessment can be conducted. All emergency vehicles should carry pneumatic tourniquets. Combat tourniquets do not belong in the civilian EMS system. The narrower windlass tourniquets may have a higher complication rate and there is no scenario within the civilian EMS system whereby a casualty would be expected to apply their own tourniquet with one hand. There are pneumatic tourniquets which have been marketed toward the EMS system, but the windlass tourniquet still remains the primary tourniquet (Galante et al., 2013).

A training program is essential. Training on proper tourniquet application need not be extensive as the tool is simple and intuitive. Training needs to focus on the proper time to use a tourniquet. Paramedics and EMTs are trained in making critical decisions regarding the appropriate treatment in any given situation. Their job is to resuscitate and transport the casualty to a higher level of care, much the same way as the military medic. The paramedics and EMTs must be allowed to use their professional skills to determine which treatment or tool is required to maintain the life of that casualty. The military has shown the tourniquet is a lifesaving tool with few significant and fewer still lasting complications. It is only antiquated policies and continued misinformation which limits professional paramedics and EMTs from employing a tourniquet when it is required. Clinical guidelines were developed for use by combat medics to guide the use of tourniquets in the combat environment. Similar clinical guidelines need to be developed and accepted by EMT organizations to standardize care across the United States. Algorithms have already been developed (Doyle & Taillac, 2008; Lee et al., 2007; Lewis, 2013). It is time to move forward with open discussions and development of protocols.

There remain a few areas where more research is required before recommendations can be made. Although the pneumatic tourniquet is considered superior to the windlass type of tourniquet, the research is inconsistent on which windlass style performs better (Lakstein et al., 2003; Savage et al., 2013; Swan et al., 2009; Wall et al., 2013). As the windlass likely will continue to have a role in the military settings, this may be worth pursuing. The research of whether to place padding under the tourniquet is also conflicting. The operating room literature fully supports the use of padding and the AORN include padding in their recommendations (McEwen & Inkpen, 2002). In the prehospital literature, there are recommendations to use padding (Welling et al., 2006), but the combat environment research found the padding caused the tourniquet to move and loosen (Kragh et al., 2008). Attempting to place padding on a significantly injured limb might prove difficult, but further investigation is needed to determine if skin damage is a problem in emergency tourniquet use and may be lessened as it is in the operating room. And finally, very little research exists on the proper width of a pneumatic tourniquet. Although the science supports the relatively wider pneumatic over the narrow windlass, the science is less clear on an ideal width for the pneumatic tourniquet (Mittal, Shenoy, & Sandhu, 2008).

Klenerman sums up the problem with tourniquet history well in an article written in 1962. Klenerman, a surgeon by trade, states the tourniquet is the "instrument of choice" for surgery on the limbs and the pneumatic tourniquet has made complications rare. Yet, when he moves to talking about any use of the tourniquet outside the operating room he states, "There is no place for the tourniquet as a first aid measure for acute hemorrhage." For a justification, he states, "Simple tool though the tourniquet may be, its application carries many potential dangers, and it should only be entrusted to skilled hands." By skilled, he is referring to surgeons. This was written in 1962. It is time to relook at this perception and acknowledge that our highly trained and exceptionally professional paramedics and EMTs also have skilled hands.

DISCLAIMER

The views expressed are those of the authors and do not reflect the official policy or position of the Uniformed Services University of the Health Sciences, the Department of the Defense, or the United States government.

REFERENCES

Akata, T., Kanna, T., Izumi, K., Kodama, K., & Takahashi, S. (1998). Changes in body temperature following deflation of limb pneumatic tourniquet. *Journal of Clinical Anesthesia, 10*(1), 17–22.

Bailey, H. (1941). *Surgery of modern warfare*. Edinburgh, United Kingdom: E&S Livingstone.

Basic Medical Specialist Manual 91B. (1975). U.S. Army Medical Department Center and Schools.

Beekley, A. C., Sebesta, J. A., Blackbourne, L. H., Herbert, G. S., Kauvar, D. S., Baer, D. G., . . . Holcomb, J. B. (2008). Prehospital tourniquet use in Operation Iraqi Freedom: Effect on hemorrhage control and outcomes. *The Journal of Trauma, 64*(2 Suppl.), S28–S37; discussion S37. http://dx.doi.org/10.1097/TA.0b013e318160937e

Blackwood, M. (2001). Royal Army Medical Corps, 3rd Corps Medical Society. Treatment of wounds from fire trench to field ambulance. 1916. *Journal of the Royal Army Medical Corps, 147*(2), 230–235; discussion 229.

Böhler, L. (1956). *The treatment of fractures* (Vol. 1; H. Tretter, H. B. Luchini, F. Kreuz, Trans.). New York, NY: Grune & Stratton.

Brodie, S., Hodgetts, T. J., Ollerton, J., McLeod, J., Lambert, P., & Mahoney, P. (2009). Tourniquet use in combat trauma: U.K. military experience. *Journal of Special Operations Medicine*, *9*(1), 74–77.

Bushell, A, Klenerman, L., Davies, H., Grierson, I., & Jackson, M. J. (1996). Ischemia-reperfusion-induced muscle damage: Protective effect of corticosteroids and antioxidants in rabbits. *Acta Orthopaedica Scandinavica*, *67*(4), 393–398.

Calkins, D., Snow, C., Costello, M., & Bentley, T. B. (2000). Evaluation of possible battlefield tournquet systems for the far-forward setting. *Military Medicine*, *165*, 379–384.

Chaudry, I. H., Clemens, M. G., & Baue, A. E. (1981). Alterations in cell function with ischemia and shock and their correction. *Archives of Surgery*, *116*, 1309–1317.

Chisolm, J. J. (1861). Hemorrhage in gunshot wounds. In *A manual of military surgery, for the use of surgeons in the Confederate army* (pp. 169–171). Richmond, VA: West & Johnson.

Chiu, D., Wang, H. H., & Blumenthal, M. R. (1976). Creatine phosphokinase release as a measure of tourniquet effect on skeletal muscle. *Archives of Surgery*, *111*(1), 71–74.

Clifford, C. C. (2004). Treating traumatic bleeding in a combat setting. *Military Medicine*, *169*(12 Suppl.), 8–10, 14.

Cosmas, G. A., & Cowdrey, A. E. (1992). *The medical department: Medical service in the European Theater of Operations*. Washington, DC: Center of Military History.

Crenshaw, A. G., Hargens, A. R., Gershuni, D. H., & Rydevik, B. (1988). Wide tourniquet cuffs more effective at lower inflation pressures. *Acta Orthopaedica Scandinavica*, *59*, 447–451.

Doyle, G. S., & Taillac, P. P. (2008). Tourniquets: A review of current use with proposals for expanded prehospital use. *Prehospital Emergency Care*, *12*(2), 241–256. http://dx.doi .org/10.1080/10903120801907570

Fitzgibbons, P. G., Digiovanni, C., Hares, S., & Akelman, E. (2012). Safe tourniquet use: A review of the evidence. *Journal of the American Academy of Orthopaedic Surgeons*, *20*(5), 310–319. http://dx.doi.org/10.5435/JAAOS-20-05-310

Flatt, A. E. (1972). Tourniquet time in hand surgery. *Archives of Surgery*, *104*, 190–192.

Galante, J. M, Smith, C. A, Sena, M. J., Scherer, L. A., & Tharratt, R. S. (2013). Identification of barriers to adaptation of battlefield technologies into civilian trauma in California. *Military Medicine*, *178*(11), 1227–1230.

Gersdorff, H. V. (1967). *Feldtbuch der Wundtartzney*. Retrieved from http://www.nlm.nih.gov/exhibition/historicalanatomies/gersdorff_bio.html

Gilliatt, R. W., Ochoa, J., Rudge, P., & Neary, D. (1974). The cause of nerve damage in acute compression. *Transactions of the American Neurological Association*, *99*, 71–74.

Graham, B., Breault, M. J., McEwen, J. A., & McGraw, R. W. (1993). Occlusion of arterial flow in the extremities at subsystolic pressures through the use of wide tourniquet cuffs. *Clinical Orthopaedics and Related Research*, *286*, 257–261.

Great Britain Army Medical Services. (1918). *Injuries and diseases of war*. London, United Kingdom: His Majesty's Stationary Office.

Gross, S. D. (1861). *A manual of military surgery, or hints on the emergencies of field, camp and hospital practices*. Philadelphia, PA: J.B. Lippincott.

Haimovici, H. (1979). Muscular, renal, and metabolic complications of acute arterial occlusions: Myonephropathic-metabolic syndrome. *Surgery*, *85*, 461–468.

Haljamäe, G., & Enger, E. (1975). Human skeletal muscle energy metabolism during and after complete tourniquet ischaemia. *Annals of Surgery*, *182*, 9–14.

Heppenstall, R. B., Scott, R., Sapega, A., Park, Y. S., & Chance, B. (1986). A comparative study of the tolerance of skeletal muscle to ischemia: Tourniquet application compared with acute compartment syndrome. *Journal of Bone and Joint Surgery*, *68*(6), 820–828.

Hernandez, A. J., Almeida, A. M., Fávaro, E., & Sguizzato, G. T. (2012). The influence of tourniquet use and operative time on the incidence of deep vein thrombosis in total knee arthroplasty. *Clinics (Sao Paulo)*, *67*(9), 1053–1057.

Hirota, K., Hashimoto, H., Kabara, S., Tsubo, T., Sato, Y., Ishihara, H., & Matsuki, A. (2001). The relationship between pneumatic tourniquet time and the amount of pulmonary emboli in patients undergoind knee arthoscopic surgeries. *Anesthesia & Analgesia*, *93*, 776–780.

Horlocker, T. T., Hebl, J. R., Bhargavi, G., Jankowski, C. J., Burkle, C. M., Berry, D. J., . . . Schroeder, D. R. (2006). Anesthetic, patient, and surgical risk factors for neurologic complications after prolonged total tourniquet time during total knee arthroplasty. *Anesthesia & Analgesia*, *102*, 950–955.

Hughes, C. W. (1954). *Hemorrhage*. Washington DC: US Army Medical Service Graduate School Walter Reed Army Medical Center.

Irving, G. A., & Noakes, T. D. (1985). The protective role of local hypothermia in tourniquet-induced ischaemia of muscle. *Journal of Bone and Joint Surgery British Volume*, *67*(2), 297–301.

Jacobson, M. D., Pedowitz, R. A., Oyama, B. K., Tryon, B., & Gershuni, D. H. (1994). Muscle functional deficits after tourniquet ischemia. *American Journal of Sports Medicine*, *22*(3), 372–377.

Kam, P. C., Kavanagh, R., & Yoong, F. F. (2001). The arterial tourniquet: Pathophysiological consquences and anaesthetic implications. *Anaesthesia*, *56*(6), 534–545.

Kelly, C., Creagh, T., Grace, P. A., & Bouchier-Hayes, D. (1992). Regional hypothermia protects against tourniquet neuropathy. *European Journal of Vascular Surgery*, *6*, 288–292.

Kheirabadi, B. S., Terrazas, I. B., Hanson, M. A., Kragh, J. F., Jr., Dubick, M. A., & Blackbourne, L. H. (2013). In vivo assessment of the Combat Ready Clamp to control junctional hemorrhage in swine. *Journal of Trauma and Acute Care Surgery*, *74*(5), 1260–1265. http://dx.doi.org/10.1097/TA.0b013e31828cc983

Klenerman, L. (1962). The tourniquet in surgery. *Journal of Bone and Joint Surgery*, *44-B*, 937–943.

Klenerman, L. (2003). *The tourniquet manual—Principles and practice*. London, United Kingdom: Springer Publishing.

Klenerman, L., Biswas, M., Hulands, G. H., & Rhodes, A. M. (1980). Systemic and local effects of the application of a tourniquet. *Journal of Bone and Joint Surgery*, *62*(3), 385–388.

Kohro, S., Yamakage, M., Arakawa, J., Kotaki, M., Omote, T., & Namiki, A. (1998). Surgical/tourniquet pain accelerates blood coagulability but not fibrinolysis. *British Journal of Anaesthesia*, *80*(4), 460–463.

Kotwal, R. S., Butler, F. K., Gross, K. R., Kheirabadi, B. S., Baer, D. G., Dubick, M. A., . . . Bailey, J. A. (2013). Management of junctional hemorrhage in tactical combat casualty care: TCCC guidelines? Proposed change 13-03. *Journal of Special Operations Medicine*, *13*(4), 85–93.

Kragh, J. F., Jr., Baer, D. G., & Walters, T. J. (2007). Extended (16-hour) tourniquet application after combat wounds: A case report and review of the current literature. *Journal of Orthopaedic Trauma*, *21*(4), 274–278. http://dx.doi.org/10.1097/BOT.0b013e3180437dd9

Kragh, J. F., Jr., Littrel, M. L., Jones, J. A., Walters, T. J., Baer, D. G., Wade, C. E., & Holcomb, J. B. (2011). Battle casualty survival with emergency tourniquet use to stop limb bleeding. *Journal of Emergency Medicine*, *41*(6), 590–597. http://dx.doi.org/10.1016/j.jemermed.2009.07.022

Kragh, J. F., Jr., O'Neill, M. L., Walters, T. J., Jones, J. A., Baer, D. G., Gershman, L. K., . . . Holcomb, J. B. (2011). Minor morbidity with emergency tourniquet use to stop bleeding in severe limb trauma: Research, history, and reconciling advocates and abolitionists. *Military Medicine*, *176*(7), 817–823.

Kragh, J. F., Jr., Swan, K. G., Smith, D. C., Mabry, R. L., & Blackbourne, L. H. (2012). Historical review of emergency tourniquet use to stop bleeding. *American Journal of Surgery*, *203*(2), 242–252. http://dx.doi.org/10.1016/j.amjsurg.2011.01.028

Kragh, J. F., Jr., Walters, T. J., Baer, D. G., Fox, C. J., Wade, C. E., Salinas, J., & Holcomb, J. B. (2008). Practical use of emergency tourniquets to stop bleeding in major limb trauma. *Journal of Trauma*, *64*(2 Suppl.), S38–S49; discussion S49–S50. http://dx.doi.org/10.1097/TA.0b013e31816086b1

Kragh, J. F., Jr., Walters, T. J., Baer, D. G., Fox, C. J., Wade, C. E., Salinas, J., & Holcomb, J. B. (2009). Survival with emergency tourniquet use to stop bleeding in major limb trauma. *Annals of Surgery*, *249*(1), 1–7. http://dx.doi.org/10.1097/SLA.0b013e31818842ba

Laffin, J. (1999). *Combat surgeons*. Wiltshire, United Kingdom: Sutton.

Lakstein, D., Blumenfeld, A., Sokolov, T., Lin, G., Bssorai, R., Lynn, M., & Ben-Abraham, R. (2003). Tourniquets for hemorrhage control on the battlefield: A 4-year accumulated experience. *The Journal of Trauma*, *54*(5 Suppl.), S221–S225. http://dx.doi.org/10.1097/01.TA.0000047227.33395.49

Le Dran, H.-F. (1749). *The operations in surgery of Mons. Le Dran* (T. Gataker, Trans.). Retrieved from http://books.google.com/books?id=Eww3AQAAMAAJ&lpg=PP8&ots=B2Gu081nPu&dq=operations%20in%20surgery%20of%20mons&pg=PP5#v=onepage&q=operations%20in%20surgery%20of%20mons&f=false

Lee, C., Porter, K. M., & Hodgetts, T. J. (2007). Tourniquet use in the civilian prehospital setting. *Emergency Medicine Journal*, *24*(8), 584–587. http://dx.doi.org/10.1136/emj.2007.046359

Lewis, P. C. (2013). Tourniquets: Translating military knowledge into civilian care. *Journal of Emergency Nursing*, *39*(6), 595–601. http://dx.doi.org/10.1016/j.jen.2013.08.011

Longmore, T. (1895). Treatment of gunshot wounds. In *Gunshot injuries: Their history, characteristic features, complications, and general treatment, with statistics concerning them as they have been met with in warfare* (pp. 770–772). London, United Kingdom: Longmans, Green and Co.

Mabry, R. L. (2006). Tourniquet use on the battlefield. *Military Medicine*, *171*(5), 352–356.

MacLeod, G. (1862). *Notes on the surgery of the war in the Crimea with remarks on the treatment of gunshot wounds*. Philadelphia, PA: J. B. Lippincott.

Majno, G. (1975). *The healing hand: Man and woman in the ancient world*. Cambridge, MA: Harvard University Press.

Maughon, J. S. (1970). An inquiry into the nature of the wounds resulting in killed in action in Vietnam. *Military Medicine*, *135*, 8–13.

McEwen, J. A. (1981). Complications of and improvements in pneumatic tourniquets used in surgery. *Medical Instrumentation*, *15*, 253–257.

McEwen, J. A., & Casey V. (2009, May). *Measurement of hazardous pressure levels and gradients produced on human limbs by non-pneumatic tourniquets*. Paper presented at the Proceedings of the 32nd Conference of the Canadian Medical & Biological Engineering Society, Calgary, Canada.

McEwen, J. A., & Inkpen, K. (2002). Safety: Preventing skin injuries. *The Surgical Technologist*, 7–15.

McEwen, J. A., Kelly, D., Jardanowski, T., & Inkpen, K. (2002). Tourniquet safety in lower leg applications. *Orthopaedic Nursing*, *21*(5), 55–62.

McLaren, A. C., & Rorabeck, C. H. (1985). The pressure distribution under tourniquets. *Journal of Bone and Joint Surgery*, *67*, 433–438.

Middleton, R. W., & Varian, J. P. (1974). Tourniquet paralysis. *The Australian and New Zealand Journal of Surgery*, *44*(2), 124–128.

Mittal, P., Shenoy, S., & Sandhu, J. S. (2008). Effect of different cuff widths on the motor nerve conduction of the median nerve: An experimental study. *Journal of Orthopaedic Surgery and Research*, *3*, 1.

Mohler, L. R., Pedowitz, R. A., Lopez, M. A., & Gershuni, D. H. (1999). Effects of tourniquet compression on neuromuscular function. *Clinical Orthopaedics and Related Research*, (359), 213–220.

Mohler, L. R., Pedowitz, R. A., Myers, R. R., Ohara, W. M., Lopez, M. A., & Gershuni, D. H. (1999). Intermittent reperfusion fails to prevent posttourniquet neuropraxia. *Journal of Hand Surgery*, *24*(4), 687–693.

Nakahara, M. (1984). Tourniquet effects on muscle oxygen tension in dog limbs: Experiments with cooling and breathing intervals. *Acta Orthopaedica Scandinavica*, *55*, 576–578.

Nitz, A. J., & Matulionis, D. H. (1982). Ultrastructural changes in rat peripheral nerve following pneumatic tourniquet compression. *Journal of Neurosurgery*, *57*(5), 660–666.

Niven, M., & Castle, N. (2010). Use of tourniquets in combat and civilian trauma situations. *Emerging Nurse*, *18*(3), 32–36; quiz 37.

Noordin, S., McEwen, J. A., Kragh, J. F., Jr., Eisen, A., & Masri, B. A. (2009). Surgical tourniquets in orthopaedics. *Journal of Bone and Joint Surgery*, *91*(12), 2958–2967. http://dx.doi.org/10.2106/JBJS.I.00634

Ochoa, J., Danta, G., Fowler, T. J., & Gilliatt, R. W. (1971). Nature of the nerve lesion caused by a pneumatic tourniquet. *Nature*, *233*(5317), 265–266.

Ochoa, J., Fowler, T. J., & Gilliatt, R. W. (1972). Anatomical changes in peripheral nerves compressed by a pneumatic tourniquet. *Journal of Anatomy*, *113*(Pt. 3), 433–455.

Odinsson, A., & Finsen, V. (2006). Tourniquet use and its complications in Norway. *Journal of Bone and Joint Surgery*, *88*(8), 1090–1092. http://dx.doi.org/10.1302/0301-620X.88B8.17668

Ojanen, R., Kaukinen, L., Seppälä, E., Kaukinen, S., & Vapaatalo, H. (2003). Single dose of acetylsalicylic acid prevents thromboxane release after tourniquet ischemia. *The Journal of Trauma*, *54*(5), 986–989. http://dx.doi.org/10.1097/01.TA.0000051589.20214.5A

Olivecrona, C., Lapidus, L., Benson, L., & Blomfeldt, R. (2013). Tourniquet time affects postoperative complications after knee arthroplasy. *International Orthopaedics*, *37*, 827–832.

Oragui, E., Parsons, A., White, T., Longo, U. G., & Khan, W. S. (2011). Tourniquet use in upper limb surgery. *Hand (New York)*, *6*, 165–173.

Otis, G. A., & Huntington, D. L. (1883). Wounds and complications. In Barnes JK (Ed.), *Medical and surgical history of the war of the rebellion: Surgical history* (Vol 2, Pt. 3, p. 880). Washington DC: Government Printing Office.

Parmet, J. L., Horrow, J. C., Berman, A. T., Miller, F., Pharo, G., & Collins, L. (1998). The incidence of large venous emboli during total knee arthroplasty without pneumatic tourniquet use. *Anesthesia & Analgesia*, *87*(2), 439–444.

Patterson, S., & Klenerman, L. (1979). The effect of pneumatic tourniquets on the ultrastructure of skeletal muscle. *Journal of Bone and Joint Surgery*, *61*(2), 178–183.

Patterson, S., Klenerman, L., Biswas, M., & Rhodes, A. (1981). The effect of pneumatic tourniquets on skeletal muscle. *Acta Orthopaedica Scandinavica*, *52*(2), 171–175.

Pedowitz, R. A. (1991). Tourniquet-induced neuromuscular injury: A recent review of rabbit and clinical experiments. *Acta Orthopaedica Scandinavica Suppl*, *245*, 1–33.

Petit, J. L. (1718). A novel surgical instrument. *Min Acad R Sci*, 252–253.

Pneumatic Tourniquets, Application, and Use. (2011). *Standards guidelines and position statements for perioperative registered nursing practice*. Retrieved from http://www.ornac.ca/downloads/ORNAC_Standards_10th_Edition_2011-Section_3-Tourniquets,_Smoke_Evacuators_and_Incident_Reporting.pdf

Richey, S. L. (2007). Tourniquets for the control of traumatic hemorrhage: A review of the literature. *World Journal of Emergency Surgery*, *2*, 28. http://dx.doi.org/10.1186/1749-7922-2-28

Santavirta, J., Höckerstedt, K., & Niinikoski, J. (1978). Effect of pneumatic tourniquet on muscle oxygen tension. *Acta Orthopaedica Scandinavica*, *49*(5), 451–459.

Savage, E., Pannell, D., Payne, E., O'Leary, T., & Tien, H. (2013). Re-evaluating the field tourniquet for the Canadian Forces. *Military Medicine*, *178*(6), 669–675.

Schultheiss, D., & Jonas, U. (1998). Johannes Scultetus (1595–1645). Urologic aspects in the "Armamentarium chirurgicum." *European Urology*, *34*(6), 520–525.

Schwartz, A. M. (1958). The historical development of methods of hemostasis. *Surgery*, *44*, 604–610.

Sebesta, J. A. (2006). Special lessons learned from Iraq. *Surgical Clinics of North America*, *86*(3), 711–726.

Swan, K. G., Jr., Wright, D. S., Barbagiovanni, S. S., Swan, B. C., & Swan, K. G. (2009). Tourniquets revisited. *The Journal of Trauma*, *66*(3), 672–675. http://dx.doi.org/10.1097/TA.0b013e3181986959

Swanson, A. B., Livengood, L. C., & Sattel, A. B. (1991). Local hypothermia to prolong safe tourniquet time. *Clinical Orthopaedics and Related Research*, (264), 200–208.

Taylor, D. M., Vater, G. M., & Parker, P. J. (2011). An evaluation of two tourniquet systems for the control of prehospital lower limb hemorrhage. *The Journal of Trauma*, *71*(3), 591–595. http://dx.doi.org/10.1097/TA.0b013e31820e0e41

Tuffier, M. (1915). Contemporary French surgery. *British Journal of Surgery*, *3*, 100.

Tuttle, A. D. (1927). *Handbook for the medical soldier*. New York, NY: Wood and Company.

U. S. Surgeon General's Office. (1944). *Manual of therapy: European theater of operations*. United States: Author.

Wakai, A., Wang, J. H., Winter, D. C., Street, J. T., O'Sullivan, R. G., & Redmond, H. P. (2001). Tourniquet-induced systemic inflammatory response in extremity surgery. *The Journal of Trauma*, *51*(5), 922–926.

Wakai, A., Winter, D. C., Street, J. T., & Redmond, P. H. (2001). Pneumatic tourniquets in extremity surgery. *Journal of the American Academy of Orthopaedic Surgeons*, *9*(5), 345–351.

Wall, P. L., Duevel, D. C., Hassan, M. B., Welander, J. D., Sahr, S. M., & Buising, C. M. (2013). Tourniquets and occlusion: The pressure design. *Military Medicine*, *178*(5), 578–587.

Walters, T. J., & Mabry, R. L. (2005). Issues related to the use of tourniquets on the battlefield. *Military Medicine*, *170*(9), 770–775.

Wangensteen, O. H., & Wangensteen, S. D. (1978). *The rise of surgery from empiric craft to scientific discipline*. Minneapolis, MN: University of Minnesota Press.

Watson-Jones, R. (1955). *Fractures and joint injuries* (4th ed.). London, United Kingdom: Livingstone.

Welling, D. R., Burris, D. G., Hutton, J. E., Minken, S. L., & Rich, N. M. (2006). A balanced approach to tourniquet use: Lessons learned and relearned. *Journal of the American College of Surgeons*, *203*(1), 106–115. http://dx.doi.org/10.1016/j.jamcollsurg.2006.02.034

Welling, D. R., McKay, P. L., Rasmussen, T. E., & Rich, N. M. (2012). A brief history of the tourniquet. *Journal of Vascular Surgery*, *55*(1), 286–290. http://dx.doi.org/10.1016/j.jvs.2011.10.085

Wolff, L. H., & Adkins, T. F. (1945). Tourniquet problems in war injuries. *Bulletin of the US Army Medical Department*, *37*, 77–84.

Younger, A. S., McEwen, J. A., & Inkpen, K. (2004). Wide contoured thigh cuffs and automated limb occlusion measurement allow lower tourniquet pressures. *Clinical Orthopaedics and Related Research*, *428*, 286–293.

Index

NOTE: Page references followed by *f* and *t* denote figures and tables, respectively.